Official Reserves and Currency Management in Asia: Myth, Reality and the Future

Geneva Reports on the World Economy 7

International Center for Monetary and Banking Studies (ICMB)

International Center for Monetary and Banking Studies
11 A Avenue de la Paix
1202 Geneva
Switzerland

Tel (41 22) 734 9548
Fax (41 22) 733 3853
Website: www.icmb.ch

Centre for Economic Policy Research (CEPR)

Centre for Economic Policy Research
90-98 Goswell Road
London EC1V 7RR
UK

Tel: +44 (0)20 7878 2900
Fax: +44 (0)20 7878 2999
Email: cepr@cepr.org
Website: www.cepr.org

British Library Cataloguing in Publication Data
A catalogue record for this book is available from the British Library

ISBN: 1 898128 90 1

Official Reserves and Currency Management in Asia: Myth, Reality and the Future

Geneva Reports on the World Economy 7

Hans Genberg
Hong Kong Monetary Authority

Robert McCauley
Bank for International Settlements

Yung Chul Park
Seoul National University, Seoul

Avinash Persaud
Intelligence Capital Limited & Investment, London

ICMB INTERNATIONAL CENTER
FOR MONETARY
AND BANKING STUDIES

CIMB CENTRE INTERNATIONAL
D'ETUDES MONETAIRES
ET BANCAIRES

International Center for Monetary and Banking Studies (ICMB)

The International Center for Monetary and Banking Studies was created in 1973 as an independent, non-profit foundation. It is associated with Geneva's Graduate Institute of International Studies. Its aim is to foster exchange of views between the financial sector, central banks and academics on issues of common interest. It is financed through grants from banks, financial institutions and central banks.

The Center sponsors international conferences, public lectures, original research and publications. It has earned a solid reputation in the Swiss and international banking community where it is known for its contribution to bridging the gap between theory and practice in the field of international banking and finance.

In association with CEPR, the Center launched a new series of *Geneva Reports on the World Economy* in 1999. The five subsequent volumes have attracted considerable interest among practitioners, policy-makers and scholars working on the reform of international financial architecture.

The ICMB is non-partisan and does not take any view on policy. Its publications, including the present report, reflect the opinions of the authors, not of ICMB or of any of its sponsoring institutions.

Centre for Economic Policy Research (CEPR)

The Centre for Economic Policy Research is a network of almost 700 Research Fellows and Affiliates, based primarily in European universities. The Centre coordinates the research activities of its Fellows and Affiliates and communicates the results to the public and private sectors. CEPR is an entrepreneur, developing research initiatives with the producers, consumers and sponsors of research. Established in 1983, CEPR is a European economics research organization with uniquely wide-ranging scope and activities.

CEPR is a registered educational charity. Institutional (core) finance for the Centre is provided by major grants from the Economic and Social Research Council, under which an ESRC Resource Centre operates within CEPR; the Esmée Fairbairn Charitable Trust and the Bank of England. The Centre is also supported by the European Central Bank, the Bank for International Settlements, 22 national central banks and 45 companies. None of these organizations gives prior review to the Centre's publications, nor do they necessarily endorse the views expressed therein.

The Centre is pluralist and non-partisan, bringing economic research to bear on the analysis of medium- and long-run policy questions. CEPR research may include views on policy, but the Executive Committee of the Centre does not give prior review to its publications, and the Centre takes no institutional policy positions. The opinions expressed in this report are those of the authors and not those of the Centre for Economic Policy Research.

About the Authors

Hans Genberg is Executive Director, Research at the Hong Kong Monetary Authority and Director of the Hong Kong Institute for Monetary Research. At the time of writing, he is on leave from the Graduate Institute of International Studies in Geneva, Switzerland where he has been Professor of International Economics since 1979. Until February 2005 he was also Head of Executive Education at FAME (The International Center for Financial Asset Management and Engineering) in Geneva. A Swedish national, Mr. Genberg holds a PhD in Economics from the University of Chicago.

Mr. Genberg's teaching and research has dealt primarily with international finance, monetary economics and macroeconomics. His publications include *Asset Prices and Central Bank Policy* (ICMB/CEPR, 2000) – co-authored with S. Cecchetti, J. Lipsky, and S. Wadhwani – as well as articles in major professional journals such as *Econometrica*, the *Journal of Monetary Economics*, and the *Journal of International Economics*.

Yung Chul Park is Research Professor and Director of the Center for International Commerce and Finance at the Graduate School of International Studies of Seoul National University. He currently serves as co-Chairman of the Public Fund Oversight Committee of the Korean government. He was a member of National Economic Advisory Council (2003–4), Ambassador for International Economy and Trade at the Ministry of Foreign Affairs and Trade (2001–2), and Chairman of the Board of the Korea Exchange Bank (1999–2001). He previously served as the Chief Economic Advisor to the President of Korea (1987–8), as President of the Korea Development Institute (1986–7), as President of the Korea Institute of Finance (1992–8), and as a member of the Central Bank of Korea's Monetary Board (1984–6). He also worked for the International Monetary Fund (1968–1974). He has written and edited several books, including *Economic Liberalization and Integration in East Asia*, and *The Financial Development of Japan, Korea and Taiwan*.

Avinash D Persaud is Chairman of two London-based investment houses: Intelligence Capital Limited specializes in structuring finance for large projects and Elara Capital Limited focuses on mid-cap corporates in emerging markets. Persaud is a Member of Council of the London School of Economics, a Trustee of the Overseas Development Institute and a founding director of the Global Association of Risk Professionals. He is a Visiting Scholar at the ECB. Previously he has been a managing director of State Street Corporation, Visiting Scholar at the IMF and Gresham Professor of Commerce. He is the only individual to have won both major essay competitions in global finance: the Jacques de Larosiere Award (First, 2000) from the IIF and the Amex Bank Award (Bronze, 1994). He is known for developing the EMU Calculator, theories of liquidity black holes and investors' shifting risk appetite and what has become known as the Persaud Paradigm of risk management: the observation of safety creates risk.

Robert N McCauley serves as the Chief Representative at the Bank for International Settlements' Representative Office for Asia and the Pacific in Hong Kong. Recent work on Asia has included analyses of capital flows, regional financial integration, bond and foreign exchange markets, effective exchange rates, foreign currency bank deposits, monetary policy, and foreign banks' domestic currency operations. He co-edited BIS Paper 15, *China's Capital Account Liberalisation: International Perpsectives* based on a joint BIS-SAFE seminar. After joining the BIS in Basel in October 1994, he co-authored a monograph on bond market volatility. He also published several works on the euro, including the Princeton Essay, *The Euro and the Dollar*. Before joining the BIS, he worked for 13 years for the Federal Reserve Bank of New York, serving at times as chief economist for the interagency committee of bank supervisors that rates country risk. There he wrote on international comparisons of the cost of capital, foreign bank lending to US corporations and the unprofitability of foreign direct investment in the US. In 1992 he taught 'International Finance and the Multinational Firm' at the University of Chicago's Graduate School of Business. In 1999, MIT Press published his co-authored book, *Dodging Bullets: Changing US Corporate Capital Structures in the 1980s and 1990s*.

Contents

List of Conference Participants

Edmond Alphandery	Chairman, Supervisory Board CNP – Assurances, Paris
Markus Arpa	Deputy Head, Foreign Research Division, Oesterreichische Nationalbank, Vienna
Jeanne Barras-Zwahlen	Senior Economist, Asian Department Crédit Suisse Private Banking, Geneva
Vít Bàrta	Advisor to Vice-Governor Czech National Bank, Prague
Ric Battellino	Assistant Governor, Financial Markets Reserve Bank of Australia, Sydney
Jarle Bergo	Deputy Governor Norges Bank, Oslo
Rémy Bersier	Managing Director, Head Market Group II Crédit Suisse Private Banking, Geneva
Marc Büdenbender	Head, Public Policy Analysis UBS AG, Zurich
Julian Callow	Chief European Economist Barclays Capital, London
Pochih Chen	Chairman Taiwan Thinktank, Taiwan
Benoît Coeuré	Deputy Chief Executive Ministry of Economy, Finance and Industry, Paris
Pierre Darier	Partner Lombard Odier Darier Hentsch & Cie, Geneva
Jacques Delpla	Director, Economist Barclays Capital, London
Slobodan Djajic	Professor, International Economics Graduate Institute of International Studies, Geneva
Zdenek Drabek	Advisor, Research Department World Trade Organisation, Geneva
Olivier Garnier	Head of Strategy & Economic Research Société Générale Asset Management, Paris
Hans Genberg	Executive Director, Research Hong Kong Monetary Authority, Hong Kong
Miranda Goeltom	Senior Deputy-Governor Bank Indonesia, Jakarta

Liping He	Professor, Economics Normal University, Beijing
Hugo Frey Jensen	Head of Financial Markets Danmarks Nationalbank, Copenhagen
Karen Johnson	Director, International Finance Division Federal Reserve Board, Washington, DC
Alexander Karrer	Ambassador, International Finance and Monetary Division Swiss Federal Department of Finance, Bern
Ulrich Kohli	Alternate Member of the Governing Board, Department I Swiss National Bank, Zurich
Jean-Pierre Landau	Director for France European Bank for Reconstruction and Development, London
Kryzysztof Majczuk	Head of Financial System Department National Bank of Poland, Warsaw
Donald Malicki	Deputy Director, Foreign Exchange Department Narodowy Bank Polski, Warsaw
David Mayes	Advisor to the Board Bank of Finland, Helsinki
Robert N. McCauley	Chief Representative, Representative Office for Asia and Pacific Bank for International Settlements, Hong Kong
Gilles Moëc	Head of International Economy Division, Research Banque de France, Paris
Akio Mikuni	President Mikuni & Co Ltd., Tokyo
Carlo Monticelli	Senior Director, International Financial Relations Ministry of Economy and Finance, Rome
Lars Nyberg	Deputy Governor Sveriges Riksbank, Stockholm
José-Antonio Ocampo	Under Secretery-General for Economic and Social Affairs United Nations Economic and Social Council, Geneva
Yung Chul Park	Director, Center for International Trade and Finance Seoul National University, Seoul
Avinash D. Persaud	Chairman Intelligence Capital Limited & Investment, London Director GAM London Limited, London
Jean Pisani-Ferry	Director Bruegel, Brussels

Richard Portes	President CEPR, London Professor of Economics London Business School, London
Eli Remolona	Deputy Chief Representative, Office for Asia and the Pacific Bank for International Settlements, Hong Kong
Hermann Remsperger	Member of the Board Deutsche Bundesbank, Frankfurt
Hélène Rey	Professor Princeton University, Princeton, NJ
Jean-Jacques Rey	Honorary Executive Director National Bank of Belgium, Brussels
Märten Ross	Deputy Governor Bank of Estonia, Tallinn
Neal Soss	Chief Economist Crédit Suisse First Boston Ltd., New York
Alexander Swoboda	Professor, International Economics Graduate Institute of International Studies, Geneva
Angel Ubide	Director of Global Economics Tudor Investment Corporation, Washington, DC
Ignazio Visco	Central Manager for International Affairs Banca d'Italia, Rome
Sushil Wadhwani	Chief Executive Officer Wadhwani Asset Management LLP, London
Mikio Wakatsuki	Chairman Axa Japan Holding Co. Ltd., Tokyo
William R. White	Economic Adviser, Monetary and Economic Department Bank for International Settlements, Basel
John Williamson	Senior Fellow Institute for International Economics, Washington, DC
Pawel Wyczanski	Deputy Director, Financial System National Bank of Poland, Warsaw
Charles Wyplosz	Professor, International Economics Graduate Institute of International Studies, Geneva
François Zenner	Head of Front Office and Treasury, Banking Operations Central Bank of Luxembourg, Luxembourg
Jean Zwahlen	Vice-President Union Bancaire Privée, Geneva

List of Tables

List of Figures

List of Boxes

Acknowledgements

The authors would like to thank San-Sau Fung and Michela Scatigna for research assistance, Stephen Arthur for help converting graphs, and Andrew Tsang for help with collecting and processing data.

A number of individuals provided valuable comments on the arguments developed in the report. Among them we would like to single out Claudio Borio, Barry Eichengreen, Gabriele Galati, Bob Mundell, John Nugee, Sushil Wadhwani, Bill White, John Williamson, Martin Wolf, and Charles Wyplosz. The comments made by participants in the ICMB/CEPR conference in Geneva on 6 May 2005, at which the report was first presented, also provided us with many ideas for improvements and clarifications of our arguments.

The views expressed in this report are entirely our own, and should not be taken to represent those of our employers or of the individuals mentioned above.

Foreword

The accumulation of foreign exchange reserves in East Asia has reached heights that could not have been imagined during the crisis of 1997–8, yet it continues. Are the causes in the economic structures of these countries or their policies, or is this just the inevitable counterpart of the immense United States current account deficit? Or are Asian surpluses and US deficits both the consequence of a 'world savings glut' whose main source is the major emerging market countries?

International macroeconomists and economic policy-makers have widely differing perspectives on these issues. Some say there is a new, unofficial 'system' that resembles the Bretton Woods period; that it is benign; and that there are strong incentives for the major players, the US and China, to maintain it. Others argue that Asian exchange rates are greatly undervalued and China should lead with a substantial appreciation, then move to a market-determined exchange rate, taking other major Asian countries with it. But perhaps the 'new Bretton Woods system' is really not a system at all, just a brief historical conjunction that will soon fall apart. That in turn, with a shift in the composition of Asian reserves away from the dollar, could lead to changes in the major exchange rates big enough to have serious macroeconomic consequences.

This seventh publication in the series of *Geneva Reports on the World Economy* offers an assessment by a team of authors with academic, official sector and market experience. Their comprehensive analysis takes into account the recently announced change in China's exchange rate policies. It offers a unique, Asian-oriented perspective on global economic imbalances. The report sets out alternative possible trajectories of adjustment and argues that a return to the economic policy coordination of the 1980s (Plaza and Louvre) is the way to reach the preferred adjustment path. They conclude by supporting greater explicit coordination of monetary and exchange-rate policies in East Asia, though they recognize that region-wide monetary integration, EMU-style, is at best many years away.

ICMB and CEPR are delighted to provide a forum for the authors to put forward this distinctive view of East Asian international financial policies. We are confident that it will be widely read and discussed. It should give policy-makers, academics and the informed public a more sophisticated understanding of these front-page issues.

Tommaso Padoa-Schioppa
Richard Portes

22 August 2005

Executive Summary

International reserves in seven East Asian economies stood at US$2.3trn at the end of 2004. This means that some 60% of total international reserves in the world economy were held by economies representing only about 40% of world GDP. In addition to being large, the reserve levels are likely to continue to increase in the coming years.

Is this accumulation of reserves the consequence of East Asia's high saving rate, deliberate undervaluation of currencies in the region leading to large current account surpluses, or is it due to the need for the United States to finance its external imbalance, or yet again to capital inflow in the region in anticipation of currency revaluations? Will appreciation of the renminbi and other East Asian currencies in itself be a solution to the Unites States' external imbalance? If not, what other policies would be helpful? What will happen to long term interest rates and G-3 exchange rates if East Asia, the United States and the EU do not make any policy changes? Will a more flexible exchange rate system in China lead to some diversification of international reserve holdings away from the US dollar towards the euro or the yen? These are the questions addressed in this report.

While it is beyond doubt that the level of reserves in the region is larger than most measures of reserve adequacy, we dispute the notion that the reserve build-up is driven by deliberately undervalued exchange rates. In fact, an examination of external payments data shows that the increase in reserves, particularly in China, has been due principally to FDI and speculative capital inflows and not only to current account surpluses. Countries with well-developed institutional investors might be able to turn such capital inflows around in the form of offsetting private capital outflows. However, in the absence of such capacity, it can be argued that it is appropriate for the authorities to intervene in the foreign exchange market to prevent a sharp appreciation that would have the potential to cause domestic deflationary pressures.

As a means to promote a better allocation of Asia's official reserves, we support the establishment of an Asian Investment Corporation. It would pool a portion of these reserves and manage them on commercial grounds as a national wealth fund. This fund would have greater freedom than is currently the case to invest in less liquid, longer-term and, where appropriate, Asian assets.

Data also show that the current account surplus in Asia and the deficit in the United States are associated with low investment rates in the former region (ex China) and a low saving rate in the latter. Reducing the current account deficit in the United States requires the national savings rate in this country to be increased. Exchange rate adjustment is not a particularly powerful method for bringing this about. From this it follows that appreciation of East Asia's currencies, including the renminbi, should not be viewed as the principal solution to global current account imbalances even if it might have a useful ancillary role to play. Moreover, the reform of the exchange rate regime in China has the potential to give the authorities more control over China's domestic economy by preserving the independence of interest rate policy and by preventing the dollar cycle from imparting inflationary and deflationary impulses to the domestic price level.

Regarding the composition of official reserves both in terms of currency and instrument, the report documents the dominance of the US dollar assets in such reserves, well beyond the relative size of the US economy. However, the report argues that, compared to the effective size of the dollar area (measured as that part of the world which has more stability in its dollar exchange rate), it was not excessive before the recent changes in the Chinese exchange rate regime. Although it is too early to be sure how the new Chinese exchange rate regime will function, if the renminbi effectively joins the already evident regional tendency for currencies to be managed relative to a basket of currencies, then the ground may be laid for some more diversification of official reserves out of the US dollar. This is due to more balanced investment portfolios producing less variable returns in domestic currency when the currency is managed against a basket of currencies.

What consequences will such diversification have for exchange rates and interest rates? The standard answer is that the dollar will weaken and the interest rates on long-term US government securities will increase as the demand for dollar assets, and Treasury paper in particular, declines. On closer scrutiny the answer is less certain, however. At the theoretical level the report shows that the impact on exchange rates and interest rates depends on how close substitutes euro (or yen) denominated assets are for dollar denominated assets. It also shows that reserve diversification on the part of, say, the People's Bank of China is analytically equivalent to sterilized interventions in the foreign exchange market by the European Central Bank or Japan's Ministry of Finance. Since it is often argued that such interventions are of only limited effectiveness, then reserve diversification, being analytically equivalent, would not be expected to have a large influence either. The existing empirical evidence is inconclusive.

Data on reserve composition shows that diversification has already taken place out of US Treasury bills into longer-dated US government and other obligations. It has been suggested that this increased demand for longer-dated securities through heavy central bank intervention may have served to hold down long-term interest rates. We review the evidence and find that it is also far from conclusive.

Our analysis suggests that the United States, the EU and East Asia could place the global economy on three possible trajectories of adjustments depending on how the three regions manage macroeconomic policies. One scenario is that East Asia grows out of its burgeoning trade surplus, which we suggest is unlikely. Another scenario involves the adoption of non-market solutions, obviously one that should be avoided at all cost. The report favours a third scenario. We argue that global coordination of expenditure-reducing/increasing policies and exchange rate adjustments between East Asia, the United States and the EU will be necessary to achieve the least-cost adjustment to the current account imbalance between the three. To this end this report proposes another Plaza Accord among the three regions for policy adjustments and co-ordination.

Monetary policy in East Asia is already quite accommodative, so it cannot be expected to take the lead in stimulating domestic demand. Fiscal policy, for its part, is subject to long-term constraints in the largest Asian economies. Exchange rate adjustments alone will be only of limited value, however useful they may be in monetary terms.

This of course does not mean that East Asian economies should sit on the sidelines. They should step up their market oriented structural and institutional reform that will lead to more reliance on domestic demand for growth and will facilitate direct integration of the private sector into the global financial system.

Coordination of policy among East Asia, the United States and the EU may be difficult in practical terms, but efforts in this regard will help diffuse the pressure of those supporting the non-market solutions. If nothing else, this should concentrate policy-makers' minds on changes that pose difficulties form a national perspective but that help relieve the risks inherent in an ongoing widening of imbalances.

Looking further into the future, the report examines the prospects for Asian monetary integration and argues that region-wide monetary unification is far off since the three largest economies – China, Japan and South Korea – are unlikely to relinquish domestic monetary independence. However, this does not mean that countries in East Asia will retreat from their pursuit of monetary integration. They could certainly expand and consolidate the Chiang Mai Initiative as a regional liquidity support system and a regional forum for policy dialogues as they have agreed to do. This strengthening of the system may in the long run reduce the demand for reserves for self-insurance in the region and keep East Asia's initiative for regional financial and monetary integration alive.

China's and Malaysia's prospective management of their effective exchange rate will bring their practice in line with that of their neighbours and permit closer coordination of monetary and exchange rate policy in the region. With East Asian exchange rates now all reacting to each other, currency appreciation poses less risk of a loss of competitiveness or deflation to an individual economy. China has the ability, as well as an interest, to join discussions that facilitate broadly joint exchange rate moves. In the absence of comprehensive monetary cooperation, the economies, small as well as large, in the region may find it in their interest to deepen their policy dialogue to take full account of the repercussions of monetary and exchange rate policies on each other.

1 Introduction and Summary

This 7th *Geneva Report on the World Economy* focuses on the recent rapid build-up of official reserves in Asia, its relationship with current account imbalances and exchange rate policies in East Asian countries, and the implications of reserve management for exchange rates and interest rates. A great deal has been written on these subjects recently, much of it from the perspective of the sustainability of the current account deficit of the United States. Our focus is more on the motivations and constraints facing East Asian countries, but the necessary equality between deficits and their financing implies views on how global imbalances can best be redressed.

We start in Chapter 2 by reviewing the size of official reserve holdings in East Asia. It is well known that these reserves are very large relative to traditional measures of reserve adequacy. Such measures are, however, not necessarily appropriate as they do not take into account the insurance motive for holding reserves, an important consideration in East Asia following the crisis in 1997–8. Nevertheless, even adjusting for such a motive, it is difficult to rationalize the sharp build-up in recent years as the pursuit of a particular level of reserves rather than as a by-product of other policies.

The chapter goes on to argue, however, that official reserve holdings should not be judged independently of the balance sheet position of the countries as a whole. If for institutional or other reasons, the private sector is not able to channel foreign asset accumulation into foreign securities, it may be appropriate for the official sector to do so in its place. This is particularly the case when foreign exchange inflows are the consequence of capital account surpluses. An appropriate response to external capital inflows that are driven by temporary expectations of a currency appreciation may be to accumulate external claims rather than to permit an unmanaged real appreciation. When the private sector is not allowed to perform, or is otherwise incapable of performing, this function, the central bank can do it as its agent.

We thus dispute the notion that the reserve build-up in the region is driven by deliberately undervalued exchange rates. From this it follows that even successful pressure on the accumulating countries, in particular China, to revalue their currencies is unlikely to accomplish its stated aim. That is, taken in isolation, Asian currency appreciation will narrow the current account imbalance between the United States and the rest of the world to only a limited extent. Moreover, pushed to the extremes argued for by some of its proponents, a large effective appreciation may lead a country that follows it into a deflationary trap much like that which Japan has been caught in since the sharp appreciation of the yen in the mid 1990s.

From this perspective we discuss the implications of the exchange rate reform measures announced by the People's Bank of China on 21 July 2005. The reforms entailed a 2% immediate appreciation of the renminbi relative to the US dollar, the move to a basket-based exchange rate policy, and the possibility of gradual adjustment in the value of the basket. Since the greater flexibility of the exchange rate and the basket-based policy will permit greater scope for macroeconomic stabilization policies, we welcome them from a domestic perspective. We point out, however, that the measures are unlikely by themselves to solve the current account imbalance between Asia and the United States, even if they lead other Asian countries to permit more appreciation of their dollar exchange rates and thereby lead to a significant effective depreciation of the US dollar. Finally, we caution that there are still risks that speculative capital inflows into China will persist. In fact, it may be argued that some technical aspects of the measures, notably the ± 0.3% intraday trading rate of the renminbi vis-à-vis the US dollar, could encourage even greater capital inflows than before.

In Chapter 3 we turn to the composition of official reserves in terms of both currency and instrument. We document the dominance of the US dollar in the currency composition, but argue that compared with the effective size of the dollar area (measured as that part of the world which keeps the dollar exchange rate stable), it was not excessive before the recent changes in the Chinese exchange rate regime. Although it is too early to be sure how the Chinese authorities will manage their system, if the renminbi joins the already evident regional tendency for currencies to be more stable in effective than in bilateral dollar terms, then the ground may be laid for some more diversification of official reserves out of the US dollar.

One of the concerns that have been raised in connection with the large reserve holdings of Asian central banks, is the potential consequences of a significant diversification of these reserves away from the US dollar towards the euro. It is often asserted as obvious that such diversification would have major effects on exchange rates. Yet it is also assumed, sometimes by the same individuals, that sterilized intervention in the foreign exchange market by the Fed, the ECB or Japan's Ministry of Finance (MoF) will not have appreciable impacts on exchange rates in view of the huge volume of transactions in the private sector. We show that diversification of Asian central banks and sterilized intervention by the Fed, ECB or the Japanese MoF are equivalent in their impact on balance sheets. Thus, the effect of each on exchange rates should therefore be the same. The empirical evidence in studies of this question is inconclusive as to what exactly this effect is.

A less known development is the increasing duration of official reserve portfolios which has come about as a result of diversification out of short-term US Treasury bills into longer-dated US government and other obligations. It has been suggested that this increased demand for longer-dated securities through heavy central bank intervention may have served to hold down long-term interest rates. We review the evidence and conclude that it is far from conclusive.

The topic of Chapter 4 is what we call the trans-Pacific imbalance, namely the current account deficit in the United States and the surplus in East Asia. Although this imbalance has neither been significantly larger nor shown a particularly different time pattern from the imbalance between the United States and the rest of the world, it has received a lot of recent attention. Arguably it is the proximate reason for legislative proposals in the US Senate to impose across-the-board tariffs on goods from China, as well as for the pressures from US officials on the Chinese authorities to reform their exchange rate system.

We show that a global coordination of policies to either reduce or increase expenditure will be necessary to achieve the least-cost adjustment to the current account imbalance between the United States, East Asia, and Europe. If such policies are implemented, real exchange rate adjustments will follow. We also argue, and present supporting evidence, that the converse is not true, i.e. autonomous exchange rate adjustments are not effective as a solution for the imbalances, and they are potentially damaging for economic growth in East Asia and elsewhere. Furthermore the frequent calls for such adjustments are in fact a significant reason for recent reserve build-ups in the region. Finally, the use of trade embargoes and tariffs as a surrogate for fundamental economic adjustments is also likely to be very costly for the world economy.

While greater domestic demand in East Asia – particularly in Japan and China – would be helpful from the perspective of narrowing current account imbalances and slowing the growth of official reserves, constraints related to budgetary positions (Japan) and demographic factors (China) have limited the scope and effectiveness of fiscal policy actions. The use of monetary policy to stimulate domestic real expenditures has likewise been hampered by the zero interest rate bound in Japan and the concern for asset price inflation elsewhere.

Until the recent change in China's exchange rate system, the extent of exchange rate adjustments in East Asia had been restrained by the fear that an appreciation vis-à-vis the US dollar, and hence vis-à-vis the renminbi, would lead to a loss of competitiveness relative to China. To be sure, some currencies, notably the South Korean won and the Thai baht, had been allowed to appreciate, but the fixed RMB/US$ rate had put a brake on the size of the adjustments. With the greater flexibility of the renminbi, it is likely that other currencies in the region will also see larger movements with respect to the US dollar as they follow, at least partly, the fluctuations of the Chinese currency. In this way East Asia will contribute to the adjustment that will be necessary if the trans-pacific imbalance is to be reduced. It is now incumbent on the other side of the imbalance, the United States, to make expenditure policy adjustments that complement the currency adjustments in East Asia.

The report ends with a brief assessment of what monetary and financial arrangements in Asia may look like in the long term future when the current controversies have been resolved and when China's renminbi has become a freely convertible currency. Using the process of monetary unification in Europe as an example we argue that a comprehensive monetary union in East Asia is unlikely. The yen, the won, and the renminbi are likely to remain independent currencies for the foreseeable future. In view of increasing economic and political ties between Mainland China, Hong Kong and Taiwan, it is probable that the Hong Kong dollar and the new Taiwan dollar will be tightly linked with the renminbi. The fate of the other currencies in the region – in particular those of Indonesia, the Philippines, Singapore and Thailand – will depend in part on the experience with the policy of inflation targeting that these countries are currently engaged in. If this policy strategy delivers sustained economic growth combined with price stability with no more attention to the exchange rate than in New Zealand or the United Kingdom, support for far-reaching changes in currency areas may be limited. If, on the other hand, management of the currency is thought to be necessary to attain stable and low inflation and other domestic objectives, it is possible that some form of currency cooperation in South East Asia, possibly with China, will become a reality. Judging by the time it took for the euro to be created, the currency map of the region will still contain many small currencies for the foreseeable future. But then again, perhaps East Asia will surprise the rest of the world also in the area of monetary unification, as it has in so many other areas of economic development.

2 Asia's Reserve Accumulation: Description, Causes and Dangerous Remedies

2.1 Introduction

Asian central bank reserves have grown far and fast in five years. At the end of 2004, the combined foreign exchange reserves of six Asian countries, including the reserves of the Hong Kong Monetary Authority, stood at $2,355bn[1]. There is a popular narrative that puts Asia's accumulation of foreign exchange reserves at the heart of today's large global imbalances, previously characterized by the twin deficits in the United States. According to this story, Asian governments are keeping their exchange rates undervalued in pursuit of export led growth (Dooley et al., 2003). Through various policy targets and mechanisms, the authorities in Asia are selling local currency for foreign exchange, boosting their reserves. Were it not for this activity, the story goes, Asian exchange rates would appreciate and Asia's current account surpluses would disappear, reducing their counterpart - the record US current account deficit. The implication is that this 'Asian mercantilism' is against the spirit of the open trading system and a force restraining aggregate demand in the world economy.

This increasingly dominant story also suggests that as long as Asian countries are intent on an export-led strategy, which hinges on pegging their exchange rates to the dollar at undervalued levels and sterilizing the monetary impact of the resulting trade surpluses, they will accumulate US dollar reserves and in so doing, finance US deficits. Large global imbalances are therefore more sustainable than traditionally envisaged. US deficits are merely the endogenous response of markets to excess-savings in Asia and the rest of the world (Bernanke, 2005). Many investors have lost money interpreting the US current account deficit as a signal to sell dollars. They think they have been unlucky, but they may just be wrong.

An off-shoot of this narrative is that this Asian mercantilism is also against Asia's best interests. It does not make sense for fast-growing but relatively poor countries to lend cheaply to the richest country in the world (Wolf, 2005). Yet this is effectively what happens when the central bank of an emerging economy builds up dollar reserves beyond what may be required to provide financial security. It is therefore in everyone's interests, so the story concludes, that Asian governments are weaned off undervalued exchange rates.

If moral suasion does not persuade Asian governments to significantly change their exchange rate arrangements[2], some argue that it is justifiable to resort to more formal mechanisms designed to inhibit what they have branded as market manipulation (Preeg, 2003; Bergsten, 2005). Indeed, the question of Asia's accumulation of dollar reserves has become a politically live issue. The stakes are high. China is threatened by Congressional bills that would place stiff tariffs on its exports to the United States if the renminbi does not appreciate significantly versus the dollar[3].

There is a danger that the politics is clouding the analysis. This chapter asks whether what we observe in Asia fits these popular stories, especially with regards to reserves, exchange rates and current account positions. In Section 2.2, we describe the reserve build up in Asia. In Section 2.3, we look at its causes. We find that the popular narrative, described above, is seriously lacking as a description and explanation for the reserve build up in Asia and, as we discuss in Section 2.4, for global imbalances. In Section 2.4, and discussed elsewhere in this report we look at some alternative remedies, where we feel remedies are required for today's imbalances.

We recognise that external pressures on Asian countries to revalue their exchange rates substantially is likely to persist. The timing of China's abandonment of its ten-year peg to the dollar on 21 July 2005 may well have reflected this pressure. We note that, if Asia's reserves are not driven by exchange rate undervaluation, the very large revaluations proposed by some observers could have largely unforeseen deflationary consequences for Asia directly and the rest of the world indirectly. There is a real danger that emerging Asia could end up being pushed down the same economic path travelled by Japan over the past ten years. We touch on these issues in Section 2.5 and return to discuss policy options in greater detail in Chapter 4.

2.2 Description

2.2.1 Accelerating accumulation

The accumulation of official reserves has been concentrated in Asia and the pace of reserve build up in Asia has not only been rapid, but it is accelerating. Just a single decade ago, the seven Asian central banks we have referred to earlier held \$509bn in central bank reserves, or just 36% of global central bank reserves. More than 50% of the rise in reserves over the past ten years occurred since 2002, see Figure 2.1 and Table 2.1. If this pace of reserve accumulation were to continue Asian reserves would represent over 75% of global reserves within five years[4].

Figure 2.1 Combined foreign exchange reserves of seven Asian countries and share of global reserves, 1995–2005

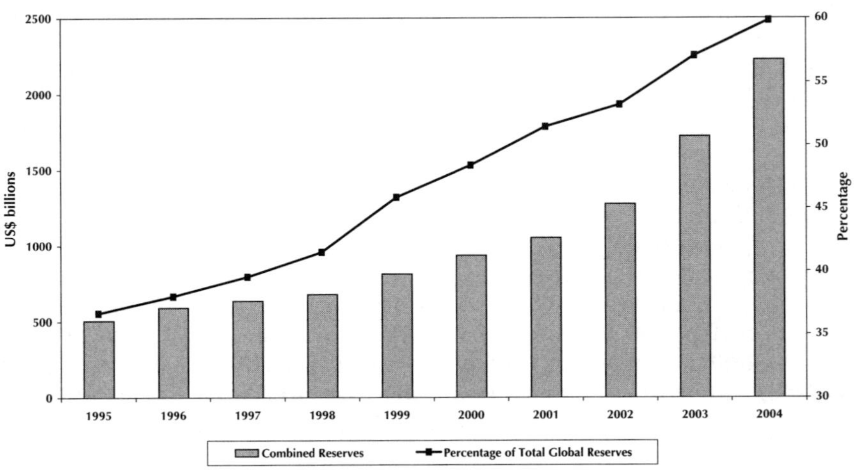

Source: IMF.

In Asia, the accumulation of reserves has been further concentrated in just two countries: Japan and China. For analytical purposes, we believe the reserve accumulation in Asia is best broken down into three groupings: Japan in a group of its own, China and Hong Kong in a second group and South Korea, Singapore, Taiwan and India in a third. (This last group, minus India, is similar to the Newly Industrialized Asian Economies classification used by the IMF.) These three groups have a different 'story' in terms of exchange rate arrangements so it is interesting that they have a remarkably similar profile in their reserve accumulation (see FIgure 2.2).

Figure 2.2 Foreign exchange reserves of three Asian groups, 1995–2005

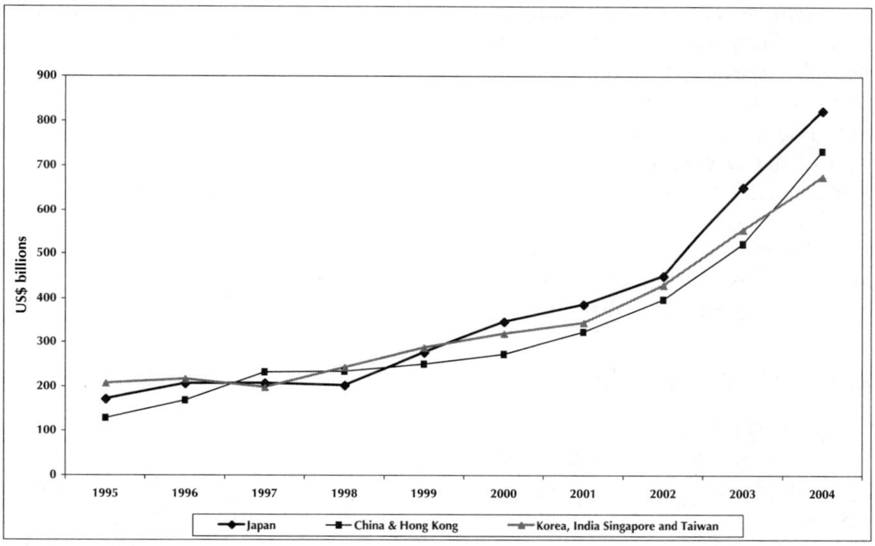

Source: IMF.

Table 2.1 Gross international reserves of selected countries ($bn)

		2001	2002	2003	2004
China	level	212.6	286.4	403.2	609.3
	change	+47.1	+74.8	+116.8	+206.1
Taiwan	level	122.2	161.7	206.6	241.7
	change	+16.5	+39.6	+45.1	+35.1
Korea	level	102.7	121.3	155.2	198.8
	change	+6.6	+18.6	+33.9	+43.6
India	level	51.0	71.9	107.5	134.5
	change	+11.5	+20.9	+35.6	+27.0
Total	level	445.4	641.3	872.5	1184.3
	change	+81.7	+153.9	+231.4	+311.8

Source: Asian Development Outlook, 2005, ADB.

2.3 Causes of the reserve build up

2.3.1 Reserve build-up and exchange rate arrangements

While the narrative about Asia's reserves is focused on emerging Asian economies with 'fixed' exchange rates, the largest single accumulation of reserves has occurred in Japan, a mature economy, without a formal exchange rate peg. Indeed, while all six countries could be considered to have managed exchange rates, only China and Hong Kong had formal pegs to the dollar over this period. Only Hong Kong is left with a dollar-peg today. The others are increasingly following both the dollar and the yen, and to a lesser extent the euro. As mentioned before, the rise in reserves does not appear to be very sensitive to the specific exchange rate arrangements, see Figures 2.2 and 2.3.

A critical element of the 'Asian mercantilist' story is that Asia's accumulation of reserves comes directly from countries linking their currencies to the dollar at undervalued levels, which generates trade surpluses. It is interesting therefore that the sharp rise in reserves since 2002 increasingly outstrips the rise in trade surpluses. The ratio of reserve accumulation to trade-surpluses is over 2 in most countries, and has been growing strongly. Trade surpluses, therefore, are not the main motor behind the recent acceleration in reserves. In 2004, they accounted for just 32% of the rise in reserves in China, see Figure 2.4[5]. In China's case, the accumulation of reserves is accounted for in part by foreign direct investment (FDI), but increasingly by 'hot money' inflows – short-term capital flows to some extent chasing an expected revaluation in the renminbi.

2.3.2 Japan and deflation

Japan slipped into deflation (falling prices) in 1995 and again from 1999 to now. Deflation is bad for real assets, but it is good for paper assets like currency and bonds. Under a deflationary environment, a ¥1000 note would buy more real assets over time. The risk is that consumers defer their spending till later when their currency can buy more. Until recently most Japanese companies have devoted their cash flow to reducing their debt rather than investing. This has tended to slow current economic activity, reduce imports and improve the current account. If Japan manages to escape from its long deflationary period it will be in large part because its households have recently reduced their saving rate.

Deflation increased the attractiveness of the yen. Moreover, whenever it looked as if Japan would resurface from deflation, international equity investors would buy Japanese equities to return to their benchmark weights on Japan. If the authorities had stood by and let capital inflows drive the yen higher, this would have added to deflationary pressures by depressing import prices and ironically undermined the recovery story that global investors were buying into. More deflation could easily have led firms to attempt to reduce debt further. The authorities thus sold yen against the dollar, stabilizing its price and, as a consequence, building up foreign exchange reserves. Japan's trade and current account surpluses therefore were not a sign that the yen should be revalued, but rather a symptom of the diversion of corporate cash flows to debt repayment and accompanying deflation., Exchange rate stabilization was argued as the appropriate response by many economists and implicitly accepted by trading partners.

Figure 2.3 Foreign exchange reserve build-up in two exchange rate arragement groups, 1995–2005

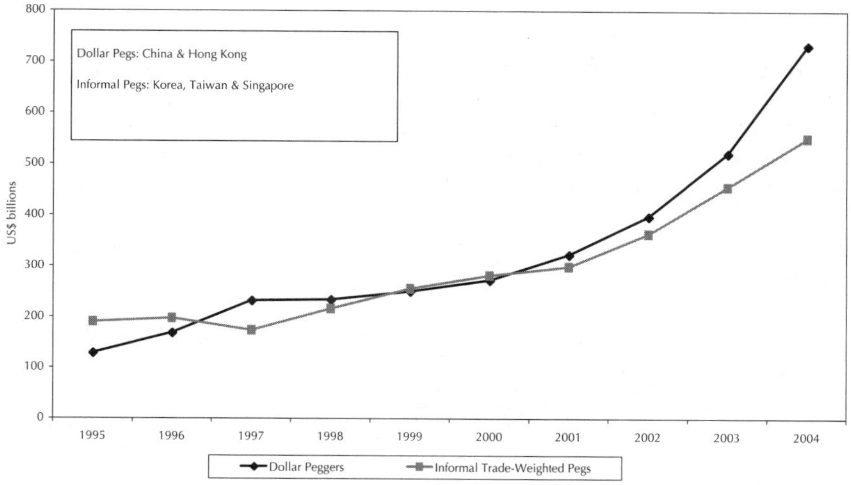

Source: IMF.

Figure 2.4 Ratio of China's annual change in reserves and annual trade ratio, 2000–2004

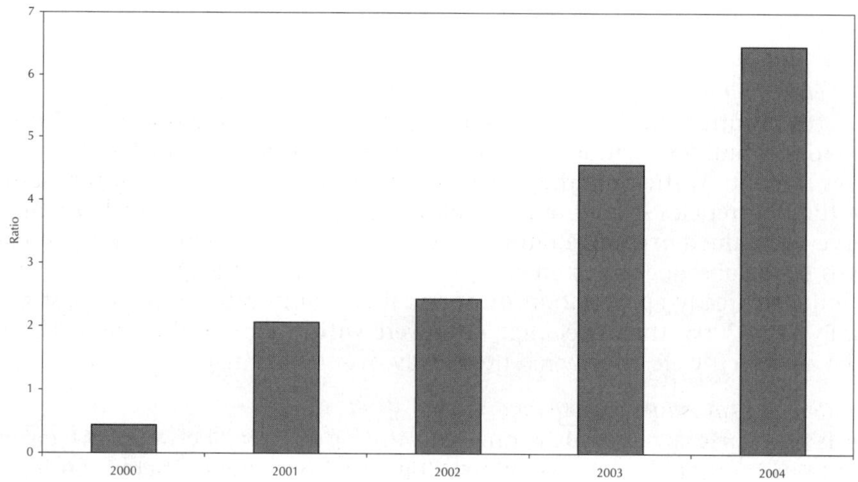

Sources: IMF; PRC General Administration of Customs.

2.3.3 The Newly Industrialized Asian Emerging Economies

The image conjured up by the allegation of exchange rate manipulation is one of countries forcing down the value of their currencies, or locking them in at levels widely considered undervalued. For example, US Treasury Secretary Rubin's adoption of the mantra that 'the US believes in a strong dollar' in June 1995 was in response to the widespread view that the US was manipulating its exchange rate lower through verbal intervention in order to support the economy. This view contributed to the dollar hitting record lows against European currencies in March 1995 well after the US economic recovery had begun. A European example of 'manipulation' might be the mini-devaluation of the Irish punt shortly before the irrevocable fixing of exchange rates for European Monetary Union in 1999. Asia's exchange rate history does not fit this image.

2.3.3.1 Emerging Asia's exchange rate history prior to 1997

While Asian policy makers are often seen as having a pathological addiction to export growth, it is important to recognize that the current policy orientation is relatively recent and in part a response to the failure of what happened before. Before the Asian financial crisis, the Asian Tigers, or the Newly Industrialized Asian Economies[6] had pursued a domestic investment orientation to economic growth. They enjoyed high investment rates and large investment flows from overseas which, in many cases, contributed to overvalued exchange rates and trade deficits, see Table 2.2.

Table 2.2 Current account positions of the crisis countries prior to the Asian Crisis as % of GDP

	1995	1996	1997
Korea	-2.0	-4.9	-4.8
Taiwan	-2.1	+4.0	+2.7
Hong Kong, SAR	-3.9	-1.1	-3.2
Singapore	+16.8	+15.7	+15.4
Malaysia	-10.0	-4.9	-4.8
Indonesia	-3.3	-3.3	-1.8
Thailand	-7.9	-7.9	-2.0
Philippines	-4.4	-4.7	-3.9

Source: IMF World Economic Outlook, May & October, 1998.

2.3.3.2 Emerging Asia's exchange rates post-1997

It is worth pointing out that the devaluations of 1997–8 were not desired policy devaluations, but devaluations that were forced upon these countries when their reserves ran out. At the time they were chastised in some quarters for not 'letting go' of their currencies sooner rather than using up reserves in a failed attempt to preserve overvalued exchange rates. The crisis economies where the central bank reserves have subsequently risen sharply – South Korea, Singapore and Taiwan – have enjoyed steady appreciation in nominal exchange rates over the past three years. By June 2005, their exchange rates were within 25% of their pre-crisis levels – levels which were considered hopelessly overvalued in 1997.

2.3.3.3 Savings-investment imbalance

There is of course a national income accounting identity between the current account position (or net exports) and savings less investment. There is an important distinction to be made however between the trade surplus being rooted in an increase in savings or a decrease in investment and what may have caused those changes. If local and global welfare were the main considerations and a trade surplus arose as a result of a recession which reduced imports, boosting aggregate demand would be a far better policy response than revaluing the exchange rate.

Another important observation that does not fit with the Asian mercantilist story is that Asia's current account surpluses have been associated with a post-crisis decline in investment rates as a percent of GDP while savings rates have remained relatively stable or have even declined (Figures 2.5 and 2.6). This is especially the case for the Newly Industrialized Asian economies. (In China in contrast the investment rate has gone up, chasing a rizing savings rate and raising questions about the quality of the investment). In this group of countries it is possible to explain the investment short-fall by the overhang of surplus capacity following

Figure 2.5a Investment rates relative to 1995 values

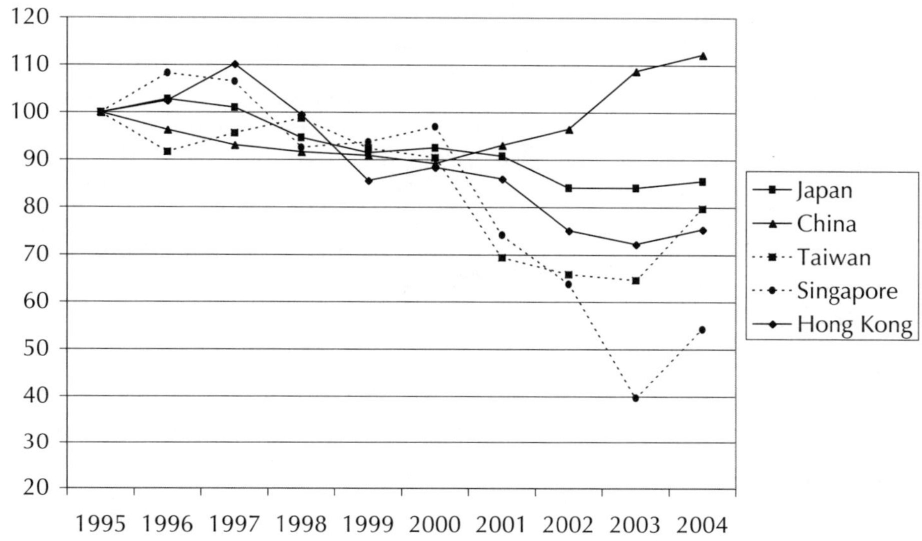

Figure 2.5b Investment rates relative to 1995 values

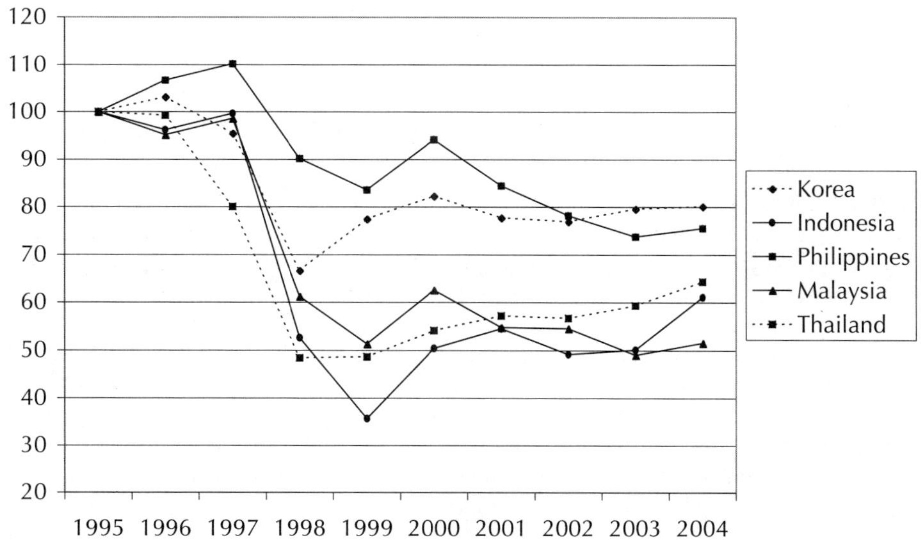

Figure 2.6a Savings rates relative to 1995 values

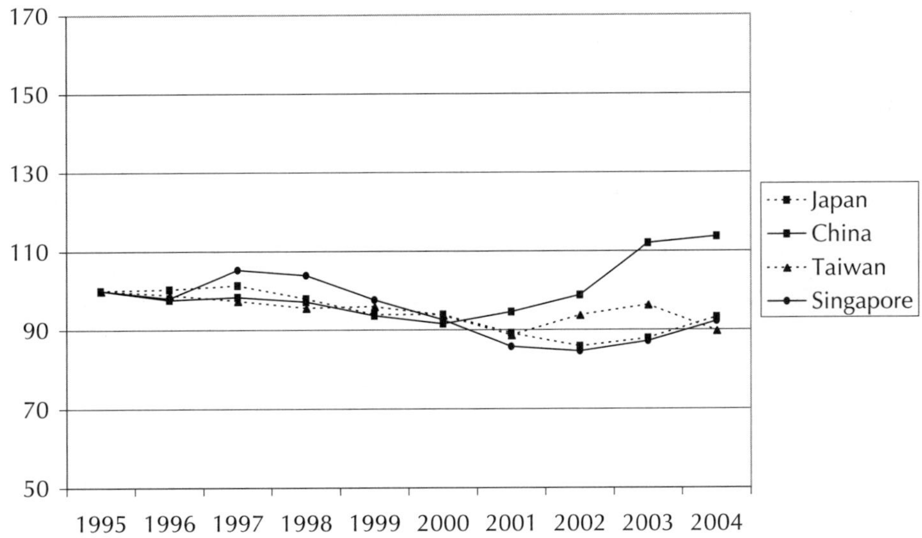

Figure 2.6b Savings rates relative to 1995 values

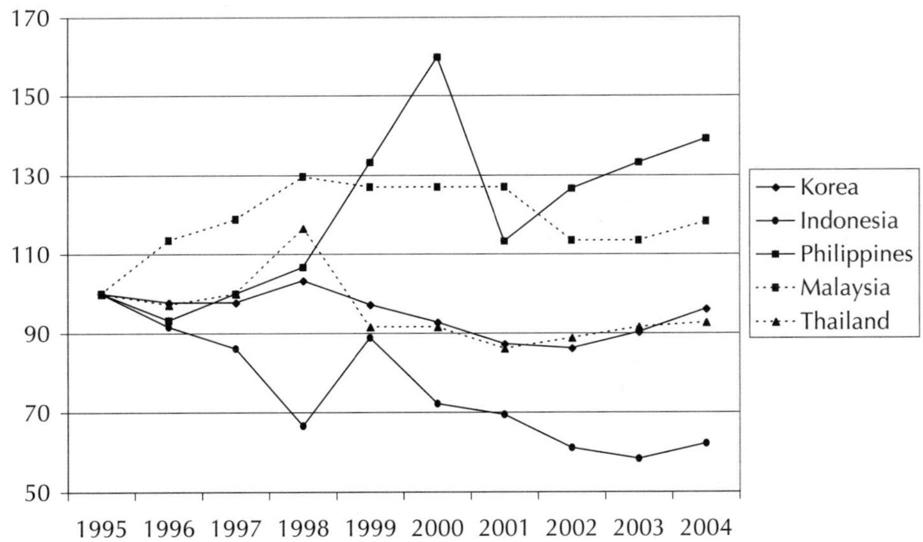

the mid-1990s investment boom, a post-crisis global recession and strong economic uncertainty. Weakness in domestic investment normally points to overvalued, not undervalued, exchange rates.

In a mature financial system it is not automatic, and arguably a little perverse, to revalue the exchange rate in response to this fall-off in domestic investment. What we would expect to see is that the surplus on the current account would be offset by an outflow on the capital account as the private sector exports excess domestic savings abroad. For whatever reason, Asian countries do not yet have mature financial systems and institutions, including regulatory institutions, which would permit the easy re-cycling of current account surpluses into capital account exports. (It is an open question whether India or China for example are ready for an aggressive easing of capital controls).[7] Consequently, the public sector has performed an intermediation function.

The national balance sheets in both Asia and Europe reflect an increase in overseas assets in response to the domestic investment short-fall, but in Asia, with under-developed financial markets, this is achieved by the public sector building official foreign currency reserves, not the private sector building up private foreign currency assets.

2.3.4 China

2.3.4.1 'Hot money'.

An increasing proportion of the reserve build up in China relates to the neutralizing of 'hot money' inflows and foreign direct investment, see Table 2.3. Over the ten years in which the renminbi was pegged at 8.28, it was only in the last two and a half years that market expectations priced-in a revaluation (in the renminbi non-deliverable forwards). Up to 2000, the market had consistently priced in a devaluation of up to 20% in the middle of the Asian Financial Crisis. The market, now convinced that the renminbi may revalue significantly, did not think so just a few years ago.

Table 2.3 Approximate 'hot money' inflows into China ($bn)

	Reserve increase	less FDI	less current account	= Hot money
2004	206	60	70	+76
2003	117	53	45	+19
2002	74	52	35	-13
2001	47	46	17	-16

Source: ADB Annual Outlook, 2005.

Between 2001 and 2004 there was little change in the trade surplus to trigger this change in sentiment. One change was the decline of US dollar interest rates against the backdrop of stable renminbi interest rates which made renminbi assets more attractive. But on top of this came expectations, especially after the Dubai G-7 meeting of September 2003 that at some point the Chinese authorities would allow a large revaluation of the renminbi. These expectations led the Chinese corporate sector to repatriate dollars and to borrow dollars in order to delay payment for imports and accelerate receipts form exports. To some extent, the reserve build up that is increasingly used as the reason why Asian countries in general, and China in particular, should revalue significantly has been driven by this external discussion of a revaluation. The history of the Japanese yen between 1985-1995 shows a similar nexus between external political pressure for revaluation, hot money inflows and either exchange rate appreciation or further political pressure to which we return in Section 2.5.

2.3.4.2 FDI and the Dutch disease

In terms of foreign direct investment flows, what China is experiencing is analogous to the 'Dutch disease'. In the late 1950s, natural gas was discovered in the North Sea off the coast of the Netherlands. The expected long-run increase in GNP caused upward pressure on asset prices, including the currency which was eventually revalued in 1960. However, because the benefits of the gas discovery took some time to come, the revaluation caused not just a switch in investment from the 'on-shore' to the 'off-shore' oil economy, it caused a net decline in current activity as Dutch manufacturers failed to compete with the stronger exchange rate.[8]

The lesson is that where exchange rates 'overshoot' as a result of the mis-match between fast moving asset markets and slow moving goods markets, accommodating upward pressure on the exchange rate could lead to a downturn in economic activity.

Access to China's army of cheap labour provides superior return on capital for foreign companies. This causes a scramble today to own those future income streams. FDI is 'front-loaded', but the higher income stream that would support the flood of FDI today will only arrive after some time. (Indeed, for a while, China developed a reputation amongst corporate treasurers as a place where the logic of investing was obvious but profits were quite elusive.) In this context, an exchange rate appreciation would reduce current activity in favour of future expected activity. One solution to this problem is to limit the exchange rate response to this capital inflow through sterilization, or at least partial sterilization, of FDI.

2.3.4.3 China and sterilization

There is a difference between speculative capital flows and persistent trade surpluses. Most would agree that the former, which represents almost half of the reserve build up in 2004, should be sterilized, and the latter, which represents just a third of the reserve build up, should not. Critics argue that by sterilizing its 'intervention' to maintain its dollar-renminbi peg, China was not following a classical fixed exchange rate system where trade-balances affect the money supply and inflation so that the real-exchange rate adjusts. Sterilization, not so much the peg, is evidence of the export orientation they say (Wolf, 2005). However, these issues are not as straight forward as they may first seem which is why most countries, including Japan and the United States, tend to sterilize any intervention as a matter of course.

Operating a fixed-exchange rate system makes sense for an open, emerging economy, but this does not mean that domestic monetary conditions must be allowed to reflect volatile capital flows. It would seem to us that it is right for China to sterilize hot money inflows. It may also be right to sterilize part of its FDI.

2.4 Asian exchange rates and global imbalances

Much pressure on China to revalue its exchange rate was applied in the name of reducing global imbalances[9]. But the protagonists could never offer an economic model that showed how a revaluation of the renminbi would do that. In fact, most general equilibrium models of the world economy concur that a revaluation of the renminbi, on its own, would only have a minor impact on the US current account deficit[10]. In addition there is a matter of arithmetic; China is simply too small to be responsible for US deficits or to be able to correct them. Journalists like to regale us with stories of the 700% rise in Chinese shoe exports this year following the scrapping of the old quotas, but these high percentage growth rates hide the fact that China is starting from a low base, and while it dominates in a number of low margin sectors, it is virtually absent from others.

To capture the full dynamics of current developments it is perhaps useful to put them in a slightly longer time perspective. The period from the Asian financial crisis in 1997 to date witnessed a deterioration of the US current account deficit by $529bn. We might expect that after the collapse of many exchange rates in Asia during the crisis that there would be an offsetting rise in Asia's current account surplus. Indeed, the Newly Industrialized Asian Economies improved their current account position by $124.8bn since 1997, or just 23.5% of the US deterioration. This is significant relative to the small economic size of this group of countries and reflects their shift from domestic to export orientation over this period, but it is less than a quarter of the deterioration of the US deficit. Over the same period, China's current account position improved by $35.6bn, or just 7% of the deterioration in the US position (see Table 2.4). This is small in absolute terms but also when considering that China's share of world GDP-ex-US is 16.7%.

Table 2.4 Changes in current account balances, 1997–2004

	$bn	% of US	% of world GDP ex US
United States	-529.0	100.0	26.4
NIAE* + China	+160.5	30.2	21.1
Russia + Mid. East	+160.0	30.1	6.7
NIAE	+124.8	23.5	4.4
Middle East	+103.0	19.4	3.5
Japan	+75.2	14.2	8.7
Latin America	+72.6	13.7	9.5
Euro area	-64.1	-12.1	19.3
Russia	+57.0	10.7	3.2
China	+35.7	6.7	16.7
India	+5.1	0.9	7.4

Notes: *Newly Industrialized Asian Economies.
Source: IMF World Economic Outlook, May 2005.

Where is the equal off-set? Between 1997 and 2004, the major oil exporters of the Middle-East and Russia saw an improvement in their current account positions of $160bn, equivalent to 31% of the deterioration in the US deficit. This is substantially higher than this group's 6% share of world GDP-ex-US. Add Latin America, another region dominated by commodity exporters and the current account improvement by this group of commodity exporters accounts for $231bn or 44% of the deterioration of the current account position in the Unted States, even though this group's GDP was only 16% of the world-ex-US.

2.4.1 Causes of global imbalances

If currency adjustments on their own are ill-suited as cures of current account imbalances, it follows that currency misalignments are unlikely causes, as opposed to consequences, thereof. Global imbalances are better thought of as the result of the relationship between monetary and fiscal policy, on the one hand, and private investment and consumption, on the other.

The current account deficit in the United States is equal to the excess of spending over income, which in turn relates in part to a loose fiscal and monetary stance. Initially, the excess spending was due to private investment in the dot com boom of 1998–2000. In the wonderful vision of hindsight, the bust would have been less traumatic if the boom had been more contained. Following the dotcom crash, the adjustment to national spending that we might have expected to witness was offset by substantial fiscal and monetary boosts. Over time low interest rates began to support asset markets and the financial system convinced the personal sector to borrow and to consume on the back of higher asset prices.

This excess spending creates a current account deficit that puts US dollars in the hands of foreigners.. They have a choice of how to use these dollars. They could spend them today, in part buying US goods and narrowing the deficit, or they could spend tomorrow and save today by buying overseas assets instead. The propensity to spend as opposed to save would depend on three factors: (1) the quality of investment opportunities at home; (2) the concern policy makers have for domestic over-heating; and (3) the degree of consumers' risk aversion, determined in part by factors such as ageing, the structure of social security systems, unemployment, recent calamities, etc.

In the case of China, the authorities have faced the dilemma posed by a high and rising private savings rate. Either investment spending must grow at breakneck speed, raising questions about the quality of the investment, the risk of rising non-performing loans and thus financial stability. Or investment spending lags behind and the excess saving is vented to the rest of the world in the form of a trade surplus. The Chinese are following the second route.

As a consequence of some or all three of the factors listed above, Asian emerging market economies chose largely to invest their surplus dollars in foreign assets. Because the financial markets are under-developed in these economies, the intermediation has been effected by central banks who have invested their reserves in what they know best as liquidity managers: low-risk, high-liquidity assets, mostly dollar-denominated. An Asian central bank buying a US mortgage-backed security or agency note epitomises the overall flow. In this way, excess-spending and trade deficits in the United States are sustained while US private liabilities and foreign official assets rise.[11]

There are some moralizing arguments about who is really to blame and what is exogenous or not. The key question, however, is what exactly is wrong with the current financial arrangements and what should be done about them.

2.4.2 Problems and possible remedies

We see two problems, neither of which are best alleviated by exchange rate changes. The first is whether emerging market economies should run surpluses and own foreign assets when there are better returns to domestic investment. The traditional model is that emerging markets are opportunity-rich and capital-poor and so international capital should finance trade deficits. Rich, more slowly growing economies should be the ones sending capital to provide better returns for their pensioners. While this makes sense in theory, the traditional model has never worked very well in practice, principally because of the fickleness of international capital. Investors exhibit regular large swings in risk appetite that often lead international capital flows to stop and reverse in an undiscerning manner.[12]

Emerging market surpluses can be seen as testament to the distrust of this traditional system. However, it is not clear that this second-best solution is faring badly. We are experiencing an unprecedented period of strong growth in emerging markets with greater stability than is often observed. High growth rates have led to tight supply conditions for commodities. Amid capacity constraints in Asia, it would be a brave economist to say that emerging markets would be unambiguously better off by spending more and increasing their dependence on international capital markets.

If there is an appetite for improving the efficiency of the self-insurance route that emerging economies are essentially following, it is through the creation of more international pooling arrangements. This tends to be thought of regionally and to involve regional political objectives, but of course this is not good insurance as crises are often regional in nature[13]. In general, regions and countries should consider pooling arrangements with their neighbours, but also with regions and countries that offer offsetting risks. On this view, oil exporters should consider pooling reserves with oil-importers; manufacturing exporters should pool with service exporters, etc..

The second, more pressing, problem with the global financial system is growing macro-prudential concerns. At the level of individuals, in the United States, or of surplus emerging market economies, balance sheets have seldom looked better. The wealth-to-income ratio of US households has climbed to 5.4, not far from its peak value of 6.2 in 1999 and above its long-run (1960–2003) average of 4.8. In Asian emerging markets, official reserves now cover around 12 months of imports, up from six months just two years ago[14]. But there is a tremendous concentration of risks in US property and the financial flows surrounding it. If that market turned, it could take a toll on consumption and financial institutions' risk-taking. Any US monetary policy loosening in response, could lower local currency returns on official reserves.

There are three remedies that should be considered. The first is a balanced array of macroeconomic and structural changes in major economies. Further US monetary policy tightening may serve to moderate asset valuations and help to keep investors discerning about the projects they finance. Fiscal and other policy changes in Asia are discussed in Chapter 4. Structural changes in Europe and Japan that raise the long-run growth potential are needed as well, though their near-term effects could prove perverse.

The second remedy is that emerging markets split their reserves into two, a liquidity portfolio and a separate national wealth portfolio. The latter would operate with a a diverse benchmark of currencies, liquidity and credits to beat. By diversifying their assets they are likely to improve returns and reduce risks. A separate agency may be required because central bankers are conservative liquidity managers, not long-term asset managers focused on long-run returns that are often best achieved through the strategic ownership of a diverse group of illiquid assets. However, this agency could be closely connected to reserve managers at the central bank or part of the central bank, as in Norway. It may be that a pooling of some portion of the wealth portfolios into an Asian Investment Corporation (AIC) would make sense.

The process might also help to moderate asset market bubbles globally as capital, given rein for choice, becomes more discerning. A separate wealth portfolio can follow a diverse currency benchmark even when the domestic currency is pegged to the dollar – though this would affect the relative scale of the liquidity and wealth portfolios. That said, the move towards currency baskets as reference points in Asia and elsewhere will tend to permit more diversified assets. The good news is that both processes are well under way (see Chapter 3).

There is a risk that there will be a scramble by small reserve managers to diversify before speculation of diversification by the big holders of reserves reduces the value of their portfolio. This scramble would not be in the interests of neither the small and large holders of dollar reserves, nor US consumers. In these circumstances, the players could consider a Central Bank Dollar Sales Agreement that limits the size and pace of diversification. Truman (2005) has proposed such an agreement, and we offer elements of a draft in Box 2.2.

2.5 Avoiding dangerous remedies

2.5.1 Is China embarked on the same path as Japan?

The large exchange rate revaluations being urged on China could prove dangerous in their monetary effects. Asia today shares some unfortunate similarities with Japan in the early to mid-1990s. Then as now, there was a tendency to view the US deficit as an Asian problem caused by restrictive trade practices. In the absence of such practices, Japanese consumers would buy more imports, the story went. To open Japanese markets, the appreciation of the yen was encouraged, which in turn encouraged capital flows into the yen making a yen appreciation harder to resist. The yen's appreciation turned the screw on the deflation that Japan was already suffering from the decline of asset prices and the consequent loss of wealth in the household, banking and corporate sectors. It was not the only factor, but was a contributing factor to the deflationary cycle that Japan fell into from 1995 to today. It should be noted that China's economy is more open than that of Japan, and tradable food and manufactures bulk larger in its consumption basket. As a result, a substantial revaluation in effective terms could more easily tip China into deflation.

2.5.2 China's new exchange rate regime

On 21 July 2005 the People's Bank of China announced the abandonment of the ten-year old dollar-renminbi peg and the adoption of a more flexible arrangement where the renminbi would be able to move up to 0.3% per day and the reference would not be the dollar but the basket of major currencies (see Box 2.1).

The dollar peg brought some stability benefits but it did not served to stabilize China's price levels or inflation. It delivered deflation when the dollar was rising in the first quarter of 2002 and has delivered commodity-price led inflation more recently. Thus, the Chinese commitment to greater flexibility in exchange rate management is quite credible in that such flexibility could be seen as serving the cause of macroeconomic stability in China. Exchange rate flexibility presents a new policy tool that could help China negotiate a moderation of economic growth to more sustainable levels without tipping the economy into deflation This would be no easy task at the best of times and it will be made a little easier by having more policy tools available.

The new flexibility may be used by the Chinese authorities to stabilize the effective exchange rate and thereby limit the deflationary and inflationary impulses arising from the dollar's movements. Further, the exchange rate may be allowed to appreciate in effective terms to reinforce other measures in the face of inflationary pressures. On this view, the management of the effective exchange rate may join interest rate control, credit constraints, reserve requirements, lower loan-to-value limits and other measures to tighten monetary and credit policy. Such Chinese exchange rate management could resemble features of the Singaporean approach, but, given still binding Chinese capital controls, would not place the effective exchange rate in the centre of monetary policy, as does the Singporean policy.

Box 2.1 Announcement by the People's Bank of China

Public Announcement of the People's Bank of China on Reforming the RMB Exchange Rate Regime
21 July 2005

With a view to establishing and improving the socialist market economic system in China, enable the market to fully play its role in resource allocation as well as to put in place and further strengthen the managed floating exchange rate regime based on market supply and demand, the People's Bank of China, with authorization of the State Council, is hereby making the following announcements regarding reforming the RMB exchange rate regime:

1. Starting from July 21, 2005, China will reform the exchange rate regime by moving into a managed floating exchange rate regime based on market supply and demand with reference to a basket of currencies. RMB will no longer be pegged to the US dollar and the RMB exchange rate regime will be improved with greater flexibility.
2. The People's Bank of China will announce the closing price of a foreign currency such as the US dollar traded against the RMB in the inter-bank foreign exchange market after the closing of the market on each working day, and will make it the central parity for the trading against the RMB on the following working day.
3. The exchange rate of the US dollar against the RMB will be adjusted to 8.11 yuan per US dollar at the time of 19:00 hours of July 21, 2005. The foreign exchange designated banks may since adjust quotations of foreign currencies to their customers.
4. The daily trading price of the US dollar against the RMB in the inter-bank foreign exchange market will continue to be allowed to float within a band of ±0.3 percent around the central parity published by the People's Bank of China, while the trading prices of the non-US dollar currencies against the RMB will be allowed to move within a certain band announced by the People's Bank of China.

The People's Bank of China will make adjustment of the RMB exchange rate band when necessary according to market development as well as the economic and financial situation. The RMB exchange rate will be more flexible based on market condition with reference to a basket of currencies. The People's Bank of China is responsible for maintaining the RMB exchange rate basically stable at an adaptive and equilibrium level, so as to promote the basic equilibrium of the balance of payments and safeguard macroeconomic and financial stability.

There are risks, however. The new exchange rate regime could lead to an appreciation of the renminbi beyond what the authorities hope for and enough to push the economy into deflation. The significance of the announcement to revalue the renminbi by an initial 2.1% from RMB8.28:US$1 to RMB8.11:US$1 is not the scale of this first step[15] but the scale of what the new regime makes possible. We have not had sufficient time to observe how the authorities will operate the new regime, but on paper at least, the new exchange rate arrangement could be seen as an encouragement to speculation. A currency with large upside potential in the long run if the pressure proves too much for the authorities and limited downside in the short run if it does not, has similar characteristics to the narrow bands of the European Exchange Rate Mechanism which proved vulnerable to speculation[16]. Still, it is remarkable, given that many believe that the renminbi is 30-40% undervalued, that the tiny initial revaluation did not fuel expectations of further revaluations . The spot exchange rate was closer to the one-year non-deliverable forward after the change than before – a very rare observation in depeggings.

Limiting the rise of the effective exchange rate is likely to be the objective of the Chinese authorities since a large appreciation would threaten deflation[17]. Judging from recent experience this should be possible provided speculative capital flows do not accelerate. In this respect it would be helpful if external political pressure and threats of trade sanctions ceased. Policy tools that the Chinese authorities may consider to help offset upward pressure on the exchange rate include a loosening of capital outflow controls and a reduction of domestic interest rates in the event of inflation dropping toward zero. Neither is a straightforward option while the authorities grapple with a fragile financial system and an over-heating property market.

2.6 Conclusion

The cause of a large portion of Asia's current account surpluses is a domestic investment short-fall, not a deliberate attempt to devalue the exchange rate in search of export led growth. Indeed, we note that commodity exporters (in the Middle-East, Russia and Latin America) have seen a far greater improvement in their current account positions than Asia or China since the Asian financial crisis of 1997–8 forced many Asian currencies lower.

Consequently, the frequently proposed solution of a very large appreciation of the Chinese renminbi and other Asian currencies is a dangerous irrelevance. An irrelevance because savings-investment imbalances are not solved by exchange rate changes (Obstfeld and Rogoff, 2004). Dangerous, because revaluations could even worsen the investment short-fall in Asia and because bets on revaluation that induce hot money inflows into Asian economies, have made the circumstances more difficult by augmenting a reserve build-up well beyond current account surpluses. A large proportion of the most recent accumulation of dollar reserves relates to these speculative flows and not growing current account surpluses as many seem to believe.

The pattern of today's global imbalances is at odds with the traditional model of emerging markets running trade deficits financed by international capital inflows. But the traditional model never worked well. The international capital markets often proved fickle, delivering first feast, then famine. The current approach of self-insurance with large reserves seems inefficient and second-best, but has secured a period of stable economic growth and outperformance by emerging markets as a group. The traditional model needs to be reassessed.

The current recycling of international capital flows may therefore be more sustainable than many imagine. But it does carry increasing risks at the macro-prudential level in the United States, where debts have risen rapidly and in emerging markets where assets have grown rapidly. The safest course of action to moderate these risks would be a balanced array of macroeconomic and structural measures. Further risk mitigation will come from a greater diversification of assets in Asia. Before the private sector is in a position to take a greater role in managing national investment and savings balances, we recommend the establishment of wealth portfolios invested by long-term asset managers focused on long-run returns. Such returns are often best achieved through the strategic ownership of a diverse group of less liquid assets. There is a danger that this diversification process set off a scramble to get out of dollar assets. Proposals for a Central Bank Dollar Sales Agreement may be considered to mitigate this risk.

Finally, we are concerned that while the current system of financial flows may be more sustainable than it first looks, it may not be politically sustainable. There is a risk that mounting US deficits may lead to protectionist pressures that could lead to a retreat of global trade or beggar-thy-neighbour policies sold as an answer to 'Asian mercantilists'.

Box 2.2 Draft Central Bank Dollar Sales Agreement

'In the interest of clarifying their intentions with respect to their US dollar holdings, the above institutions welcome the US authorities continued commitment to a stable and strong US dollar and the reduction in unsustainable imbalances and consequently make the following statement:

1. The US dollar will remain an important element of global monetary reserves.
2. The above institutions will not enter the market as sellers, with the exception of already decided sales.
3. The US dollar sales already decided will be achieved through a concerted programme of sales over the next five years. Annual sales will not exceed approximately 5% of reserve holdings.
4. The signatories to this agreement have agreed not to expand their use of dollar futures and options over this period to effect further sales.
5. This agreement will be reviewed after five years.'

Figure 2.7 Ratio of foreign exchange reserve growth to current account surplus

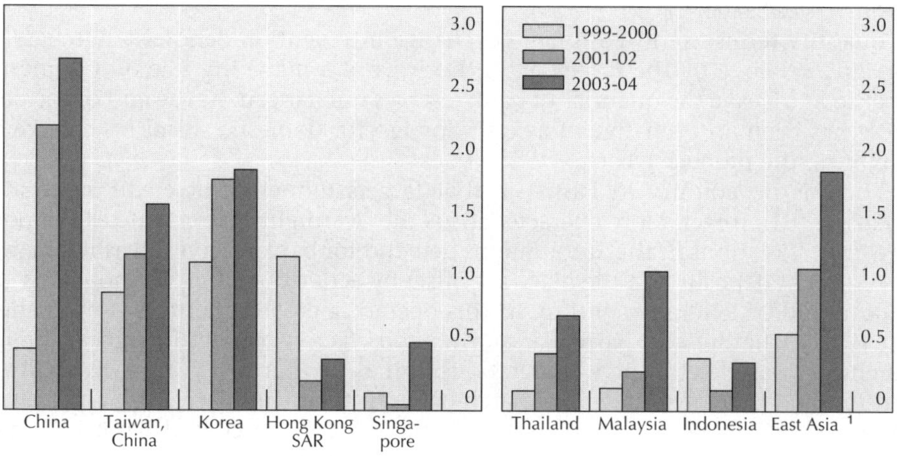

Note: East Asia (EA) is defined as the countries shown.
Sources: IMF, *International Financial Statistics*, national data; BIS calculations

Appendix 2.1 Sterilization: effectiveness and cost

For many observers, one of the most puzzling features of the reserve build-up in East Asia has been the apparent ease in handling the monetary consequences of large purchases of foreign exchange. Various expectations seem not to have been met: that monetary control would be lost; that preventing a loss of monetary control would push up interest rates; and that the expense of preventing a loss of monetary control would rapidly undermine the policy of resisting exchange rate appreciation by accumulating large reserves. These expectations reflect to a considerable extent the experience with exchange-rate based stabilizations in Latin America.

This appendix draws on Ho and McCauley (2005) to discuss three questions. What does sterilization mean under monetary policy regimes not focused on the quantity of money? What effect has sterilization had on interest rates in East Asia? What has sterilization cost the relevant authorities?

For those immediately involved, sterilization has implied the build-up and near constant refinancing of a very large stock of domestic currency debt. It can have the feel of a labour of Sisyphus. The burden of this argument is that the authorities in East Asia have risen to the considerable technical challenges. Monetary control has generally been maintained. The weak investment spending that underlies the current account surpluses in much of the region (and that has led the authorities to be so concerned to maintain the thrust of net exports) has meant that the banking system can readily accommodate the sterilization debt. This 'room' in the banking system, along with the generally short-term tenor of the chosen sterilization instruments, prevented the sterilization process from raising interest rates. Finally, the running cost of sterilization has been generally negative or very low in East Asia, owing to the generally low inflation and low real interest rates (again reflecting weak investment). Even where it is highest, in Korea and India, the costs at their worst in March 2004, before the Federal Reserve embarked on its current tightening cycle, look manageable.

Defining sterilization

In quantity terms, sterilized foreign exchange intervention denotes a purchase of foreign exchange by the monetary authority and a matching sale of a domestic asset so as to leave the quantity of bank reserves unchanged. At the end of the day, there has been an exchange of assets – foreign for domestic – and no change in liabilities,-the monetary base.

There is no country in East Asia that targets monetary or credit aggregates exclusively, however. More characteristic is the overnight interest rate as the policy target. Variations in the autonomous demand for bank reserves – cash demand, government deposits and the like – are offset by active operations (if not by use of deposit and/or lending facilities). In this operating environment, it is not coherent to ask whether one particular autonomous factor, namely foreign exchange purchases, was offset by active operations. It may be that in a year of heavy intervention that there is some broad match between their cumulative size and that of the main offsetting operation (mostly issuance of some central bank liability). Monetary control, however, does not require that there be 'full' sterilization.

For instance, in 1989 the Federal Reserve acquired $12.6bn in foreign currency in a year in which its net liabilities rose by $11.1bn. Evidently, very little of the increase in foreign exchange holdings was sterilized. In fact, it just happened that the drain of additional demand for cash (which varies from year to year but is always positive) just about matched the injection from foreign exchange purchases, and other factors netted to zero. In the market for overnight bank deposits, federal funds traded normally in relation to the Federal Reserve's targets. Operationally, there was full sterilization, but a naive juxtaposition of two items on its balance sheet would conclude the contrary.

More generally, in the current operating environment for most central banks, the question concerning sterilization is whether the overnight (or other short-term) interest rate was maintained at the targeted level. An examination of short-term interest rates in relation to announced intentions suggests that in this sense sterilization was the norm.

Interpreting China along these lines presents a challenge. There are elements of quantity targeting, with excess reserves as the operating target. There is also an interest rate corridor for interbank rates defined by the rate of remuneration on excess reserves at the bottom of the corridor and the rediscount rate at the top (Ma and McCauley, 2004). Thus, one can analyse whether purchase of foreign exchange was associated with an enlargement of excess reserves or whether interbank rates moved out of the corridor. Given the mixture of elements, amid the development of instruments, it is possible to read the data to suggest difficulty, or not much difficulty, in dealing with the monetary consequences of the accumulation of reserves by China.[18] For sure, the unusual device of paying interest, albeit at a rate that has been lowered over time, on excess reserves means that there is an aspect of automatic sterilization in the system: interbank rates cannot fall to zero.

The deeper question is whether a concern for further capital inflows has inhibited central banks from raising targeted interest rates when their inflation goals would have otherwise required it. Fear of increased capital flows has been argued to have applied a brake on the Chinese authorities' raising interest rates last year. However, the difficulty in specifying their operating procedures has a counterpart in the difficulty of pinning down their inflation goals, so it is hard to know by what standard to judge the policy path chosen. Elsewhere, the interest rate cuts by the Bank of Korea in 2004 in the face of an inflation threat and strong capital inflows might be interpreted as a case of policy constrained. The interpretation offered in the body of this report, however, is different: interest rate cuts were combined with letting the won strengthen in a package intended to cool inflation and rebalance demand away from exports to consumption and investment.

Interest rate effects

At the outset, it should be recognized that the purchase of foreign exchange represents an increase in the monetary base. If this exceeds the need for bank reserves, given any reserve requirements and operational needs, the tendency is for short-term interbank yields to fall towards zero. Nevertheless, the Latin American experience has led to expectations among some observers that sterilization leads to higher money market interest rates, attracting further capital flows, further foreign exchange purchases, further sterilization, and so on. In the context of monetary operations focused on stabilising a short-term rate, the possible pressure on interest rates would take the form of a steepening yield curve. Two factors have prevented this expectation from being generally realized in East Asia in recent years.

First has been the generally weak state of investment demand. This has had as its counterpart weak demand for bank loans from the corporate sectors that have been running financial surpluses. While East Asian banking systems have widened the market for mortgage and credit card lending to households, there has generally been plenty of room on banks' balance sheets for the sterilization debt.

Second has been the short-duration debt sold by the authorities. In Japan, the MoF's three-month bills, which are used to finance the marginal reserve holdings, could put upward pressure on near-zero interest rates in 2003–4, but, from an international perspective, it would take an electron microscope to observe the resulting interest rate rises. In India, too, government paper has been used to sterilise Reserve Bank of India purchases of foreign exchange (with the government building up a blocked account at the central bank). The government paper has had only a small share of paper with a maturity of over one year. Elsewhere, the central bank liabilities that are used to sterilize the foreign exchange reserves are mostly of short-term.

The exceptions are Taiwan, Korea and, to a lesser extent, China. Apparently, the issuance system in the first case is tap issuance at posted yields. In such a system, the two-year maturity paper is issued only if there is demand for it at the posted rate, so it can keep yields from falling but it cannot pressure yields upwards. In Korea, however, the Bank of Korea's auctions of one- and two-year monetary stabilization bonds can put pressure on bond yields. In early 2005, for instance, fairly heavy issuance combined with somewhat improved outlook for domestic demand led to a sharp rise in bond yields. The People's Bank of China has been extending maturities of its bills out to one- and two-year maturity, apparently at times pressuring yields upwards in a not well integrated money market.

Given generally short-term sterilization debt and monetary operations focussing on stabilizing overnight or short-term interest rates, monetary policy expectations thus constrain the effect of East Asian sterilization operations on yields. This may be in contrast to more quantitative monetary policy as used to be practised in the Latin American countries. Another difference working in the same direction is the greater development of money (not to mention bond) markets in Asia in recent years compared with their counterparts in Latin America in the same period. Less segmented money markets would anchor three-, six- and nine-month paper more closely to the short-term policy rate.

Costs of sterilization

In inflation-prone economies pursuing a strategy of exchange-rate based stabilization of inflation, sterilization can prove a costly and thus self-defeating exercise (Calvo, 1991). Again, the recent state of affairs in East Asia differs from the Latin American circumstances that have given rise to expectations that sterilization is a very costly operation. Even when US policy rates were held to 1%, major reserve holders Japan, Taiwan and Singapore had short-term interest rates below or at US levels. For China, Malaysia and Thailand, short-term interest rates exceeded those in the United States by little enough so that the combination of short-term sterilization debt and medium-term investment of official reserves (given the steep US yield curve) reduced carrying costs to low or even negative levels.[19] Of the major reserve accumulators, Korea and India had interest rates far enough above US rates that the question of sterilization costs of macroeconomic significance arose.

Before turning to the estimates of these costs for these two countries, let it be clear that not only the cases chosen, but also the date chosen and the baseline chosen share a worst case character. We focus on March 2004, the last quarter before the Federal Reserve started to raise dollar short-term interest rates. And we will measure the cost of the entire stock of reserves, before turning to the more reasonable baselines of reserve holdings.

Computing sterilization costs requires that a counterfactual be squarely faced. What are the foregone opportunities of holding safe but low-yielding foreign reserve assets? If the central bank were to cease holding foreign assets, what would it hold instead? And how much of a gain would this alternative bring? Generally, instead of holding a unit of foreign assets (earning x%), the authorities could have held more domestic asset (earning y%), or redeemed costly liabilities (saving z%), or done a combination of the two. More specifically, however, the alternative(s) chosen ought to respect the composition of the relevant authorities' balance sheet and the realities of institutional constraints.

Table 2.A.1 Estimated holding cost (per year) for Korea

	Dec 2002	Mar 2003	Dec 2003	Mar 2004
Quantities (% of 2003 GDP):				
Net foreign assets	16.08	17.96	21.42	22.54
Foreign liabilities	4.23	4.51	5.83	9.21
Yield differentials over US Treasury 2-5 year (%):[1]				
MSB 1-year	2.02	2.27	2.14	2.06
Government bond 5-year	2.41	2.47	2.47	2.48
Government bond 3-year	2.61	2.66	2.27	2.23
MOFE's gains from alternative (% of 2003 GDP):				
Pay off bonds associated with				
FX acquisition	010	0.11	0.14	0.23
BOK's gains from alternatives (% of 2003 GDP):				
Pay off MSBs, then acquire 3-year bonds	0.36	0.43	0.47	0.47
Switch all to 3-year bonds	0.42	0.48	0.49	0.50

Notes: 1 Average over the previous 12 months.

Table 2.A.2 Estimated holding cost (per year) for India

	Dec 2002	Mar 2003	Dec 2003	Mar 2004
Quantities:				
Net foreign assets (% of 2003 GDP)	12.50	13.17	16.98	18.28
Yield differentials over US Treasury 2-5 year (%):[1]				
Indian government securities 5-year	3.46	3.62	3.03	2.75
RBI's gains from alternative (% of 2003 GDP):				
Switch all to 5-year securities	0.43	0.48	0.52	0.50

Notes: 1 Average over the previous 12 months.

We estimate the stock opportunity costs for Korea and India using institutionally appropriate assumptions (Tables 2.A.1 and 2.A.2).[20] For Korea, we assume that the Ministry of Finance and the Economy's alternative to holding its share of foreign reserves is to redeem the corresponding amount of so-called foreign exchange stabilization bonds outstanding, while the Bank of Korea's alternative is first to pay off all outstanding so-called monetary stabilization bonds and then to invest the remainder of the proceeds of selling the foreign reserves by acquiring the benchmark three-year government bond. For India, we assume that the alternative is five-year government securities.[21]

On the unrealistic baseline alternative of no foreign exchange reserves, Korea and India could have saved carrying costs of something like 0.7% and 0.5% of GDP, respectively. Recall that this statement applies to the perfect storm period of high reserves and very low US dollar interest rates. Retaining the focus on this date, what would the cost be on a more realistic baseline?

The problem with answering this question is that there is no agreement on 'necessary' or 'warranted' reserves that would permit a measure of the cost of 'excessive' reserves as a remainder. Our approach therefore is to let the reader 'roll his own', so to speak, by ranking criteria for reserve adequacy from universally accepted (three months of import cover), to very broadly accepted (100% coverage of short-term external debt), to sometimes proposed (100% backing for foreign currency liabilities of the domestic banking system to residents) to what accepted (a third of the stock of foreign-held portfolio investments), to rarely accepted. This hierarchy of hypothetical warranted reserves yields estimates of the cost of 'excess' reserves. For Korea, these range from 0%, on the broadest notion of warranted reserves, to 0.5% of GDP on the most restrictive, down from 0.7% (Table 2.A.3).

Table 2.A.3 Carrying cost of 'excess' reserves for Korea, March 2004

Concept of 'warranted reserves'	'Warranted reserves' $bn	'Excess reserves' $bn	Cost of 'excess reserves' as % of GDP
Three months imports	63	100	0.48/0.51
Three months imports plus short-term external debt	123	40	0.27/0.30
Three months imports plus short-term external debt plus Korean foreign currency deposits in Korean banks	141	22	0.21/0.24
Three months imports plus short-term external debt plus Korean foreign currency deposits in Korean banks plus one-third of foreign holdings of Korean equities	169	-5	0

Notes: Cost calculated by subtracting the 'warranted reserves' (evaluated at 1140 KRW/USD) from the stock of $174bn in Bank of Korea foreign assets. First number is based on alternative of paying off monetary stabilization bonds first; second figure is based on alternative of switching all to 3-year bonds.

Source: Ho and McCauley (2005).

3 Investment of Asia's Foreign Exchange Reserves

A popular model in global financial markets holds that Asian central banks have been propping up the US dollar and holding down long-term US interest rates by the manner in which they have been investing their foreign exchange reserves. Were the Asian central banks to step back from the foreign exchange market, it is widely thought, the dollar could plunge and US long-term interest rates would rise sharply. Those who hold this view can point to the market action in the hours after the Chinese announcement of 21 July 2005: the dollar fell by about 2% against the yen and 0.4% against the euro in the hours after the Chinese announcement, while the US long bond yield rose by 10 basis points in New York trading, equivalent to a surprise on the monthly non-farm payrolls of $80,000–$90,000.

Aspects of this model must be correct. Most observers would accept that the generally sterilized intervention of East Asian central banks has enjoyed success in resisting the appreciation of their currencies. In other words, the US dollar would have been weaker against Asian currencies in the absence of the heavy management of the latter. This effect can be seen on the US dollar real effective exchange rate graph as the relative stability of the 'other important trading partners' index, as compared with the sharp appreciation of the major trading partners, including Europe, Canada and Australia (or that of the overall index which averages the major and other currencies).

What effect has this relative stability of the emerging market currencies over the last three years had on the dollar's overall effective exchange rate? Three answers can be given, ranging from none, to some, to a great deal. Some observers seem to consider that the relative stability of the 'other' currencies since the beginning of 2002 has simply displaced dollar weakness onto more flexible currencies like the euro, the pound sterling and Canadian and Australian dollars. This perspective sees currency management in Asia and Latin America as leaving the overall value of the US dollar unaffected.

Others seem to assume that the major currencies would have appreciated by the same extent had the emerging currencies been allowed to appreciate. On this view, if the emerging currencies had appreciated to the level seen before the Asian crisis, then the overall US dollar index would have already traded at the end of 2004 close to its real effective lows of the mid-1990s and 1980 (given the weight on the other currencies of about 40% in the overall index).

Still others assume that the Asian central banks both buy and hold US dollars, and therefore see the Asian officials as supporting the dollar against their own currencies both when intervening and against the major currencies when investing. This last scenario sees the Asian officials doing most to prop up the dollar. It depends critically, however, on a strong assumption that the Asian central banks cannot or do not diversify out of the dollar. The evidence reviewed below on the currency composition of reserves does not seem consistent with this last view.

Figure 3.1 Measures of the US real effective exchange rate[1]

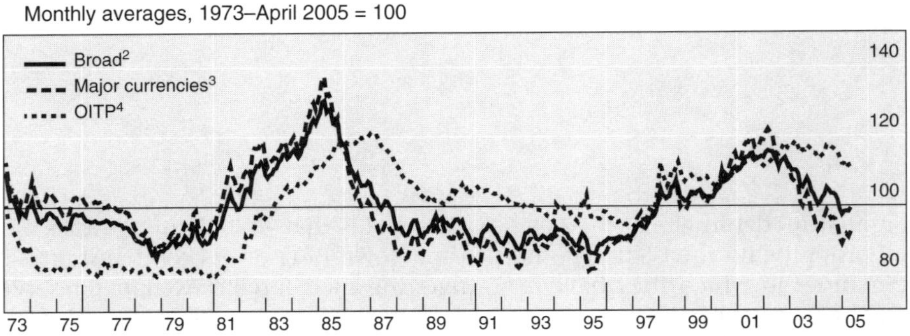

[1] In terms of relative consumer prices. [2] Twenty-six currencies of those economies whose bilateral shares of US trade exceeded 0.5% in 1997. [3] Seven (Australian dollar, Canadian dollar, euro, yen, pound sterling, Swedish krona and Swiss franc) of the 26 currencies in the broad measure. [4] Other important trading partners: the remaining 19 currencies in the broad measure.

Source: Board of Governors of the Federal Reserve System

Again, an aspect of the model would command wide agreement on the interest rate effect of Asian central banks' investment. In particular, that excesses of savings over investment in Asia tend to hold down global interest rates would seem uncontroversial. A parallel thesis is that the current account surpluses of oil exporting countries are tending to hold down global interest rates. Chapter 2 has emphasized, however, that the reserve build-up in East Asia has increasingly reflected capital inflows into Asia rather than current account surpluses. If the investment of Asian reserves, and not the smaller current account surpluses, is to be taken as the measure of the effect on long-term interest rates, the popular model carries a heavier burden than is often recognized. Circuits of international capital flows, as well as net savings flows, must be seen as holding down US interest rates.

For both the effect of Asian reserve managers' choice of currency and choice of instrument, the key question is the degree of substitutability of assets of different currency or maturity in private portfolios. In a world of perfect substitutability, these choices make no difference. If private holders of US and European government bonds consider these to be perfect substitutes, then official switches from dollars to euros would be offset by private sales with no effect on the equilibrium exchange rate or interest rates in either bond market. For example, given expectations of, say, a 1% per year depreciation of the dollar, any incipient rise in US yields or decline in the dollar resulting from official switches from dollar-denominated bonds to euro-denominated bonds would suggest higher returns on the dollar bonds and thus would encourage willing private purchases of them. Similarly, if investors in fixed income markets treat instruments of different maturities as perfect substitutes (consistent with the expectations hypothesis of the yield curve), then official switches from bills to bonds would be offset by private sales of bonds for bills with no effect on interest rates. In particular, any incipient decline in the bond yield resulting from a central bank bid would suggest higher yields from holding and rolling over bills and thus would induce private purchases of bills.

This chapter first reviews the investment of official foreign exchange reserves by currency. It does not appear that the share of dollar reserves has risen in a manner implied by the assumption that Asian central banks simply buy and hold dollars. Instead, the dollar share of global foreign exchange reserves seems to be broadly consistent with the dollar zone's share of global GDP. Further, even though the Asian reserve build-up has carried official reserves invested in the US dollar to a very large sum, central banks are still far from predominant in holding the global dollar exposure. Judging from the US international balance sheet, official reserves contain less than half of the rest of the world's net dollar claims on the United States.

Returning to the official reserve portfolio, the possibility of an overhang of dollars arises from the fact that the dollar bloc was tending to shrink even before the recent changes in currency management by China and Malaysia. Analytically, any resulting diversification of official reserves away from the dollar is shown to have a portfolio effect equivalent to that of sterilized intervention in the major currency pairs. If the assumption of perfect substitutability between high quality debts denominated in the dollar, euro and the yen just described is thought to be unrealistic over the possible scale of such diversification, then various policies, listed below, can be considered to limit its impact on foreign exchange rates. This part of the chapter closes with a reminder that the scale of official reserve holdings is small in relation to the stocks of privately held assets. Thus, it is easy to overstate the role of official portfolio management in determining exchange rates and long-term interest rates.

The chapter then reviews the instrument composition of official foreign exchange reserves, focusing on dollar reserves. Even though official reserve managers have been accepting more risk over time in the pursuit of higher yields, they still concentrate their holdings in relatively safe assets compared with their private counterparts. If reserve managers were playing as important a role in global asset pricing as is often ascribed to them, one might expect to see that spreads between their favoured safe, public-sector paper, on the one hand, and riskier corporate paper, on the other, had widened. Instead, risk spreads actually tended to narrow over the years of the big official reserve build-up, casting doubt on their importance. The question of the effect of official reserve portfolio management on US long-term interest rates is more often posed. A review of various analyses of this question suggests that the evidence is rather mixed.

Taken together, the arguments of this chapter suggest that the popular model systematically exaggerates the importance of official reserve managers.

3.1 The currency composition of official foreign exchange reserves

This section first provides data and caveats concerning the composition of foreign exchange reserves by currency, and questions the widespread view that the dollar share is too high. It proposes that the share of the world output accounted for by the US dollar bloc is an appropriate basis for assessing the dollar share in official reserves. The portion invested in dollars is then put into perspective by a comparison with the rest of the world's net exposure to the dollar, and it is shown that officials hold less than half of this exposure. Returning to the composition of reserves by currency and recognizing the continuing shrinkage of the dollar zone, the analysis turns to the implications of any diversification of reserves away from the dollar. An equivalence theorem is argued: such diversification is similar in its balance sheet aspects to sterilized intervention in a major currency pair. This section concludes with a review of policies that have been proposed or implemented over the years to deal with a perceived overhang of dollars (or gold) in reserve portfolios.

3.1.1 The US dollar's continued dominance in official foreign exchange reserves

It must be recognized at the outset that pinning down the currency composition of official foreign exchange reserves is not a straightforward task. There has always been the problem of reserve holders who are not members of the IMF: formerly the Soviet Union and still Taiwan, China. It is not clear that all IMF members are always forthcoming about their situation: Prasad and Wei (2005) do not appear to be well informed on the composition of Chinese reserves. Financial market analysts have identified another problem that may be more significant: the reporting of cash positions rather than exposures, including forward positions. While the Asian financial crisis of 1997–8 highlighted the risk of authorities reporting substantial foreign exchange reserves while having sold dollars forward against domestic currency, recently analysts have suggested that unreported forward sales of dollars against the euro or yen could confound the interpretation of the data on reserve composition.

Bearing in mind these caveats, it appears that the dollar has persisted as the overwhelming currency of choice in official foreign exchange reserve holdings. In mid-2004, it seemed that almost two-thirds of official foreign exchange reserves were dollar-denominated. Reports of the death of the dollar in this role have been vastly and repeatedly exaggerated (Frankel, 1995).

3.1.2 Is the US dollar's share in official foreign exchange reserves too high?

This persistence of the dollar as the preponderant reserve currency stands in contrast to the US economy's share or the US dollar's share in most global financial markets. Since World War II, the US economy's share of world GDP at PPP exchange rates has fallen, reaching only 21.1% in 2004 (IMF, 2004). The US share of global trade is even lower.

In global financial markets, the dollar's share does not seem to lend support to the official weight on the dollar. For instance, in March 2004, the US dollar's share of outstanding international bonds and notes not issued in the home currency was only 44% (ECB, 2005, pp.13-14).

One factor working to keep the dollar share of official reserve holdings high is the vehicle role of the US dollar. The dollar remained on one side of 89% of foreign exchange transactions in April of 2004 (BIS, 2005b). Despite the expectations of some that the euro would develop quickly into a vehicle currency, only 9% of foreign exchange transactions featured the euro on one side and a currency other than the US dollar on the other.[22]

This vehicle role of the dollar means that most central banks in the world need to lay hands on dollars to intervene in the spot foreign exchange market. The few exceptions seem largely to be in central Europe, where some currencies trade against the euro with as much or more depth than trading against the dollar.

A priori, it would seem that the dollar's vehicle role would be more important at low levels of reserve holdings. A central bank with modest foreign exchange reserve holdings might well hold a high fraction of dollars to be prepared to intervene. Even in this case, just as long-term securities can normally be lent out against cash to obtain liquidity, so, too, euro or yen can normally be swapped at any time of the day to provide dollar liquidity. Nevertheless, one can imagine that, as a central bank graduates from modest foreign exchange holdings to larger holdings, and an investment portfolio is split out from the liquidity portfolio, the dollar share would fall. In this model, the evolution of the dollar share of world reserves would depend on the distribution of growth across adolescent holders (with strong liquidity considerations) and mature holders (with more investment considerations). For the latter, it would seem unlikely that the dollar share needs to be above one half for liquidity reasons.

This model does not fit the data, however. The concentration of world reserve growth in East Asia, as described in Chapter 2, implies that liquidity considerations should have had ever less bearing on the investment of the marginal reserve dollar. An appeal to the dollar's vehicle role as a prop for the high share of dollars in foreign exchange reserve holdings, therefore, seems increasingly problematic.

Thus, considering the size of the US economy, its role in global financial markets and even its outsized vehicle role in the foreign exchange market, it seems hard to rationalize a share of official reserves of almost two-thirds. Before the conclusion is drawn that this share is inexplicably too large, let us consider the share of the dollar zone in world GDP.

The dollar zone of the world economy may be defined as the US economy plus those economies whose currencies track the dollar, like Hong Kong, or show only idiosyncratic variation against the dollar, like Mexico.[23] From this perspective, the relative size of the US economy, however, is too narrow a measure of the motive to hold dollars. Following Frankel and Wei (1994), Bénassy-Quéré (1996), and Kawai and Akiyama (1998), a dollar zone, may be operationalized as including currencies whose movements show little or no sympathy with movements of the Deutschemark/euro or yen against the dollar. It used to include the whole Western Hemisphere, most of Asia outside of Japan, the Middle East, anglophone Africa and much of the former Soviet Union. According to Kawai (2002), the dollar bloc so defined amounted to 45% of the world economy in 1990–9 (using current dollar GDP).

We have extended this work by computing the share of world GDP accounted for by the G3 currency zones. We regress changes in the dollar exchange rates of 46 economies that collectively account for 89% of world GDP on changes in the dollar against the Deutsche mark/euro and yen. We take the product of the estimated coefficients for the Deutsche mark/euro and yen and the respective economy's share of world GDP at PPP exchange rates (based on year 2000 data), as computed by the IMF (2004), to derive its contribution to the euro and yen zones. For instance, if the pound sterling on average appreciates by about 0.7% for every 1% appreciation of the euro against the dollar, then we add 70% of the UK's GDP to the euro area and 30% to the dollar area. The use of GDP measured at PPP tends to boost the dollar's share as compared with Kawai's result, not least because of China. We have distributed the remaining 11% of world GDP in accordance with the shares derived for the 89%.

Judging by the figure, the dollar share in foreign exchange reserves is not far from the share of the dollar zone in global GDP. It is easy to rationalise a 57% share of the dollar in official foreign exchange reserve portfolios. Indeed, the share of the dollar in reserves outside of Japan lines up remarkably closely to the dollar zone's share of global GDP: 57% compared with 59%.

The last two observations for the dollar share of reserves and world GDP would be still closer together if we exclude Japan's reserves. Clearly, one factor that has helped to maintain the dollar share of reserves over the last three years is the rapid

Figure 3.2 Global reserve composition and size of currency blocs (%)

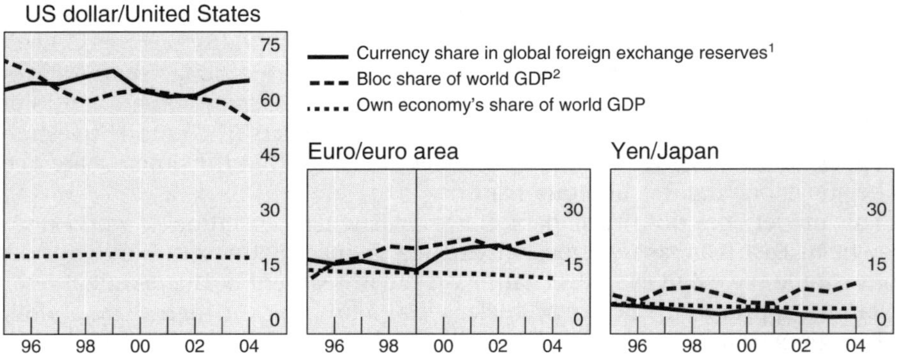

[1] At constant 2003 exchange rates; 2004 figure as at June. Prior to 1999, holdings in Deutsche marks, French francs and Dutch guilders used as a proxy for euro holdings. [2] Bloc share estimated as the own economy's share of PPP GDP, plus the elasticity-weighted share of all other countries' PPP GDPs. The elasticities are calculated as the coefficients in a regression of weekly changes in the domestic currency/ US dollar exchange rate against a constant, the yen/dollar and the euro/dollar (prior to 1999, Deutsche mark/dollar) exchange rates, during the corresponding year.

Source: IMF; BIS calculations

growth of Japanese holdings of foreign exchange reserves and their concentration in dollars. The valuation changes reported by the Bank of Japan for the years 2001-2003 suggest something close to a 90%–10% split in favour of the dollar over the euro (Bank of Japan, 2002; 2003; 2004). As the Japanese authorities have emphasized, they are buy-and-hold investors, which makes sense in terms of the central role of the yen and the size of Japanese reserves. Thus, it is interesting to examine the currency composition of global foreign exchange reserve holdings excluding those of Japan. If we subtract Japan's reserve holdings in mid-2004 of \$800bn from the global total of \$3.3trn, we are left with \$2.5trn. If we subtract Japan's assumed dollar holdings of \$720bn from the global total of \$2.15trn, we are left with \$1.43trn. This suggests a 57% dollar share for the world excluding Japan. This is just below the 59% dollar share of world GDP in 2004.

When this paper was presented in May, a discussant challenged the authors to provide a theoretical justification for use of the major currency zones' shares of the global economy as a benchmark for official reserve composition. One answer is that it is no worse than the extant empirical alternative, namely the US economy's share of the world economy (Eichengreen and Frankel, 1996; Eichengreen, 1998). Indeed, it might be that the US economy share works empirically because it serves as a smooth proxy for the more volatile dollar zone share.

A more satisfactory answer can be given in terms of a mean-variance choice of the currency composition. If the numeraire for a systematic approach to the choice of the currency in foreign exchange reserves is the domestic currency, then for any given country outside the G-3, it will minimize the variance of the value of the reserve portfolio to match its composition with the expected movement of the home currency against the major currencies. This is true whether the co-movement of the domestic currency with the euro or yen against the dollar is an outcome of exchange rate policy (as in Hong Kong or Singapore) or more of a market process (as in the United Kingdom). The minimum variance portfolio will not in general be the optimal choice, but in aggregate may not be a bad approximation.

The observed relationship between the orientation of the domestic currency to major currencies and the currency composition of reserves provides some support to this benchmark, moreover. Of course, most countries do not disclose the currency composition of their reserves, but 19 have done so. Figure 3.3 plots the reserve composition against the currency orientation. The European countries cluster in the upper right of the graph, tending to have relatively low weights on the dollar-and correspondingly high weights on the euro. Economies like Canada and Israel, whose currencies share less co-movement with the euro have higher weights on the dollar. Hong Kong, with its dollar peg, and Colombia and the Philippines, with strong dollar orientation, put relatively little weight on non-dollar currencies. Australia and New Zealand are outliers, but the strong co-movement of their dollars and the euro is a fairly recent development.

3.1.3 Implication for the global distribution of dollar exchange rate risk

Figure 3.3 Reserve composition vs exchange rate sensitivity

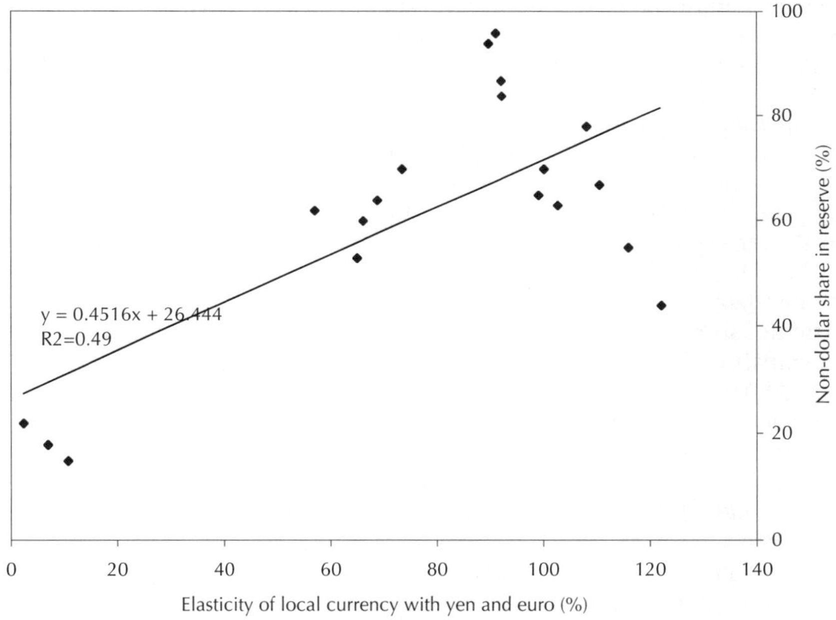

A frequently posed question is: how much of the US current account deficit are foreign officials financing? The BIS *75th Annual Report* in 2005 (Graph V.6, p 82) reported that dollar reserve growth represented about 4% of US GDP and the US current account deficit reached about 6% of GDP. One might say that officials financed two-thirds of the deficit. If this reasoning regarding the flows of finance and deficits is applied to the stocks of official dollar reserve holdings and US net international liabilities, a strange result is obtained. One could say that of the US net international liability position of $2.5trn (Abaroa, 2004), 76% or $1.9 trn had been financed by foreign officials. This juxtaposition conveys the impression not just of heavy reliance on official flows in recent years, but systematic and continual reliance on them to finance the accumulated current account deficits since the early 1980s.

This impression, however, is misleading. There were substantial dollar reserve holdings even when the United States still held net international assets. The relevant deficits that officials have helped to finance by adding dollars to their portfolios are larger than US current account deficits by the net acquisition of foreign currency assets by US corporations, institutional investors and households.

Recent work on international balance sheets has highlighted the accumulation of gross positions in domestic and foreign currencies that are quite substantial in relation to GDP (Tille, 2002, 2004; Gourinchas and Rey, 2005; McCauley, 2005). The norm for industrial countries, whether net creditors or debtors, is a short position in the domestic currency and a long position in foreign currencies. Such a position is implied by Kindleberger (1965), who described the United States as systematically issuing short-term (dollar) liabilities and accumulating long-term (generally foreign currency denominated) assets.[24] It appears that, as the US economy moved into current account deficit in the 1980s, the rest of the world accommodated the shift by accumulating not only sufficient dollar claims on the US to finance continuing US investment in foreign securities and corporate assets, but also enough to finance the US excess of spending on goods and services over receipts (i.e., the current account deficit).

The upshot is that the United States has a net short position in US dollars that stands at a multiple of the US net international liability position. This net short position can be defined as dollar-denominated liabilities to the rest of the world less dollar-denominated claims on it. According to Tille (2004), the United States has a net short position in the US dollar amounting to $7.2trn at the end of 2003. This far exceeds the already cited net international liability position of $2.5trn, that is, all external liabilities less all external assets, with the difference accounted for by the net US holdings of foreign currency assets. Of the corresponding net long position in the US dollar of the rest of the world, central banks held $1.9trn, or just over a quarter. This suggests a more modest role for official holdings of dollars than the above juxtaposition of official dollar holdings and the US net international liability position.

The net short position in dollars implies that a weak dollar gives rise to valuation gains in US portfolios, as emphasized by Tille (2002, 2004), Gourinchas and Rey (2005) and Cline (2005). By the same token, the rest of the world suffers an exchange valuation loss when the dollar declines. Central banks are on the hook for over a quarter of the loss.

Europe and Asia differ in who bears the losses from dollar depreciation. In Europe, relatively small official reserves imply that any valuation loss from dollar depreciation is concentrated in the private sector, especially the corporate sector. There, foreign exchange losses drain firms' capital and thereby prolong the ongoing deleveraging, leading to caution in investment and hiring. This hinders any increase in absorption relative to output. This in turn slows current account adjustment, which can only encourage the belief that the dollar needs to depreciate further. In Asia, the foreign exchange valuation losses from a weak dollar are concentrated in the public sector, as highlighted by Higgins and Klitgaard (2004). The fact that the public sector bears this risk in Asia can safely be presumed to reduce the behavioural response to and exchange losses. Unless taxpayers see through the veil of the state and fully respond to exchange losses on official reserves (Ricardian equivalence), the socialization of exchange risk attenuates the pressure on spending from the wealth losses caused by dollar depreciation.

Still, the losses in the public sector occasionally come into public view. For instance, the Japanese prime minister Junichiro Koizumi was asked in the spring of 2005 at parliamentary question time about the public losses on a depreciating dollar. He gave not the official answer – it is the job of the public sector to absorb these losses, which are in any case unrealised – but rather suggested the possibility of diversification. Similar statements by the authorities in other countries, which at times have led to dollar declines, seem utterly inexplicable unless due account is taken of some hazy understanding in the political realm of the fiscal risks entailed by the long dollar position.

Thus, while policy makers in Europe can take comfort from the fact that official losses from dollar depreciation are limited compared with those in Asia, the private incidence of the dollar risk in Europe may restrain absorption in Europe. The public bearing of the dollar exchange rate risk in Asia may in contrast limit such a perverse response of absorption to a weak dollar.

This brings us to a result contrary to that of Tille (2002, 2004) and Gourinchas and Rey (2005). They emphasize the contribution of a weak dollar to US valuation gains on international assets to the stabilization of the US net international investment position ('debt relief from a weak dollar'). We emphasize instead that the negative wealth effects in the rest of the world from a weak dollar can restrain absorption there and thereby retard the rebalancing of global demand away from the United States needed to narrow the US current account deficit. On the US side, valuation gains on foreign currency assets have in recent years added to the much larger wealth gains associated with rising house and equity prices. These wealth gains, of course, have tended to increase absorption and widen the current account deficit.

3.1.4 Could an official dollar 'overhang' be developing?

It was argued above in Section 3.1.2 that it is far from obvious that there was a dollar overhang in official portfolios at the end of 2004. If one conceives of dollar reserves as reflecting the size of the US economy, it is all but impossible to imagine a sharp fall-off in the dollar's share. In contrast, the size of the currency zones can change quite quickly. Consider the two largest movements in the estimated share of the dollar zone in world GDP, both drops, in 1997 and 2004. The first showed the combined effect of the continued stabilization of European currencies against the Deutsche mark and the increase in sympathy of East Asian currencies with the yen that occurred during the Asian crisis. In 2004 the decline in the dollar zone's share of global GDP was even more balanced between the euro and the yen zone. Within Europe, tighter relationships between the euro and sterling as well as Central European currencies contributed. East Asia's drift away from the dollar benefited both the euro and yen zones (Ho et al., 2005).

The dollar zone seems to be shrinking again substantially in 2005. The euro area may be expanding eastward to the edges of continental Europe. The Brazilian currency seems to be showing more co-movement with the euro against the dollar this year (BIS, 2005c, p.88). If the effective exchange rate as a 'reference' in China's newly announced exchange rate policy proves to be important, then the change in the orientation of the renminbi could lower the dollar share of the world economy by 5-10% (on these PPP measures). This in turn would tend to move the rest of East Asia further away from the dollar, continuing the trend already evident (Ogawa and Ito, 2002).

The upshot is that, even though there has been no obvious dollar overhang in global official portfolios, one could be developing if the US dollar zone's share of the world economy to continue to shrink. Thus, it is worth considering analytic aspects of the diversification of official portfolios away from the dollar.

3.1.5 The equivalence of reserve diversification and sterilized intervention

An important insight into the question of the effect of reserve managers' diversifying away from the dollar is that its balance sheet effect is analytically equivalent to that of sterilized intervention in the major currency pairs. Indeed, since, for instance, sales of US dollars by the Russian central bank for euros cannot possibly signal a shift in either Federal Reserve or eurosystem monetary policy, reserve diversification is a cleaner case of a portfolio shift than most cases of sterilized intervention. The equivalence of reserve diversification and sterilized intervention is important because its recognition forces a consistency in views of the two. It appears that many analysts who would dismiss sterilized intervention as unimportant attach great importance to the possibility of reserve diversification.

Box 3.1 The concerted intervention to support the euro in September 2000

Consider a case of sterilized intervention; say when the Federal Reserve bought €1.50bn dollars against $1.34bn on 22 September 2000 (Fisher, 2000). The Federal Reserve must have added the US dollars sold to the autonomous factors increasing bank reserves, have taken into account any changes in demand for such reserves and then drained the difference by selling securities from its portfolio under an agreement to repurchase them at some future date. Insofar as the purchase of euros has not been since reversed, it resulted in a permanent increase in bank reserves. Such an increase would otherwise have normally been effected through the purchase of a coupon-bearing long-term Treasury security. The euros purchased may be assumed to have been invested in European government securities.

Stepping back, the sterilized intervention in this case resulted in the Federal Reserve expanding its balance sheet (ultimately to accommodate growing cash demand) against European government securities rather than US government securities. From the standpoint of the rest of the world, the consequence was €1.50bn lower holdings of European government bonds and an equivalent amount more in holdings of US Treasury securities.

The European Central Bank intervened the same day, buying perhaps €2bn against $1.8bn.[1] Its purchase of euros threatened a shortage of euros in the money market. In order to prevent this shortage, the eurosystem stepped up its repurchase agreements in its 'main refinancing operations'. In the end, the rest of the world ended up holding the dollar investment that the ECB had formerly held, perhaps a US Treasury note. At the same time euro area banks ended up borrowing more euros from the eurosystem through repurchase agreements. Thus the rest of the world ended up holding more US dollar-denominated bonds and holding less net short-term euro investments.

Because the US and European authorities were intervening on the same side, these two sets of transactions sum to perhaps a €3.5bn shift towards holding dollar paper from holding euro paper on the part of the global private sector. What difference would such sterilized intervention make? For the answer, see Box 3.2.

1 The consolidated financial statement of the Eurosystem shows a rise in claims in foreign currency of €21 billion and a rise in revaluation accounts of €23bn in the week of 29 September 2000. See ECB Monthly Bulletin October 2000, pp.6* and 7*.

Box 3.2 The efficacy of sterilized intervention

It is important to emphasize the adjective 'sterilized'. Just as Bundesbank and Federal Reserve intervention was sterilized (Dominguez and Frankel, 1994; Weber, 1994), so too are the Eurosystem and Federal Reserve interventions sterilized. Under conditions of short-term interest rate targeting, sterilisation means that the central bank does not allow its sale or purchase of foreign currency to affect its targeted short-term rate. What effect do such interventions in the foreign exchange market have?

Starting with Jurgensen (1983) and continuing for at least another ten years (Edison, 1993), the answer was 'not much'. Two mechanisms have been identified: the portfolio balance effect and the monetary policy signalling effect. The first asks what needs to happen to make private portfolio managers accept the €3.5bn shift toward dollar holdings? The answer has tended to point to asset stocks of tens of trillions of dollars and euros and to invoke a prejudice of very high if not perfect substitutability between dollar and euro securities. The conclusion was that a very small, perhaps not measurable, rise in US interest rates relative to euro interest rates and/or a slight rise, again perhaps not measurable, in the euro against the dollar would make room in private portfolios for the extra dollar paper. Thus the overall effect of sterilized intervention operating through the portfolio balance effect would depend inversely on the degree of substitutability (assumed high) and directly on the scale of portfolio shift (generally small in relation to the underlying stocks of assets). Thus, the working assumption has long been that portfolio effects are so small that they could be neglected.[1]

Many observers would consider sterilized intervention potentially powerful if it signalled future monetary policy changes. In current practice, if the intervention of September 2000 foreshadowed to some extent higher interest rate settings by the eurosystem or lower interest rate settings by the Federal Reserve, then it could affect currency markets. Of course, any such signalling would not be the exclusive province of exchange market intervention, but would be shared with monetary policy statements, Congressional testimony, press conferences and other means of foreshadowing future interest rate moves. Little or even negative evidence has been found that US intervention actually signals future policy, however (Kaminsky and Lewis, 1996; Fatum and Hutchison, 1999). For the present purpose, however, it must be repeated that this effect cannot operate in the case of reserve diversification. The information that the Russian central bank might be selling dollars for euro conveys no information about the Federal Reserve or eurosystem's interest rate intentions.

The Japanese intervention in 2003–4 has dented the conventional wisdom that sterilized intervention has no effect. The scale of this intervention was such as to have not only recycled the entire current account surplus of Japan, some 2% of GDP, but also to have offset a substantial share of the flow into Japanese equities from the rest of the world. Some would argue that the portfolio effect was always known to be potentially powerful if the scale of intervention were sufficiently large: 'Anything counts in large amounts'.

One can make the same point more broadly. As noted, most discussion of the reserve build-up in East Asia accepts the presumption that the associated intervention is preventing the relevant currencies from appreciating against the dollar. If the intervention is taken to be sterilized, which we take to be the correct general presumption (Ho and McCauley, 2005), then in effect it is widely presumed that sterilized intervention is effective in East Asia.

1 Some studies have suggested an effect on the expected volatility of exchange rates rather than the level. See Galati and Melick (1999).

Box 3.1 provides a refresher course in the portfolio effects of such intervention in a major currency pair, taking as its example the intervention to support the euro in September 2000. Box 3.2 provides a refresher course on the question of the efficacy of sterilized intervention.

Reserve diversification and sterilized intervention in a major currency pair have a similar effect on private portfolios. If an Asian central bank diversifies away from the US dollar to the euro, it sells, say, a US Treasury security and then sells the dollar proceeds for euros and then invests the euros acquired in, say, a European government bond. At the end of the day, the world's private sector portfolio has to absorb more dollar paper and less euro paper. This consequence of reserve diversification is identical to that of the eurosystem's and Federal Reserve's intervention of 22 September 2000. The effect one ascribes to the portfolio consequence of the intervention should thus be the same effect that one ascribes to the diversification move. In particular, if the portfolio effect of the September 2000 intervention is seen as supporting the euro, then the diversification may put pressure on the euro to appreciate against the dollar. If the portfolio effect of €3.5bn in intervention was judged to be negligible, so, too, should a similar quantity of diversification.

3.1.6 Policies to manage an overhang of dollars in global portfolios

Policies to deal with a portfolio imbalance in official (or private) portfolios outside the United States could, judging from precedents, attempt to reduce the long dollar position, to redistribute it or to freeze it. First, US residents could be induced to hold fewer foreign currency assets, resulting in less dollar liabilities for the rest of the world. Any such policy would run counter to the general trend toward a diminution of home bias in portfolios. It is hard to say, therefore, what policies might have slowed down the $100bn US purchase of foreign equities in 2003-04. The policies adopted in the late 1960s, the 'interest equalization tax' and the 'voluntary credit restraint programme', hardly offer good precedents; the latter was in plain speech a type of capital control.

A second approach would be for the United States to take on exchange rate risk through the sale of government debt denominated in foreign currencies: the 'Roosa bonds' and 'Carter bonds' of the US Treasury in the 1960s and 1970s. (US sterilized intervention in the form of selling euro and yen for dollars would have the same effect of absorbing US dollar debt and releasing foreign currency debt.) It might seem odd to suggest that the United States might willingly give up the favourable circumstance of borrowing in its own currency to any extent. Two possible justifications can be offered, however. At some stage, it might be in the US Treasury's interest to be seen to place itself in a position to lose from further dollar weakness, given the influence of its own policies over the level of the dollar. The other argument that might be offered is that US tax receipts are higher because dollar profits of the US corporate sector are higher in the event of dollar depreciation. If revenues are stronger in a weak dollar scenario, then debt denominated in foreign currency can be seen as matching revenues to some extent.

A third approach, known as a 'substitution account', would allow an exchange of dollar reserves for SDR-denominated claims. The stumbling block to this in the late 1970s was getting agreement on the international sharing of the risk involved.

A fourth, less centralized way of permitting diversification out of the dollar, would be sterilized intervention by the eurosystem or the Japanese authorities. This could offset the effect on private portfolios of any hypothesized official shift to the euro or yen (see Box 3.3). Equivalent in its balance sheet effect, although possibly very different in its market dynamics, would be the suggestion at the presentation of the draft of this report that Asian central banks might swap their

Box 3.3 Reserve diversification and G-3 sterilized intervention

It follows from the above that intervention by G-3 authorities can offset any effect of diversification. In the case of intervention by the Japanese or European authorities, such offsetting intervention would also multiply global reserves. It is useful to walk through this scenario, since it reinforces the argument made above that sterilized intervention and reserve diversification resemble each other in their portfolio effect.

Hypothetically, an Asian central bank desires to switch from US dollar holdings to Japanese yen holdings. It sells a US Treasury security and uses the proceeds to buy yen, which it invests in a Ministry of Finance (MoF) bill. The Ministry of Finance resists the upward pressure on the yen that this bid for yen entails by selling yen for dollars. The Ministry then buys a US Treasury security. At the end of the day, global foreign exchange reserves have risen, and the ownership of the US Treasury security has been transferred from one central bank to another. The currency diversification by an Asian central bank has caused the official Japanese balance sheet to gross up, and resulted in a transfer of the risk attached to the long dollar position to Japan.

Asian central bank diversifies into yen and MoF intervenes

Asian central bank		MoF		US Treasury	
- US Treasuries + MoF bill		+ US Treasuries	+ MoF bill		- due to Asian central bank + Due to MoF

NB: Official foreign exchange reserves 'grossed up'

The accounts would differ for Europe, because of the institutional difference between the ownership of marginal official foreign exchange reserves. In Japan, the Ministry of Finance is the holder of additions to reserves, and finances these by issuing its own paper. In the case of Europe, the European System of Central Banks (ESCB) would be the acquirer of any dollars bought. It would sterilize any such purchases by reducing its domestic assets. In what follows this is shown as a sale of a euro area government security, but it could be just a reduction of credit extended to the banking system under the main refinancing operations, namely repurchase agreements.

Asian central bank diversifies into euro and ECB intervenes

Asian central bank		ESCB		US Treasury	
- US Treasuries + Euroland gov't		+ US Treasuries - Euroland gov't			- due to Asian central bank + due to ESCB

NB: Official foreign exchange reserves 'grossed up'

Despite the institutional difference, the symmetry of reserve diversification, on the one hand, and sterilized intervention, on the other, is evident. Again, foreign exchange reserves have been multiplied by the insertion of an intermediary between the Asian central bank and the US Treasury. Again, the long dollar position remains within the official sector, but it has been assumed by a G-3 central bank.

dollar assets for euro assets held by the European System of Central Banks (ESCB). Of course, either approach would lodge the risk of holding dollars onto the ESCB. The general point of the equivalence of debt management and sterilized intervention can be invoked again at this point however. The European governments and agencies with substantial dollar debts could refinance these debts with euro-denominated securities. An exchange, for instance, of a euro-denominated bond of the German agency KfW for its outstanding dollar-denominated bond would serve to reduce the dollar share of Asian central bank reserves to the extent of their holding of KfW's paper. To the extent that private parties hold the dollar paper, such a swap would offset a like amount of diversification by Asian central banks out of the dollar and into the euro.

The first two policies would reduce the long dollar position, but the third and fourth would redistribute it. Alternatively, an orderly marketing agreement, somewhat like that for gold, among dollar holding central banks could reduce the probability of a disorderly outcome. Truman (2005) has proposed such an agreement.

Table 3.1 Selected bond issues by euro area sovereigns and quasi-sovereigns denominated in dollars (US$bn, Jan. 2000 – May 2005)

	Total
CADES (French agency)	6.75
KfW (German agency)	44.36
Republic of Italy	52.15
Total	103.26

Sources: Dealogic; BIS

3.1.7 Why it is easy to overstate the importance of reserve diversification

Private market participants show a propensity to overstate the effect of changes in behaviour by reserve managers and to understate the effect of changes in the behaviour of firms and institutional investors. This was evident in the lead-up to the euro (McCauley (1997)). Market analysts puzzled over questions about the official sector. What would European central banks do with their presumed excess dollar holdings? Would Asian central banks shift immediately into euros? In the end, it turned out that the decline of the euro from its starting point of $1.17 to its lows near $0.80 had more to do with the behaviour of private parties. In particular, European firms' attempts to bulk up by buying US assets and global borrowers finding the euro bond market more accessible than its predecessor markets both put pressure on the euro.

Any discussion of reserve diversification thus should include a reminder that even with official reserves as large as they are, most of the cards remain in the hands of private players. Above it was noted that officials outside the United States hold well under half of the world's net long dollar position.

The same point can be made in relation to asset stocks. Focusing only on the fixed income stocks in which central bank invest most of their holdings, and neglecting the very large global stock of purely domestic bank deposits, it is very clear that central banks are bit players. Domestic and international bonds and paper, along with international bank deposits, amounted to a stock of $59trn in the middle of 2004. The IMF reported official reserves at $3.3trn at that time.

Table 3.2 Selected global fixed income stocks and official reserve holdings, June 2004 (US$trn)

	Short-term	Long-term	Total
Domestic bonds	10.1	31.1	41.2
International debt securities	2.1	10.3	12.4
International bank deposits			5.8
Total			59.4
Memo: Official reserve holdings			3.3

Notes: Bank deposits include cross-border (BIS Quarterly Review Table 3B) and local currency (Table 4B) liabilities to nonbanks and liabilities to official monetary authorities (Table 5 B). Maturity assumed to be 100% short-term.

Sources: IMF, BIS.

3.2 The instrument composition of official foreign exchange reserves

In this section we start by showing that official reserve managers now favour instruments of over one-year maturity for the bulk of their investments. This demonstration is necessarily limited to the investment of dollar reserves, owing to the unavailability of information on the investment of reserves in other currencies. Then the instrument choice of official portfolio managers is contrasted to that of private investors in US securities to make clear how risk averse official investors are. That official reserve managers do favour long-term instruments makes it possible that their investment has served to hold down US (or global) long-term interest rates. Thus the analysis then turns to both stock comparisons and time series analysis in an attempt to shed light on the hypothesis. Our conclusion is that the case for the view that central banks have held down US long-term interest rates is weaker than most treatments would suggest.

3.2.1 Official reserve managers favouring long-term instruments

If the dollar remains the currency of choice of official reserve managers, the short-term Treasury bill has decidedly lost its one-time predominant role in their choice of instrument. This is evident from available evidence on the composition of US dollar reserves by instrument. It can be presumed that much the same conclusions would hold for investments in euro and possibly yen, were it possible to put together a broad picture of official reserve holdings in these currencies.

Data on official holdings of dollars in June 2003 show that short-term instruments, including US Treasury bills, amounted to no more than 42% of identified holdings.[25] This is the result of increased holding of long-term instruments since the post-war peak of US long-term interest rates in the early 1980s.

Another salient feature of the instrument composition of US dollar reserves is the share of US Treasury securities in total holdings. This declined in the 1970s as official reserve managers diversified towards higher-yielding eurodollar bank deposits. The shift toward longer maturities over the past 20 years tended to sustain the Treasury share as official reserve managers took duration risk while eschewing credit risk by adding Treasury coupon securities to their portfolios. More recently, however, the tendency of many reserve managers to buy US agency and corporate securities, including asset-backed securities, has tended to lower the US Treasury share. By June 2003, the share in identified holdings had declined to

53%. Our best guess is that more than half of official US dollar holdings were invested in instruments other than US Treasury securities in mid-2003.

Table 3.3 Instrument composition of US dollar reserves at end-June 2003 (US$bn)

	Short-term	Long-term	Total
Treasury securities	228	653	881 (53.1%)
Other assets	472	306	778 (46.9%)
Repos and deposits in the US	112		
Commercial paper and CDs in the US	82		
Offshore deposits	278		
Agency securities		180	
Corporate bonds		21	
Equities		105	
Total	700 (42.2%)	959 (57.8%)	1659 (100%)
Memo: Share of Treasury securities in assets of the given maturity	32.6%	68.1%	
Total est. US dollar reserves at June 2003			1,830

Sources: Figures for US Treasury securities, agency securities, corporate bonds and equities are from US Treasury et al. (2004). Figures for deposits and money market paper in the United States are from the US Department of Commerce, Bureau of Economic Analysis, International Transactions Table 4. Figures for offshore US dollar deposits are from the BIS (2005a), Table 5C, and the Japanese SDDS for June 2004.

With this review of the instrument allocation of official dollar holdings in mind, it is understandable that some analysts have argued that official reserve managers have collectively become an important influence on the level of US, and perhaps euro, long-term interest rates. We return to this question below.

3.2.2 Contrasting foreign official and private holdings of US securities

Foreign official portfolio managers are very different from their private counterparts. Even if we restrict our attention to long-term securities, where investors must assume some price risk, official investors in the United States are much more risk averse than private portfolio managers. Fully 87% of the official long-term portfolio is invested in Treasury and agency securities, while less than a quarter of the private long-term portfolio is invested with such evident risk aversion. Private investors have an equity weight of over 40%, while officials come in at just above 10%.

This juxtaposition helps to make clear the implications of a country's entrusting its foreign asset investment to the official sector rather than the private sector. The purchase price of lower risk is lower returns. It is easy to understand from this the logic of central banks passing, as foreign exchange reserves grow, from liquidity portfolio management to investment portfolio management to wealth management.

3.2.3 Effect on US or global interest rates

Market participants and officials have drawn a connection between the build-up of official foreign exchange reserves, their investment in notes and bonds and the low yields on these. This section first draws on the previous section to suggest how foreign official investment might affect yields compared with the same quantity of investment undertaken in characteristic manner by private portfolio managers.

It then complements this perspective with one that focuses on the duration gap between the central bank liabilities used to finance the reserve build-up and the assets acquired. The various time series approaches to the same question are then critically reviewed. The conclusion that the investment in US bonds of the proceeds of heavy central bank intervention by Asian banks has lowered bond yields appears to have been accepted mostly through the sheer force of repetition (Roubini and Setser, 2005). Our conclusion is that the case for central banks' having materially lowered US long-term yields has yet to be made.

Table 3.4 Foreign holdings of long-term debt and equity in the United States by official and private investors, as of June 2003

	Official holdings US$bn	Official holdings % of official	Private holdings US$bn	Private holdings % of private	Total
US Treasury securities	653	68.1	463	13.1	1,116
as % of market	26.6		18.9		45.5
Agency securities	180	18.8	406	11.5	586
as % of market	3.5		7.8		11.3
Corporate bonds	21	2.2	1215	34.3	1,236
as % of market	0.3		15.4		15.7
Equities	105	10.9	1459	41.2	1,564
as % of market	0.6		8.1		8.7
Total	959	100.0	3544	100.0	4,503
as % of market	2.9		10.6		13.5

Source: US Treasury et al. (2004).

3.2.3.1 Private versus official holdings in the United States

One approach to the question of the effect of the growth of official portfolios is to compare their investment habitat with that of private investors. This comparison recognizes that official flows are not ex ante portfolio shifts but rather the consequence of a lack of private flows at given exchange rates and interest rates.[26] It is evident from the comparison of official and private portfolios in the United States drawn in the previous section that official investment would tend to lead to lower bond yields but lower equity prices.

Figure: 3.4 Holdings of long-term US securities by official and private investors (% of total portfolio, June 2003)

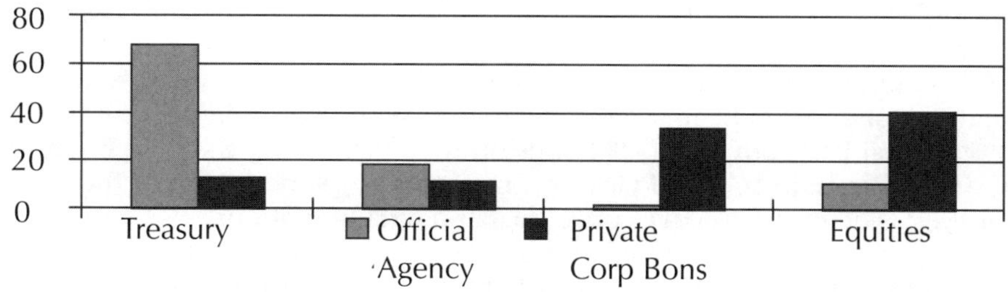

Within fixed income investments, the propensity of official reserve managers to buy Treasury and agency paper might be expected to lead to wider spreads on corporate bonds relative to Treasury and agency yields.[27] What one observed in much of 2004, however, was historically very narrow spreads.

Figure 3.5 Credit spreads (month end, in basis points)

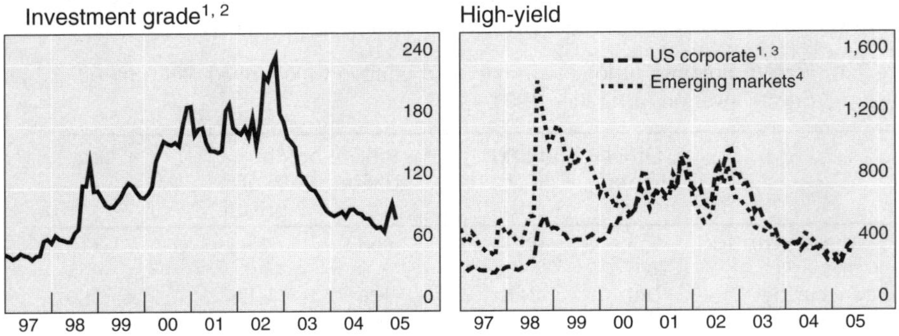

[1] Option-adjusted spreads between corporate and US government bond yields. [2] Lehman Brothers US investment grade corporate bond index. [3] Merrill Lynch High Yield Master II corporate bond index. [4] Stripped spreads between emerging market sovereign and US government bond yields; JPMorgan Chase EMBI Global.

Sources: JPMorgan Chase; Lehman Brothers; Merrill Lynch

3.2.3.2 Asian central banks' approach to asset and liability management

Another perspective on the possible effect of Asian central banks' reserve management is to consider the gap between the duration of the investment of the foreign exchange reserves, on the one hand, and the duration of the financing portfolio, on the other. With the exception of the Hong Kong Exchange Fund, central banks sterilize, or finance, additions to reserves. The key observation is that sterilization debt is generally short-term while foreign exchange reserve investments are nearly all long-term at the margin. This means that central banks have funded long bonds with cash. This would contribute to the flattening of global yield curves.

While the qualitative contribution of central banks to global yield curve flattening seems reasonable, the question can be asked how significant an influence central banks might have been. Certainly, Asian central banks are not the only players in financial markets that are financing holdings of long-term securities with short-term debt. The next section notes another way in which Asian central banks can be considered to be part of a circuit of capital flows that in effect finances long-term securities with short-term debt, in this case, both denominated in dollars.

3.2.3.3 Flow time series analysis

Several sets of analysts have used time series econometrics to assess the implication of central bank buying of US bonds on their yields. These studies essentially regress the change in US bond yields on measures of intervention or official asset acquisition. These studies have conceptual and data limitations.

Conceptually, the treatment of central bank investment as an ex ante portfolio shift is questionable. As discussed in Chapter 2, much of the recent increase in reserve holdings has had as a counterpart capital inflows into the Asian economies. A US pension fund may sell a US dollar bond in order to buy a Korean equity share, and the Korean authorities may intervene to resist the won's appreciation and invest the dollars in a US Treasury or Fannie Mae bond. There is no

Figure 3.6 Major investment banks' risk-taking

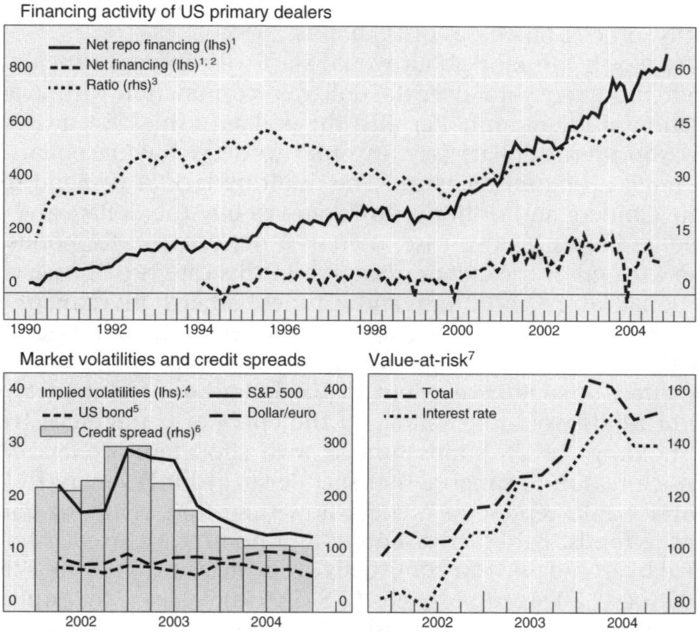

[1] In billions of US dollars. [2] Net financing ("securities out" minus "securities in") as defined in T Adrian and M Fleming, "What financing data reveal about dealer leverage", *Federal Reserve Bank of New York Current Issues*, March 2005. [3] Net repo financing as a percentage of total assets of securities dealers. [4] At-the-money call implied volatility; in per cent. [5] Ten-year. [6] Lehman Brothers Corporate Index, based on Moody's Baa ratings; in basis points. [7] Market capitalisation-weighted averages of eight large institutions' total and interest rate VaR relative to their total VaR in the fourth quarter of 2001; quarterly data, in per cent.

Sources: Federal Reserve Bank of New York; Lehman Brothers; Merrill Lynch

Figure 3.7 Hedge fund size, performance and leverage

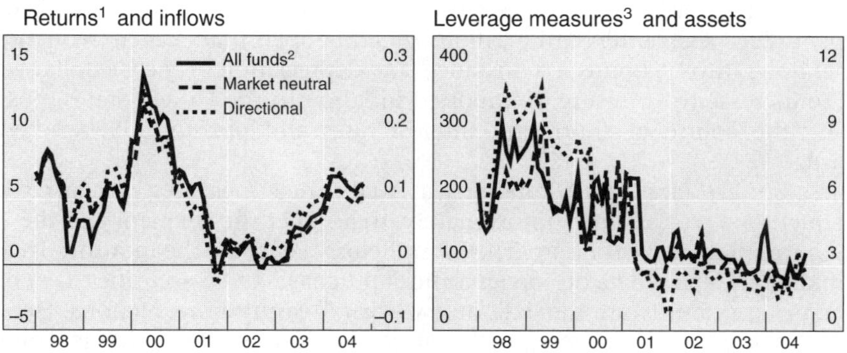

Note: The shaded areas represent hedge fund flows and stocks respectively, indicated by the left-hand scales, in billions of US dollars.

[1] Average annualised excess return across hedge funds; relative to three-month US Treasury bill yields. [2] Includes equity, market neutral and directional style families. [3] Based on the regression methodology described in P McGuire, E Remolona and K Tsatsaronis, "Time-varying exposures and leverage in hedge funds", *BIS Quarterly Review*, March 2005.

Sources: Hedge Fund Research, Inc.; BIS calculations

net demand for US dollar bonds in this circuit of capital flows. Note the possibility of reverse causation: poor economic news in the United States might lead to a decline of bond yields, a capital outflow to Asia, intervention to resist appreciation and, finally, official purchases of US bonds.

Another case worth thinking about would start with interest differentials that formerly favoured the renminbi over the dollar, in conjunction with expectations of an appreciation of the renminbi against the dollar. In this case, a Chinese firm might borrow short-term dollars (say, in order to delay buying dollars to settle imports) and build up renminbi assets. The resulting lack of demand for dollars would lead the Chinese authorities to intervene to buy the dollars and to invest them in US dollar bonds. In this case, there is a net demand for bonds. But the beginning and the end of the circuit of capital in this case is (Chinese corporate) borrowing of dollars at the short-term and (Chinese official) investment of dollars at the medium or long term. Such leveraged investment in US bonds is not a peculiar feature of the circuit of capital involving central banks.

Rather, the effect of such investment in US dollar bonds ultimately financed with short-term funds would be similar to the effect of commercial banks' and hedge funds' holdings of US bonds funded with short-term dollars. Moreover, there is not much reason to suppose that such leveraged investment in US bonds involving central banks represents a larger flow than that involving commercial banks and hedge funds. Banks' cross-border and non-local currency holdings of securities issued by non-banks, an admittedly crude measure, grew by $269bn and $549bn in 2003 and 2004, respectively (BIS, 2005a).[28] Major investment banks have been reporting higher values at risk in fixed income markets over the past several years, despite generally lower bond market volatility, consistent with increases in long positions in bonds (Figure 3.6, lower right panel). While the growth of hedge fund assets appears modest by the standards of the growth of Asian reserves, it must be remembered that hedge funds leverage up, by two or three times according to estimates based on the relationship of fund returns to asset returns (Figure 3.7).It is ironic that analysts working for banks and securities firms that are themselves very substantial leveraged bond investors put so much emphasis on central bank purchases of US bonds.

Finally, the estimates that these studies produce should be understood as at best measuring a portfolio effect, within the context of East Asian central banks' attempts to resist appreciation. Were the banks to step away from the market, and sharply reduce their intervention, more would happen than a mere reduction in official flows into US bonds. For instance, any depreciation of the US dollar would tend to increase the pressure of imported inflation in the United States, possibly altering the course of short-term interest rates and pressing US bond yields upward.

These studies face data limitations as well. Their measures of central bank investment are partial, and, unfortunately, the higher the frequency of the data, the less comprehensive they are. The most inclusive data are the monthly Treasury International Capital data on foreign official purchases of US securities. Less inclusive but also monthly are the data on two-year Treasury note auctions. Here the central bank purchases are proxied by successful 'indirect' bids, that is, competitive bids that are placed by dealers on behalf of third parties, which includes some official buyers. The monthly frequency, however, leaves few data points for time series analysis.[29] Other studies use the weekly statement of the Federal Reserve balance sheet regarding its custody holdings for foreign central banks. Not all central banks bank at the Federal Reserve, however, in part because they want to be less observable. Still, the weekly data on holdings seem to track monthly data on holdings constructed from the monthly flow data fairly well (Figure 3.8, left panel).[30]

Daily data on intervention by the Japanese authorities have been used by Bernanke et al. (2004), but these pertain only to one country and pose the problem of the gap between the acquisition of dollars and their investment, described below.

Figure 3.8 Foreign holdings of US Treasury securities (US$bn)

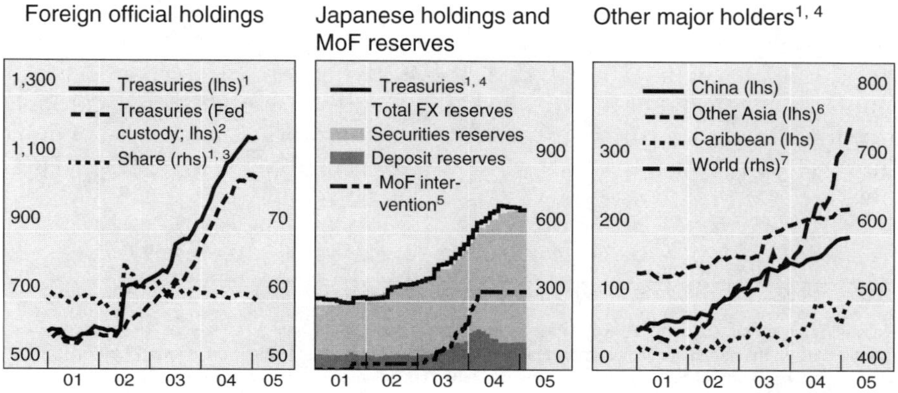

[1] TIC data. [2] Held in custody at the Federal Reserve on behalf of foreign official institutions. [3] Share, in per cent, of total foreign holdings. [4] Holdings of US Treasury securities by public and private entities. [5] Cumulative intervention since end-2000. [6] Hong Kong SAR, India, Korea, Singapore, Taiwan (China) and Thailand. [7] Excluding Japan, China, other Asia and the Caribbean.

Sources: Board of Governors of the Federal Reserve System; Japanese Ministry of Finance (MoF); Treasury International Capital System

The studies are discussed in the order of the frequency of the data used. These range from monthly for Garzarelli (2004) and the BIS (2005c), to weekly for McCauley and Jiang (2004) and BIS (2005c), to daily (Bernanke et al. (2004).

Garzarelli (2004) adds the monthly Treasury International Capital (TIC) data on official purchases of US Treasury bonds and notes, deflated by the CPI index, to a benchmark equation for the level of ten-year US Treasury yields. The benchmark equation includes the level of three-month yields in the United States and abroad (to capture monetary policy settings), the public sector deficit in the United States and abroad, US core inflation, GDP growth and the current account position. He finds that the benchmark equation puts the equilibrium US ten-year Treasury rate at 5.4% in September 2004, two standard deviations above the actual rate then. Adding the net foreign official purchases drops the benchmark equation's equilibrium rate to 5%, that is, 40 basis points lower. In this exercise, it is not clear why official foreign purchases are distinguished from private ones and why official purchases of agency notes and bonds are neglected.[31]

The BIS (2005c) takes a close look at the immediate bond market reaction to the TIC data release (Figure 3.9, middle panel). For the two years of data in the sample, January 2003 through January 2005, positive surprises in the net foreign purchases of US Treasury securities are not associated with a drop in interest rates in the two hours surrounding the release of the TIC data. Indeed, the yield on the two-year note seems to increase when large purchases are announced! 'The Treasury market was unfazed by the relatively large surprise (based on a consensus forecast) in net foreign purchase in the November 2004 TIC report, and by the $2.8bn surprise in the December report' (p. 105). Repeating the exercise with the five-year note or with just official purchases did not alter the finding of 'scant evidence that the release of data which shed light on Asian purchases of US securities tended to move yields in a predictable way' (ibid.).

Figure 3.9 Impact of foreign official investment on US Treasury yields

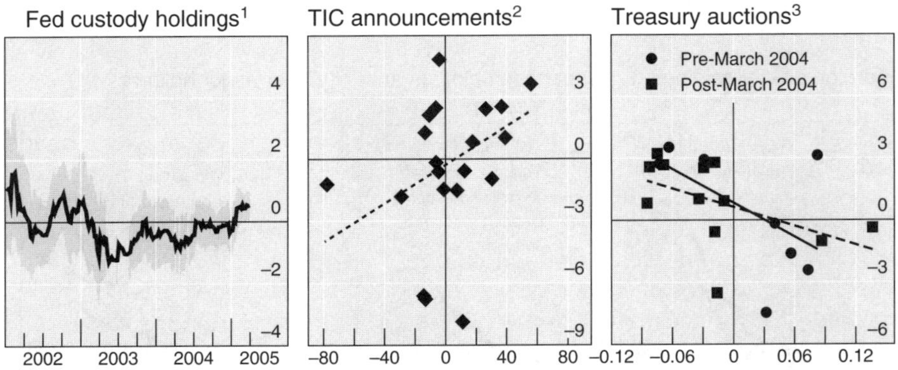

[1] Coefficients estimated from a 26-week rolling regression of the weekly change in five-year US Treasury bond yields on the change in custody holdings for foreign official accounts; in basis points per $1 billion change in foreign official custody holdings. The grey shading indicates the 95% confidence interval; the vertical shading indicates the periods in which the beta coefficient from the bivariate regression is negative and significant at the 95% level. [2] The vertical axis is the change, in basis points, in the yield on the two-year on-the-run US Treasury in the two hours surrounding the release of the TIC data. The horizontal axis is the estimated surprise in the monthly release of the TIC data, measured as the deviation from a three-month moving average of net foreign purchases of US Treasury securities; for the period January 2003–January 2005. [3] The vertical axis is the change, in basis points, in the yield on the two-year on-the-run US Treasury in the two hours surrounding the release of the US Treasury auction results. The horizontal axis is the estimated surprise in the indirect bid share, measured as the deviation from a three-month moving average of the ratio of indirect to total competitive bids accepted in the two-year auction. Pre- and post-March 2004 periods correspond to August 2003–March 2004 and April 2004–March 2005, respectively.

Sources: Board of Governors of the Federal Reserve System; Bloomberg; GovPx; TIC; BIS calculations

The BIS (2005c) also examines the relationship between surprises in indirect bidding at the two-year US Treasury note auction and yield changes on these notes after the auction (Figure 3.9, right panel). 'Prior to March 2004, a 5 percentage point upward surprise in the indirect bid share – which averaged over 40% over the May 2003 to March 2005 period – is associated with a 1.4 basis point fall in the yield on the on-the-run two-year note in the hours surrounding the release of the auction results. This result is slightly weaker when the role of other factors is taken into account, including the bid-to-cover ratio and the total auction size. After March 2004 (the last month of Japanese interventions), this effect decreased to 0.8 basis points' (ibid.). This result is only marginally statistically significant for the two-year note and insignificant for the five-year note, and the overall finding is termed 'inconclusive'.

Kasman and Malik (2004) assume that central banks invest in intermediate-term securities. Thus they take a model of the gap between three-year US Treasury securities and ten-year US Treasury securities and relate the residuals from it to the change in US Treasury securities held in custody at the Federal Reserve. They find that the 12-month change in such holdings is closely related to their measure of mispricing, with an R-squared of .87. Moreover, the magnitude of the estimated effect is quite large: a billion-dollar change is associated with a 0.61 basis point decrease in three-year yields relative to ten-year yields.

This analysis cannot be accepted as definitive, however. It is not clear for one thing that central bank investment in US securities is indeed concentrated in the 'belly' of the yield curve, as these analysts presume. The exclusion of agency securities from the analysis is not easy to understand in light of the strong diversification from US Treasury securities toward agency securities in the period of the analysis. In addition, the use of a 12-month change in custody holdings of Treasury securities raises a question regarding the time series properties of the analysis.

McCauley and Jiang (2004) regressed the change in US bond yields on the weekly change in Federal Reserve custody holdings of US Treasury and agency securities of foreign officials. They employ a rolling regression to let the data identify periods in which a statistically and economically significant change can be identified. They find that a statistically and economically significant association comes and goes in data. When the relationship was evident in the course of 2003, the point estimate of the impact hits a maximum at 1 basis point lower ten-year yield per $1bn change in foreign official holdings.

Figure 3.9, left panel, updates the regression, which is rolled forward over 26-week windows. The 2004 data do not favour the hypothesis that variations in foreign central bank buying over time have been positively associated with changes in the yield on the benchmark US Treasury note. Substitution of the five-year note for the ten-year note does not materially affect this conclusion. Indeed, the most recent data suggest that larger holdings of US Treasury and agency securities by foreign officials at the Federal Reserve are associated with higher ten-year yields!

Bernanke et al. (2004) regress the change in US Treasury bond yields on daily Japanese intervention data and find that $1bn in dollar purchases reduces US ten-year yields by a 0.73 basis points. This finding is robust to exclusion of days of major news in the United States, which reduces the parameter to 0.66 basis points. Taken at face value, the implication is that the $315bn of Japanese intervention in the five quarters ending in the first quarter of 2004 cumulatively reduced US ten-year yields by 2.0-2.3 percentage points.

One reservation regarding this finding is that it is a 'buy-on-the-rumour' result. That is, it assumes perfect knowledge of the scale of intervention in real time by market participants. In fact, the scale of the intervention was subject to much guess-work, with analysts trying to draw inferences from the Bank of Japan's published balance sheet. When the data were eventually published by the Ministry of Finance, editors assigned the stories big headlines as if the information were not known. Moreover, the analysis telescopes the considerable lag between the purchase of dollars, on the one hand, and purchase of bonds, on the other. In fact, the Japanese authorities acquired dollar deposits in banks in the first instance, and only over time invested the funds in securities, including US Treasury securities (Figure 3.7, middle panel). Finally, one wonders whether the estimated effect is constant over the sample period or whether it waxes and wanes, as above.

3.3 Conclusions

This chapter documents the dominance of US dollar assets in global official dollar reserve holdings but questions the widespread view that the dollar share is excessive. The portion of world GDP produced in an empirically defined dollar zone has tended to support the heavy share of the dollar in reserve holdings.

One of the concerns that has been raised in connection with the large reserve holdings of Asian central banks is the potential consequences of a significant diversification of these reserves away from the US dollar towards the euro. It is often asserted as obvious that such a diversification would have major effects on exchange rates. Yet it is also assumed, sometimes by the same individuals, that sterilized intervention in the foreign exchange market by the Fed, the ECB or Japan's Ministry of Finance does not have appreciable impacts on exchange rates in view of the huge stocks of privately held assets. We show that diversification of Asian central banks and sterilized intervention by the Fed, the ECB or the MoF are equivalent in their impact on balance sheets, and that the effect of each on exchange rates should therefore be the same. The empirical evidence in the literature is inconclusive as to what exactly this effect is.

Turning to the investment habits of central banks, it is clear that official reserve portfolios have come to be mostly invested in notes and bonds rather than in US Treasury bills and bank deposits. This diversification into longer-dated US government and other securities has led to suggestions that the increased demand for longer-dated US securities resulting from heavy central bank intervention may have served to hold down long-term interest rates. We review the evidence and find that it is far from conclusive.

4 East Asia and the Trans-Pacific Current Account Imbalance

In Chapter 2 we discussed the build-up of official reserves in East Asia showing that they have reached levels that are very large relative not only to traditional measures such as import cover, but also relative to what can reasonably ascribed to an insurance motive against financial shocks. We also argued, however, that the reserve levels do not reflect obvious macroeconomic policy errors in the countries concerned, but can, depending on which country we consider, be ascribed to factors related to demographic developments, institutional rigidities, and a reliance on stable exchange rates to provide nominal anchors. We also cautioned in Chapter 2 against adopting poorly targeted policies to deal with the reserve build-up.

We return now to these themes but from a different perspective, namely the origins and possible solutions to what we call the trans-pacific imbalance. By this we mean the large current account deficit of the United States during the past several years and the smaller but still sizable surpluses in East Asia. This imbalance, particularly the bilateral balance between the United States and China, is becoming a rallying point for protectionist pressure groups in the United States.

Figure 4.1 Current account balances (US$m)

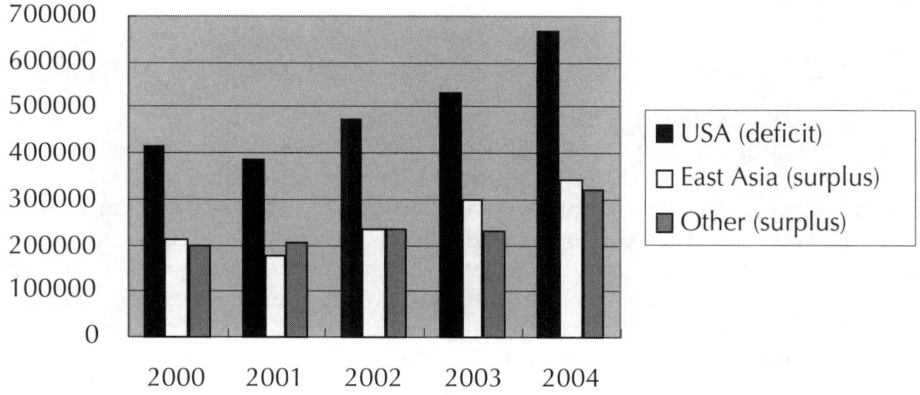

Figure 4.1 shows the current account deficit in the Unites States over the past five years and the corresponding surpluses in East Asia and the rest of the world.[32] While it is true that the evolution of surpluses in East Asia mirrors that of the deficits in the United States, the figure makes clear that the US imbalance is not

only trans-pacific. It is nevertheless the case that much of the academic and policy discussions related to this issue have focused on the relationship between the United States and East Asia.

4.1 Causes and potential consequences of the trans-Pacific imbalance

Although the US current account deficit rose to 6 per cent of its GDP in 2004, according to some economists, notably Dooley et al. (2003), this does not pose any immediate dangers because in their new Bretton Woods system it can be financed as long as East Asian countries are fixated on an export-led growth strategy. Bernanke (2005) argues that the global imbalance is not made in the US. A global saving glut forces the United States to live beyond its means. Balancing the federal budget, according to Bernanke's estimation, will reduce the US current account deficit by less than one percentage point of GDP over the medium-term.

Obstfeld and Rogoff (2004) are not as sanguine as these optimists, saying that the dollar could fall by as much as 20–40% in the process of current account adjustment in the United States. They do not, however, believe that this massive decline in the dollar would be catastrophic for Europe and Japan. Roubini and Setser (2005), on the other hand, believe that the existing imbalance, which is likely to grow further, will provoke a major financial crisis before the end of 2006.

What will happen to the imbalance if it is left unattended? Is there any market mechanism that will resolve the imbalance in an orderly manner without destabilizing the global financial system? This chapter discusses a number of possible patterns of adjustment of the imbalance, which depend on policy changes that the United States and East Asia may or may not make.

Our discussion requires a careful examination of the causes of the imbalance which in recent debates has been described in terms of three contrasting views: One is that East Asians do not consume enough, another accuses East Asian economies of manipulating their exchange rates; and the third points to the United States' growing budgetary deficit and a low private savings rate. We examine each in turn.

4.1.1 A global saving glut: is East Asia saving too much?

Bernanke (2005) believes that there is a global savings glut created largely by emerging economies. The developing world has moved from an aggregate current account surplus of $87 billion in 1996 to a surplus of $205bn by 2003. Unless emerging and developing countries invest more, they will have to transfer their excessive savings to the borrowers in advanced countries who borrow to finance their investment or consumption. Since the EU has been running a trade surplus, it is the United States that has been forced to absorb these savings. According to Bernanke, there is little the United States can do to resolve its current account deficit, as long as the rest of the world saves more than invests.

East Asia as a whole has been a net supplier of savings to the rest of the world for a long time and more so since the 1997-98 Asian financial crisis. This net-saving position of the region could be considered a problem if the region-wide high savings rate were the result of forced saving or policy measures that provided incentives to save or artificially curtailed lending for consumption. There is little evidence of forced saving with the possible exception of the Central Provident Fund of Singapore, or an incentive structure that artificially generates excessive saving.

A more compelling interpretation of the high savings rate of the region is that it is the outcome of intertemporal spending decisions of households in the context of demographic transformations and changes in social security conditions, the latter being particularly important in China. In addition, the aggregate savings rate reflects a strong self-insurance motive. East Asia's fear of exposing itself to financial crises in the future lingers on. Holdings of large reserves serve therefore as war chests to be used to fend off any speculative attack or to meet other unexpected large capital outflows. Furthermore, a lack of profitable local investment opportunities has produced a large current account surplus for the region as a whole.

Viewed from the perspective of the savings and investment balance, the excess of savings over investment – the current account surplus or net foreign investment – is not necessarily a policy problem, if East Asia's savings are invested in foreign investment projects with risk-adjusted rates of return higher than those in East Asia. However, the bulk of East Asia's excess savings has not been allocated in such a manner, as it has been channelled to the United States for the financing of its consumption. Many view this to be less desirable on the ground of global welfare than an allocation that would send East Asia's savings to other parts of the world, including keeping it in emerging markets for the financing of their own investment.

In recent years, emerging economies from other regions have in fact enjoyed narrowed spreads and unprecedented access to international capital markets, even as East Asia's savings have flowed into safer assets in the industrialized countries. A number of the issuers included in the Emerging Markets Bond Index have been upgraded to investment grade, and a substantial number of corporate and financial institution borrowers from these economies can raise funds on international capital markets. The irony is that this improved access for Latin America in part reflects the current account surpluses that imply that, in aggregate, saving is flowing out of this region.

Experience of these economies also suggests that the deregulation and opening of financial markets does not necessarily improve their effective access to them. On the contrary, capital account liberalization can increase the amplitude of cycles in domestic financial markets, causing a larger holdings of foreign reserves to be held as insurance against the possibility of sudden disruptions in the access to external finance.

Although it may sound paradoxical, reforms that have contributed to liberalizing and opening domestic financial markets appear to have weakened investment demand throughout East Asia. Banks and other financial institutions have become much more reluctant to finance long-term and risky investment projects out of concern for the quality of their asset portfolios. Governments have also refrained from expanding their own investment or supporting private investment in social infrastructure, education, research and development, rural development, public health, and the environment. Financial institutions, corporations, and governments themselves have all been preoccupied with strengthening their financial positions to insulate themselves against external financial shocks and speculative attacks. If indeed there is a glut of saving in the global economy, this may reflect the workings of international financial markets, an issue the chapter returns to in Section 4.5.

4.1.2 East Asia's exchange rate manipulation and export-led development strategy

A number of US-based economists have accused East Asian economies of rigging their exchange rates to keep their currencies undervalued in order to subsidize exports.[33] In their view, this foreign exchange market intervention is the main cause of East Asia's ballooning trade surplus. Would a real appreciation of East Asian currencies then set in motion an adjustment that would ultimately restore global balance?

At the outset it should be noted that East Asia's export-led growth strategy itself is not responsible for the reserve accumulation. Many East Asian countries ran large current account deficits before when they were promoting exports more aggressively. This experience suggests that it is too simplistic to argue that the export-led strategy is the principal cause of the growing imbalance unless it can be shown that there is a mechanism by which the strategy has led to the increase in the gap between savings and investment in East Asia. In addition, many East Asian currencies have appreciated in real, trade-weighted terms since the 1997–8 crisis, and this has not prevented export growth in the region. Finally, to our knowledge no one has presented any convincing evidence that East Asia's alleged currency manipulation can explain its growing gap between savings and investment.

During the 1970s and 1980s, a sustained export expansion in East Asia invariably created a favourable environment for business investment and powered an upturn of the economy, which then led to a large increase in imports of capital and intermediate goods and to deterioration in the current account. For a number of reasons this chain of reactions triggered by an export expansion appears to have broken down in many East Asia's emerging market economies, resulting in large and persistent current account surpluses in the region.

One possible explanation for this breakdown is that the East Asian countries, in particular the crisis-hit ones, have yet to complete the paring down of the excess capital stocks they built in the run-up to the 1997–8 crisis. From the point of view of East Asia's policy-makers, the 1997 crisis left them with a large excess stock of capital to be worked off over time. This stock adjustment together with the bursting of the IT bubble in 2001, has curtailed domestic investment demand. As already noted in Chapter 2, between 1995 and 2003, investment as a proportion of GDP fell in all East Asian countries other than China while their savings rates have remained relatively stable (see Figures 2.7 and 2.8). In Indonesia, the investment-GDP ratio in 2003 was less than a half of what it was in 1995. Malaysia saw its ratio plummet to 24.4% in 2003 from the high of 43% in 1997. Korea and Thailand experienced a similar setback, amounting to decreases of 11 and 20 percentage points of GDP, respectively, over the same period.

4.1.3 The US fiscal deficit

The international financial and monetary system at present finances the US current account deficit and the associated fiscal deficit. For Roubini and Setser (2005) this financing is 'the defining feature' of the current system. That is, the US budgetary deficit and the dependence of the rest of the world on an expansion of US domestic demand are the causes of the global imbalance. And as Roubini and Setser see it, the US fiscal deficit is likely to remain large – at more than 3.5 percent of GDP – in coming years if the tax cuts of the current US administration become permanent. They do not believe that the world's central banks are prepared to continue to finance the growing US current account deficits indefinitely: the new Bretton Woods system of Dooley et al. (2003) may last at most for another two years.

In response to Roubini and Setser's pessimistic forecast, it could be argued that a reduction in federal deficit spending runs the risk of setting off a global economic slowdown as it contracts both the US current account deficit and global aggregate demand, unless the reduction is offset by a corresponding demand increase elsewhere. Although US adjustment could create a deficiency in global aggregate demand, it does not follow that running a budgetary deficit in the United States is either an unavoidable or a desirable policy choice. The implication of the global imbalance is that the dependence on the US fiscal deficit is unhealthy and that the international economy should find other areas – regions, markets, and industries – where institutional and policy reforms could support more balanced growth of global aggregate demand.

4.2 Policy adjustments in East Asia: monetary and fiscal policy

The implication in the above section is that reviving domestic demand, in particular fixed investment, in East Asia is important if the countries in the region want to contribute to a policy strategy, preferably coordinated with the United States and the EU, to resolve the trans-pacific imbalance. In view of the severe recession and financial turmoil that a disorderly resolution of global imbalances could provoke, East Asia has every reason to participate actively in any policy adjustments on which the three regions can agree. In this section we examine what countries in the region have done in the spheres of monetary and fiscal policy to facilitate the external adjustment process. We note that monetary policy has mostly been geared towards achieving other goals and that a host of structural constraints are limiting the effectiveness and desirability of fiscal policy interventions. Maintaining the status quo hence seems to be the most likely outcome.

4.2.1 Monetary policy

Monetary policy in the region is accommodating as judged by the level of real short-term interest rates. Since the financial crisis of 1997–8 these have declined in most economies and they are now close to zero and even negative in some cases (see Table 4.1).

Table 4.1 Short-term real interest rates[1]

	1990–6	1999–2001	2002–4	2005 (Jan.–April)
Hong Kong	-3.59	8.26	1.99	1.43
Philippines	4.20	4.53	1.84	-1.39
China		5.04	1.26	0.69
Indonesia	4.27	2.71	1.18	-2.95
Malaysia	2.59	1.54	0.93	0.35
Taiwan	3.05	4.47	0.76	-0.83
Korea	7.35	2.53	0.59	0.15
Japan	2.38	0.80	0.45	0.21
Thailand	4.97	2.43	0.17	-0.66
Singapore		0.36	-0.15	1.39

Note: 1 The real interest rates have been calculated as the difference between representative short term market interest rates and the actual CPI inflation rate over the past year.

Would it be appropriate for monetary policy to be even more expansionary for the purpose of contributing to the reduction of external imbalances? For several reasons, the answer is negative. First, easing monetary policy further would increase the risk of fuelling asset price inflation (real estate inflation in particular) which could lead to another boom-bust cycle as in the run-up to the crisis in 1997. No country in the region is willing to take this risk. Second, some central banks have adopted explicit or implicit domestic inflation objectives for the conduct of their monetary policy. Further easing at this stage or a slower rise than would be indicated by inflation forecasts could endanger the attainment of these objectives. Third, yet other countries have chosen to focus on exchange rate stability which restricts the use of monetary policy for other purposes. Fourth, it is uncertain whether monetary expansion would succeed in reducing current account surpluses through the expansion of domestic demand.

The objectives of monetary policy vary from country to country in East Asia, as they are in general attendant on the choice of an exchange rate regime. In economies where the exchange rate is fixed and international capital movements are free, there can be no independent monetary policy. This is essentially the case in Hong Kong where interest rates are dictated almost exclusively by the corresponding US dollar rates. The case is similar in Singapore, where the monetary authority sets the desired effective exchange rate path so as to achieve a domestic inflation objective. In this policy environment, the authorities also have a very limited ability to set short-term interest rates, against the background of very substantial international capital mobility.

China's and Malaysia's just altered rigidly fixed exchange rates allowed scope for an independent domestic interest rate policy given porous but substantial and effective controls on international capital movements. Indeed, to prevent overheating of the economy and financial instability, the Chinese authorities have adopted both administrative measures and interest rate rises to rein in the rapid growth of credit and capital investment. These measures have achieved some success in stabilizing the general rate of inflation. Despite the tightening of credit growth, there is still excess liquidity in the system, which continues to fuel real estate speculation and asset price inflation. In view of these developments, a loosening of China's credit policy to permit more rapid growth of investment in order to restrain the current account surplus would run the risk of overheating the economy and exacerbating the non-performing loans problems at the banks as excessive investments may result in a large increase in business failures.

Four of East Asia's emerging economies – Indonesia, the Philippines, South Korea, and Thailand – have adopted explicit inflation targeting as their monetary policy regime. Subject to maintaining price stability such a policy regime may at times permit the authorities to pursue domestic output objectives. At present, however, further easing of monetary policy may not stimulate consumption and investment demand before it accelerates further the continuing asset inflation in the cases of South Korea and Thailand, and it would contribute to general inflationary pressures in Indonesia and the Philippines.

Quite apart from the issue of whether it would be in the interest of the countries in the region to adopt a more expansionary policy for the purpose of stimulating demand and thereby reducing the current account surplus, it is not a foregone conclusion that such a policy would actually succeed. Standard theory would predict that under conditions of high capital mobility the expansionary effect of monetary policy would lead to an improvement rather than a deterioration of the external balance through a depreciation of the currency. With low capital mobility, or in situations where the traded asset is equity rather than bonds, this result may be overturned and the current account could deteriorate.

If the responsiveness of corporate investment in Asia to short-term interest rates were very large, it might be reasonable to suppose that easier money would help narrow the gap between savings and investment and thereby reduce the current account surplus in the region. However, the corporate sector is producing a financial surplus in most countries in the region. This net corporate savings suggests that the cost of freshly raised bank loans or newly issued bonds might not have a strong effect on investment demand. Indeed, the persistent sluggishness of investment demand in East Asian countries (except China) in the presence of very low real interest rates suggests that traditional channels of monetary policy, in particular the cost of capital channel, may have weakened. For example, it is generally believed that this is the case in Japan, and it may also be true in Taiwan and South Korea.

The upshot of this discussion is that it would be unwise for East Asian countries to ease monetary policy at this stage for the purpose of influencing the external balance, because it is uncertain whether it would be effective and in any case it would be counter to domestic stability objectives.

4.2.2 Fiscal policy

Fiscal prudence is an Asian value that has been held in high regard, and East Asian countries have generally considered fiscal expansion as a means of stimulating domestic demand only with reluctance. In many nascent democracies in the region, fiscal policy suffers from rigidity of implementation and a long lag, since it is often necessary to go through a notoriously slow and complicated political process to obtain consensus on tax cuts or the size and distribution of government expenditure between projects, sectors, and regions. Fiscal policy can therefore easily prove to be pro cyclical. East Asian policy-makers are also determined not to follow Japan's example with a pump-priming policy that has constructed deserted highways, public buildings and other idle infrastructure, financed with a massive increase in national debt.

Whatever the desirability of restoring the current account balance, it is difficult to pressure China to adopt a more expansionary fiscal policy in view of the underlying inflationary pressures and its budgetary and extra-budgetary position. To begin with, the central government cannot easily control fiscal expenditures or organize and implement a government-spending programme without securing the cooperation of the provincial governments. Although the stated share of central government expenditure and debt in GDP is relatively small, the overall burden of China's national debt is not. If non-performing loans of state-owned banks and other financial institutions and unfunded social obligations are included, estimates of the level of the debt become large. Adding to this debt with wider fiscal deficits would obviously not be prudent. Instead, along with tightening monetary policy, the Chinese authorities have sought to curb spending of the local as well as the central government in order to restrain inflation and curb real estate speculation. The medium-term fiscal objective of the Chinese government is to keep the nominal budgetary deficit constant. Few would disagree with this objective.

As for Japan, a sensible macroeconomic policy mix would hardly include more spending for investment in infrastructure and other public projects when the country is faced with a difficult task of managing a national debt which is approaching 150% of GDP. It is beyond the scope of this study to discuss the prospect for the Japanese economy, but it is clear that fiscal policy will not be used again to revive the economy.

The exclusion of the two major players leave ASEAN states, Taiwan and South Korea as plausible candidates to expand fiscal policy in East Asia. Among the

ASEAN states, Indonesia and the Philippines are in no position to contemplate any further increase in government spending or any cut in taxes. The Indonesian government is committed to further fiscal consolidation to reduce vulnerability arising from the high level of public debt. Its objective is to achieve broad budgetary balance by 2006–7 consistent with lowering public debt to below 50% of GDP. The Indonesian government has also been engaged in fiscal reform that envisages more efficient tax administration and improvement in budget preparation and execution. The size of the public debt in the Philippines exceeds 100% of GDP, which is high and unsustainable. Before the recent political strains, the new administration had committed itself to balancing the budget by 2009 by tax increases and rationalization of expenditure.

Thailand and Malaysia have been able to bring down budgetary deficits to a manageable level, and as a result they do not have national debt problems that rule out an expansionary fiscal policy. The new government in Malaysia is seeking to reorient fiscal policy from large infrastructure projects to more broad-based stimuli. Although Thailand has room for additional fiscal stimulus, its authorities were reluctant to run a budgetary deficit. Its goal had shifted to maintaining a neutral stance in fiscal policy as the economy has enjoyed balanced growth based on the expansion of exports, consumption and investment. The recently announced set of infrastructure projects suggest considerable stimulus against the backdrop of a current account that is already registering a deficit.

South Korea, Singapore and Taiwan are all known for their fiscal conservatism. They could certainly take on a more expansionary stance on fiscal policy. Of these countries, South Korea has moved ahead with an expenditure-switching policy that combines lower interest rates and the front-loading of government spending with an exchange rate appreciation. The two other economies have not been as active as Korea has as expanding export earnings have generally supported relatively high rates of growth.

Suppose, however, that all three countries are persuaded to implement an expansionary fiscal policy. To what extent would their policy change contribute to checking the growth of East Asia's aggregate trade surplus? As a group, Singapore, South Korea and Taiwan accounted for less than a quarter of East Asia's total foreign reserves at the end of 2003. During the 2000–3 period, their combined current account surplus amounted to \$196.4bn, or slightly more than twenty percent of East Asia's total. Although these countries would benefit from fiscal stimulus, these figures suggest that expansionary policies would hardly be sufficient to bring about a significant reduction in the overall trans-pacific imbalance even if they had an impact on all of the three economies.

There is also a structural characteristic of East Asia that raises the question of the effectiveness of fiscal expansion in these emerging economies as a means of reducing the transpacific imbalance. The domestic demand expansion in ASEAN, Taiwan, and South Korea may not necessarily increase their imports from or decrease their exports to the United States. According to a simulation study based on a multi-country intertemporal general equilibrium model (Lee et al., 2004), a fiscal expansion in East Asian countries excluding Japan amounting to 2% of GDP causes current account balances to worsen by between 0.2% and 1.1% of GDP in the first year. The corresponding improvement in the US current account is a much small share of its own GDP because the combined size of the expanding countries is small relative to the United States. Another interesting result of this exercise is that the same fiscal expansion tends to increase Japan's trade surplus, which amounts to 0.11% of GDP. This result is not surprising in view of the fact that Japan is a major supplier of capital and intermediate goods for other East Asian countries. It might be fair to conclude that the effect of a fiscal expansion in East Asia excluding Japan would depend on how Japanese exchange rate policy reacted to the improvement in Japan's exports.

4.3 Adjustment of exchange rate policy in East Asia

The stability of the trade weighted exchange rates of East Asia's emerging market economies reflects the efforts of their authorities to intervene in the foreign exchange markets. Park and Wyplosz (2004) discuss a number of the objectives of their interventions. Maintaining their export competitiveness is certainly one of them, but as we have emphasized above, maintaining financial stability and providing a nominal anchor for the economy are also important.

The ten East Asian economies that include the original ASEAN countries (Indonesia, Malaysia, the Philippines, Singapore and Thailand) and China, Japan, South Korea, Taiwan and Hong Kong have piled up large amounts of reserves. These are excessive by most standards, especially since the danger of another round of financial crises has receded. In the past two or three years expectations of currency appreciation have attracted more capital inflows into the region, thereby complicating the management of exchange rates and domestic monetary conditions. Under these circumstances, some of these economies have allowed their nominal exchange rates to strengthen vis-à-vis the dollar. For example, over the six-month period beginning in October 2004, the Korean won appreciated 15%. More recently, the change in China's exchange rate regime announced on 21 July 2005 reflects the intention to permit exchange rate adjustments to play a greater role in macroeconomic management in that country.

Currency appreciation could send a signal that the East Asian policy makers are serious about making a needed macroeconomic adjustment to shift resources to the non-tradable sector over time. As long as China maintained a rigid peg to the US dollar it was difficult for other East Asian countries to contemplate appreciation on their own. Their unwillingness reflected not only the perceived desirability of having a stable exchange rate for the puropses of domestic macroeconomic and financial-stability, but also a collective action problem the East Asian economies face in coordinating their exchange rate policy (Ogawa and Ito, 2000). If the renminbi becomes more flexible de facto, this collective action problem implies that the Chinese currency will become more important for the movements of the other currencies in the region. Its importance was already presaged in the co-movement of the renminbi non-deliverable forwards and regional currencies in 2004 (Ho et al., 2005).

4.3.1 Policy impasse: collective action problem

Countries in East Asia that manage their exchange rates were reluctant to allow their currencies to appreciate as long as local trading partners and competitors did not, because doing so would lead to a loss of their shares of export markets both inside and outside the region. In particular, as long as China maintained a rigid peg of the renminbi to the dollar, other East Asian countries also resisted appreciation of their currencies vis-à-vis the dollar since China competes in both regional and global export markets.

East Asia's policy-makers admit that there is a need for a collective exchange rate policy and have even raised the possibility of creating a regional monetary union in the future. They have established institutional arrangements such as the ASEAN+3 meetings of finance ministers or their deputies, which could serve as fora for coordinating exchange rate policy among these states. However, if past experience with policy coordination among ASEAN+3 is any guide, the member countries will not be able to agree easily on any issue as complicated as coordination of exchange rate policy for two main reasons.

One problem is that Japan and China, the two major countries, which could and should provide leadership for any collective policy actions and cooperation, have not always seen eye to eye on many regional issues. Another problem is more fundamental in that the economies belonging to ASEAN+3 may not necessarily constitute an optimum currency area given the structural diversity and differences in the level of development. This suggests the likelihood of external shocks that are too asymmetric to be accommodated by a uniform monetary policy, in the event that the dismantling of capital controls rendered stabilized currencies tantamount to a common monetary policy. Even if China and Japan were able to work together, therefore, they might not be able to persuade the other ASEAN+3 countries to join any collective exchange rate system such as a common basket peg or an Asian version of the European Monetary System.

The issue is further complicated by the ambiguous position of Japan on East Asia's exchange rate policy coordination. Since the yen is a major free floating currency comparable with the US dollar and the euro, it is difficult for Japan to join any East Asian collective exchange rate arrangement for the foreseeable future. Japan's non-participation may present another hurdle for exchange rate policy coordination in East Asia.

Japan has been running a surplus in its trade with all other East Asian economies including China. The group of emerging market and developing economies, on the other hand, has been running a surplus with China, but a large deficit with Japan. Because of these different profiles of bilateral imbalances, East Asian emerging market and developing economies may be able to accept a simultaneous appreciation of their currencies and the renminbi against the dollar, but they will also be concerned that the yen appreciate against the dollar at the same time. There is some evidence in the foreign exchange market that such an outcome could be expected (Malcolm, 2005), and the reaction of the yen to the renminbi's appreciation on 21 July 2005 offers further evidence in the same direction. But since there is no guarantee that the yen will appreciate as much as other East Asian currencies do vis-à-vis the U.S. dollar, other East Asian economies will be cautious of any collective exchange rate appreciation, out of fear that their own currencies may appreciate against the yen. This would deepen their persistent structural trade deficits with Japan. To economists, bilateral trade imbalances may not matter, but to East Asia's politicians and policy-makers, they matter a lot.

4.3.2 What effect would an across-the-board appreciation of the East Asian currencies have?

To date, the demand for East Asian currency appreciation has been mostly directed at China and other regional emerging economies even though Japan accounts for almost half of ASEAN+3's total reserves and an equally large share of the region's current account surplus. The tendency to leave Japan out of the demand for appreciation reflects both the yen's float and the special consideration of Japan's continuing deflation despite zero interest rates.

Suppose for the sake of argument that the group of the original ASEAN 5, together with China and South Korea, manage to clear the hurdles to adjust their bilateral exchange rates to bring about an overall appreciation of the currencies of the group vis-à-vis the dollar. How much of a group wide exchange rate adjustment would then be needed to balance its aggregate current account? This is an empirical question, and not surprisingly there are many contending views.

The sources of contention are two interrelated empirical issues: the magnitudes of price elasticities of both imports and exports of these seven economies and the costs and benefits of the group's unilateral real appreciation. Bergsten (2005) urges China to revalue its currency by 25% and other Asian countries by half as much. This currency adjustment would reduce, it is argued, the annual US current account deficit by $50-60bn. If China and other Asian countries do not permit such a revaluation, he calls for a multilateral name-and-shame campaign against them for manipulating their exchange rates.

Cline (2005) echoes this view by suggesting that these currency manipulators should face trade penalties unless they let market forces bid up their exchange rates against the dollar. In making this demand, however, Chine contradicts the results of the simulation using his own general equilibrium model, which shows that an exogenous depreciation of the dollar generates very little external adjustment and that fiscal contraction is needed as a central part of the US external adjustment process.

Using a static real sector model that includes both tradables and non-tradables, Obstfeld and Rogoff (2004) estimate the extent of depreciation of the US trade-weighted real exchange rate that would be consistent with a closing of the US current account gap. Their results suggest that the dollar may have to depreciate anywhere from 20% to 40% depending on the rigidity of nominal prices and the degree of the exchange rate pass-through.

The simulation of a concerted revaluation of East Asian exchange rates by 10% in a multi-country intertemporal general equilibrium model (Lee et al., 2004) shows that it does not make any significant impact on the trade balances of the East Asian countries. The trade impacts of this policy for global imbalances are small with minor impacts on the current accounts of the revalued East Asian economies as well as others. The reasons are clear. The revaluation makes export goods less competitive on world markets during the period that domestic prices have not adjusted to the effective tightening of monetary policy. The revaluation also reduces domestic demand. Thus the effect of the decrease in East Asian countries' import demand is offsetting the effect of a stronger currency on exports. Whether a country is positively or negatively affected depends on the size and nature of trade with the East Asian countries and the impact of changes in the East Asian countries' demand on other countries. The demand and relative price (or competitiveness) effects tend to cancel in their impact on the trade balances of most countries. The estimation result suggests that the East Asian currency revaluation will have no effect on the U.S. current account balance.

McKibbin and Stoeckel (2004) also explore the implication of a 10% appreciation of the Chinese exchange rate. The main result is similar. Chinese revaluation has significant impacts on the Chinese economy by decreasing GDP growth by 4.1% relative to the baseline in the first year, but the effects disappear over time. The Chinese current account balance worsens by close to 0.5% of GDP but with minor impacts on the trade positions of other economies including the United States'.

As these selective but representative examples indicate, there is a large discrepancy between the results from partial-equilibrium and general-equilibrium models when they are used to evaluate the effect of exchange rate changes on global current account imbalances. This is not surprising. Whereas the letter models by their very nature must take a stand on how savings and investment rates are determined, the former typically ignore the constraint that the current account must be equal to the national savings/investment balance. Partial equilibrium calculations based on a trade balance equation simply assume that the savings/investment balance adjusts passively and without causing further repercussions. This is an incredible assumption in our view, and for this reason we see no reason to take seriously the corresponding policy recommendations with regard to exchange rate adjustments.[34]

This does not mean of course that real exchange rates will not adjust if and when the current account adjustments take place, but the size of exchange rate changes will depend on exactly how the current account adjustment comes about, for example whether it is due to an endogenous change in real interest rates, an autonomous reduction in total spending in the United States that is tilted towards traded goods, or an autonomous increase in spending in East Asia that is tilted towards non-traded goods.

If adjustments of real exchange rates are needed, it is generally believed that it is preferable to implement these through nominal exchange rate changes rather than through changes in domestic price level. This has also been recognized by Chinese policy makers of course, but while acknowledging the need to increase the flexibility of the renminbi dollar exchange rate, their actions have been constrained by a Catch-22 dilemma. As we have emphasized in Chapter 2, introducing some flexibility together with a small initial revaluation runs the risk that capital inflows continue or even increase. A larger initial move may have succeeded in restraining capital inflows, but such a policy change was not adopted presumably because of its negative impact on employment, growth and on the banking sector saddled with large amounts of non-performing loans. To make matters even more complicated, depending on how the Chinese authorities manage the exchange rate in the new regime, capital inflows may continue as external pressures for a large revaluation persist.

4.4 Intrarregional policy adjustments and coordination in East Asia

Although it is somewhat too early to judge, there is an optimistic outlook that as the current upswing in East Asia's business cycle matures, the trans-pacific imbalance may resolve itself into a transitory problem of adjustment between East Asia on the one hand and the United States and the EU on the other. This does not mean that East Asia can and should wait out until the imbalance itself and the ongoing debate on what the region should do dissipates itself. There is little disagreement that East Asian economies need to develop more competitive domestic markets and strong domestic demand in aid of the region's financial stability and growth. Any decrease in East Asia's trade surplus that follows should be regarded as a by-product.

4.4.1 Revival of demand: Japan should take the lead

One of the implications of the discussion in the two previous sections is that as long as Japan remains unable to revive domestic demand and China is labouring for a soft landing of the economy, other smaller East Asian countries individually or collectively can only do so much to curb a further increase in the transpacific imbalance, simply because the number of the economies that could reflate domestic demand and their combined economic size are small. Unless Japan is prepared to absorb more goods and services not only from the United States but also from other East Asian economies, the external pressure on the rest of East Asia to expand domestic demand will not be well received. If Japan makes headway in pulling the economy out of its decade-long slow growth, other East Asian counties will be better disposed to cooperating with Japan and the United States to make necessary policy changes.

If indeed it is critical that East Asia as a whole embraces a more domestic demand based growth strategy, Japan is the country that should take the lead. Unless Japan breaks out of its economic doldrums, one cannot have much hope for restoring balance between the two sides of the Pacific with only policy changes in the rest of East Asia. Japanese domestic demand has repeatedly faltered, and the prospect for an early recovery of the Japanese economy remains at best uncertain. There are signs that the Japanese corporate sector is completing its balance sheet repair, and is in a better position to put cash flow to work in investment. Surely, the Japanese banking system has also gone very far in completing its balance sheet repair as well. Other East Asian countries could make up for the lack of domestic demand in Japan, but only to a limited extent. This is East Asia's dilemma.

4.4.2 Exchange rate policy: China holds the key

China has now formally moved to a more flexible exchange rate regime. This should permit greater flexibility of US dollar exchange rates of East Asian currencies more generally. Their initial reactions to the 2% appreciation of the renminbi relative to the dollar bear this out. Chinese leadership has been vital because China is the largest export market and at the centre of regional trade integration in East Asia. China's remarkable growth and entry into the global trading system have produced market forces that are creating a triangular trade relationship involving, China, the United States, and Japan, together with East Asia's emerging market economies.

In this relationship, Japan and East Asia's emerging market economies export capital goods and intermediate inputs to China. China in turn uses these capital and other intermediate goods to produce a wide variety of manufactured goods that are exported to the United States, the EU and other regions. At present, it is not too much of an exaggeration to characterize the region that comprises ASEAN+3 as 'a large conveyor belt, carrying components, sub-assemblies and capital equipment to factories in China' (De Jonquieres, 2005). If trade integration in East Asia is aligned along the vertical axis with China at the end of the production line, China naturally holds the key to the exchange rate adjustment in East Asia. It remains to be seen how rapid and large this adjustment will be.

4.4.3 Consolidation of bilateral FTAs and the CMI

Another regional development in East Asia that has important implications for the management of the imbalance has been the proliferation of Free Trade Areas (FTAs). While skepticism abounds as to the advantages of bilateral FTAs over multilateral trade liberalization, there is widespread agreement that the completed and proposed FTAs will serve as building blocks for future regional trade integration in East Asia.

Regional trade integration may lessen East Asia's dependence on the US and EU markets for final goods. A continuing increase in intrarregional trade brought about by trade liberalization is expected to create new investment opportunities throughout the region including China. The new opportunities may help keep more of East Asia's savings in the region instead of lending them to other regions.

But there is a danger that this process may exacerbate transpacific trade tensions. Further integration among mostly export-oriented economies with China as the centre of gravity of a vertically integrated production process may create a huge export-oriented region, which will push out more exports than before to the rest of the world. For this scenario not to materialize, it is important that intrarregional trade in final goods is also expanded.

China and other East Asia's emerging and developing economies would be inclined to hold much lower levels of foreign reserves for self-insurance, if they had access to market and official sources of liquidity support in addition to the IMF. The Chiang Mai Initiative (CMI) established a regional currency swap arrangement to serve as a regional liquidity assistance system. If the participating countries gain confidence in the system as a source of liquidity, East Asia's precautionary reserve demand may fall. In this regard, ASEAN+3's decision to expand and consolidate the CMI into a de facto regional lending arrangement is a welcome development.

The initiative for furthering the development of bond markets in Asia by the ASEAN+3 will also help East Asian countries move into a higher gear for regional financial integration. Creating liquid and deep bond markets where East Asian firms can issue local currency denominated bonds will then increase the availability of long-term financing, which can only facilitate investment and thereby narrow the region's saving and investment gap.

4.5 Interregional policy coordination

4.5.1 Simultaneous macroeconomic policy adjustments

There is little doubt that the resolution of the transpacific imbalance requires not only East Asia's but also Unites States' policy adjustment. If outside observers believe that East Asia's emerging economies including that of China, will continue to run up surpluses on their current accounts and use these surpluses to buy up US securities, they are ignoring the ominous macroeconomic adjustment already in view that will eventually stem the growth of East Asia's surplus. If American and European policy-makers believe that unilateral policy changes in East Asia will stop the swelling of the transpacific imbalance in the short run, they are also ill advised.

Likewise, East Asian policy-makers would be ill advised to believe that it is the United States which is primarily responsible and should therefore take steps to cut down its fiscal deficit to resolve the imbalance. It is true that a smaller US current account deficit may result in a drop in real interest rates in both East Asia and Europe and that this could produce expansionary effects. But, as pointed out above, the lower cost of capital is not likely to resuscitate East Asia's weak investment demand. Given this possibility, one may argue that the best policy choice is simultaneous macroeconomic policy adjustments in all three regions: tightening of fiscal policy in the United States, continued expansionary monetary policy in Europe, and loose fiscal policy together with currency appreciation in East Asia.

4.5.2 Articulation of the demand for policy changes in East Asia.

In insisting on East Asia's currency realignment, proponents have often failed to clarify their demand. Are they asking for non-intervention in the foreign exchange market and hence unfettered free floating? Or are they demanding discrete exchange rate adjustments by East Asian de jure floaters as well as those with a fixed exchange rate system? Are they also demanding capital account liberalization at the same time? Proponents have vacillated between insistence on liberal reforms, on the one hand, and demands for short-run policy adjustments, such as a unilateral revaluation of the currencies of East Asia's emerging economies, on the other. This has weakened their voice in the reform debate.

There is no single exchange rate regime appropriate to all East Asia's emerging market and developing economies. There is no clear evidence that capital account liberalization will help sustain macroeconomic stability or growth in the short term. If outside observers believe that East Asian economies including Japan are in need of stimulating their domestic consumption and investment, then their suggestions for policy changes should be more specific in terms of the policies and institutional reform needed in individual East Asian countries. Most of all, to be effective the demand for the policy changes in East Asia will have to be accompanied by concomitant policy adjustments in both the United States and the EU and support for East Asia's efforts at regional economic integration as an intermediate step towards eventual integration with the global system.

4.5.3 A new Plaza Accord

If the continuing expansion can be sustained, then East Asia's demand for imports from outside the region will increase, reducing its overall current account surplus. China's recent import weakness is probably temporary, but a slow-down in its domestic investment will limit the overall narrowing of East Asia's current account surplus. However, this will not necessarily lead to a similar reduction in the U.S current account deficit so long as the US savings–investment gap remains unchanged. Instead, a decrease in East Asia's surplus is likely to be matched by an almost equal increase in the combined surplus of other regions vis-à-vis the United States. The resolution of the transpacific imbalance therefore requires policy coordination not only among the East Asian countries but also between East Asia, on the one hand, and the U.S. and EU, on the other.

The United States may continue not to make policy adjustments on the assumptions that the imbalance is not likely to pose any serious threat to the stability of its financial market or the global financial system and that it is not made in America. This benign neglect, however, may weaken the dollar further and put pressure on the euro to appreciate more than otherwise. In view of this need for policy coordination, the United States, the EU and ASEAN+3 could consider establishing a framework of policy coordination in which the participating countries devise interregional policy adjustments. This would focus on a scheme of domestic demand expansion and exchange rate appreciation in East Asia that would be matched by supporting policy changes in both the United States and the EU and structural reform in all three regions needed for the resolution of the imbalance. The world economy needs a new Plaza Accord, but for different objectives and with different players.

4.5.4 Resurrection of the reform of the international financial system

The large accumulation of reserves in East Asia, originally built up for self insurance, underscores the need for reform of the international financial system. This would assure the availability of short-term liquidity financing for those economies experiencing temporary balance-of-payment difficulties. Reforming the international financial system, therefore, would serve as a long run solution of the imbalance. Such reform will allay the fear of many smaller East Asian economies that they are innately vulnerable to external shocks and that international financial markets will refuse them short-term liquidity when they are faced with an unexpected and large capital outflow. If the international financial system were reformed, together with financial reform in the region it could then speed up East

Asia's integration into the global financial system.

Fearing that the required reform will not be forthcoming, emerging economies including those in East Asia, have taken the prevention of future financial crises into their own hands. Having accumulated large amounts of reserves, East Asian emerging economies feel secure about their financial positions. They risk becoming complacent about pressing ahead with their much needed structural reforms that were set in place long before.

4.6 Three scenarios

The above discussion of the scope of and instruments for policy adjustments in East Asia suggests that the United States, the EU and East Asia could put the global economy on one of the following three trajectories of adjustment, depending on how they manage macroeconomic policies,.

4.6.1 Growing-out

The most desirable scenario is that East Asia grows out of its imbalance. A growing number of market participants and policy-makers in East Asia share an optimistic outlook that after seven years of an investment slump, East Asian economies are poised to step up their spending on plant and equipment as they have worked off much of the excess capacity that they built before the 1997–8 crisis.

The ongoing export boom will serve as a catalyst for more spending on capital goods. Low interest rates and the abundance of liquidity will also stimulate consumer spending and the demand for real assets. These developments will reinforce each other to increase East Asia's overall demand for imports from outside of the region including the United States. Related to this, there is also the possibility that East Asian countries could make policy adjustments unilaterally to stimulate domestic demand possibly without making any further major exchange rate adjustment. If they are effective, East Asia's unilateral policy changes would add to the region's import demand. This increase in East Asia's import demand will in part be met by US exporters so that it could hold up further deterioration in the U.S trade account, thereby taking pressure off the weakening of the dollar.

However, this scenario has two problems. One is that in view of recent developments in both China and Japan – the two countries that account for almost 70% of East Asia's total trade surplus – East Asia's imports from other regions, in particular from the United States, may not increase as much as needed to reduce the transpacific imbalance to manageable proportions. China has been able to record a substantial trade surplus while growing 9% a year, and a possible slowdown in breakneck investment suggests that this surplus may be widening. In contrast, economic growth in Japan has faltered since the third quarter of 2004, indicating that the recovery that began a year before is petering out again. Unless Japan and China can at least prevent their surpluses from widening, growth in demand in the smaller East Asian countries alone will not make a dent in the transpacific imbalance.

Another problem is that a priori, it is uncertain whether an increase in East Asia's import demand will result in any significant improvement in the US current account balance. In a Keynesian framework, an exogenous increase in exports improves the current account balance and at the same time narrows the savings–investment gap through an income and interest rate effect. However, when the supply capacity of traded goods is constrained, as it is in the United States, and federal deficits persist, then to be effective the increase in East Asia's import demand for US-produced goods and services will have to crowd out private spending to make the US current account deficit smaller. However, if this crowding-out effect is not significant, a pick-up in East Asia's growth may not be adequate to scale down the growth of the global imbalance. What this development means is that the euro and other areas will then widen their surpluses.

In order to examine the consequences of this scenario further, assume that the world consists of the United States, the EU and East Asia. East Asia's trade surpluses with both the United States and the EU will fall as the region begins to grow faster. However, if the US budgetary deficits persist, then the US current account deficit will likewise persist and the surplus with the euro area could widen.

4.6.2 Non-market solutions

Following the line of argument advanced by Bergsten and Cline, US policy-makers may reexamine their earlier view that the current account imbalance does not put the global economy at risk. Indeed, as noted earlier, Bergsten and Cline have begun to raise the possibility of imposing restrictions on East Asia's exports to the United States. On 6 April 2005, the US Senate tacitly endorsed the so-called China Currency Bill which would impose a tariff on China equal to the supposed undervaluation of the renminbi. This is tantamount to taking a non-market solution on the part of the United States. Unable to persuade East Asian economies to make appropriate policy adjustments including exchange rate appreciation, and unwilling or unable to make the required domestic policy adjustments, the United States may resort to a more aggressive policy of restricting its imports from East Asia on the pretext of East Asia's unfair trade practices and rigging of the exchange rate. Aside from the imprudence of such a drastic action, such a non-market solution will not help resolve the imbalance. Without a change in the underlying flows of savings and investment, such policies will simply shift part of the transpacific imbalance to other regions of the world.

If the non-market solution is designed to force East Asian countries to make necessary policy change, it is not likely to succeed. Instead, it will cause trans-Pacific economic relations to deteriorate to a perilous point. The US imposition of import restrictions, including higher tariffs, could endanger the Doha round of trade negotiations and bring into question the future role of the WTO. If any non-market solution for resolving the imbalance ever comes to the fore, it will also draw more East Asian countries to an inward-looking regionalism that will encourage growing support for trade integration centering on China.

Instead of taking what amounts to retaliatory action, the United States may also consider other strategies that could diffuse the frictions. The United States could, for instance, step up its demand on East Asian economies for deregulation and opening their financial markets along with further import liberalization to make it easier for East Asia's private investors to hold more US securities in their portfolios. At the same time, the United States may look for more opportunities for negotiating bilateral free trade agreements with East Asian countries. The increase in the number of FTAs the United States can conclude with East Asian countries will not by itself resolve the imbalance, but it may defuse some of the tensions currently characterizing international economic relations.

4.6.3 Policy coordination among the United States, the EU and East Asia

The above discussion of the two scenarios underscores what appears to be an obvious conclusion that interregional policy coordination among the United States, the EU and East Asia is critical to the resolution of the global imbalance. The savings glut itself or the so-called new Bretton Woods system cannot be sustained for much longer. There is an uncomfortably high probability that the global economy could be thrown into a recession with financial turmoil unless the United States, the EU and East Asia manage to coordinate their policies to allocate East Asia's savings to more productive uses.

The cooperative efforts among the three regions will be effective if they are directed to lowering the US fiscal deficit as a proportion of GDP while expanding domestic demand in both Europe and East Asia. Even if the three-region policy coordination did not succeed in removing the imbalance, a useful step would have been taken if it at least contained its further expansion. This containment will contribute to dispelling some of the uncertainties in international financial markets such as the widely held belief among global investors that the imbalance could precipitate a large dollar depreciation, thereby leading to instability in the global financial system. The probability a regional or global financial crisis would be considerably reduced following a credible agreement on a plan for policy coordination that was seen as effective in reducing the present imbalance.

For its part, East Asia will benefit a great deal from stimulating domestic demand while letting its currencies appreciate to discourage speculative capital inflows. Deregulating capital outflows including outbound FDI, further liberalization of imports, revamping the domestic regulatory structure that constrains domestic investment and developing competitive domestic markets are some of the structural reforms they could initiate immediately. For some countries with a lower national debt-GDP ratio more aggressive expansionary fiscal policy – cutting taxes and increasing government investment in social and physical infrastructure – is in order.

A coordinated set of policy adjustments is essential because if the United States succeeds in narrowing the current account gap, it could create a global deficiency of demand unless Europe and East Asia play their parts. The United States unilateral policy adjustment could cause a precipitous fall in its demand for imports from the rest of the world. Given its high dependence on the US market, East Asia may suffer proportionately more of an economic contraction. The elasticity of substitution between many exported goods on the one hand and domestically consumed traded and non-traded goods on the other in East Asia is relatively low. The lower the elasticity, the steeper will be the slowdown.

What are then the chances of policy coordination among the three regions? Unfortunately they appear to us as worryingly small simply because of the inability of the three principal parties to play their parts in the coordination process. It is an open question whether the United States will have the political will to restrain the expansion of its budgetary deficit. Equally uncertain is whether East Asian economies will be able to get their acts together to coordinate their macroeconomic policies. While the East Asian economies are vacillating, the United States will step up its demand on East Asia for policy changes. Unable to respond to the demand in a collective manner, East Asia's emerging economies including China could continue to drift, placing themselves at the mercy of speculators moving massive sums of money in and out of the region and in doing so throwing regional as well as domestic financial markets in disarray.

5 Monetary and Exchange Rate Arrangements in East Asia in a Longer-Run Perspective

This final chapter looks beyond the current controversies and imbalances and attempts to paint a picture of monetary and financial arrangements in East Asia in a longer term perspective. Such an exercise is difficult not only because the economic forces involved are hard to predict, but also because political considerations are likely to be critical for the outcome. It may nevertheless be useful, because, as the weight of East Asia in the world economy continues to grow, the monetary and financial arrangements that emerge in the region will become increasingly important for the rest of the world.

Currently the combined GDP of the economies of East Asia is close to 90% of the euro area. Projected growth rates in the region, especially in China, indicate that a decade from now the two areas will be of about equal economic size and each will be about three quarters of the size of the US economy. The importance of intrarregional trade in East Asia has grown rapidly in recent years, and it is now similar to that in Europe.[35] There is every reason to believe that trade will be even more integrated in the future.

If trade integration has proceeded rapidly, the same can not be said for financial integration. Capital markets are fragmented, in some cases as a result of controls that limit cross-country flows, and in others by limited institutional infrastructure.

Policies in the region generally attempt to maintain some form of exchange-rate stability, even in the context of more or less explicit inflation targeting, with Japan the notable exception.[36] Although the notion of an 'East-Asian dollar standard' is not supported by empirical evidence, the trade-weighted orientation of exchange rate policy in several countries, together with the strictly fixed US dollar exchange rates of the renminbi, HK dollar, and Malaysian ringgit, implies that the dollar still plays an important role.

In this chapter we will examine how the motivations behind the current interest in monetary integration in East Asia are influenced by each of the factors mentioned above: the expansion of interregional trade, the desire to develop financial markets, and the search for appropriate monetary policy strategies. We will do so by looking at what lessons the path to European monetary integration may hold for the likelihood of a similar development in East Asia.

5.1 The long road to monetary union in Europe

The process of monetary integration in Europe was long and winding.[37] What interests us here is whether the incentives that appear to have driven that process are likely to move East Asia in a similar direction. For this reason a brief interpretation if the European experience is useful.

When the Bretton-Woods system broke down in the early 1970s, the relative stability of intra-European exchange rates was no longer guaranteed by each country's peg to the US dollar. The reaction of European governments/central banks was not to introduce floating exchange rates, but rather to seek some form of intra-European exchange rate stability. This took the form of the so-called Snake arrangement according to which fluctuations of European currencies vis-à-vis each other would be limited. The main reason for the revealed preference for intra-European exchange rate stability was a perception that floating exchange rates would be detrimental to intra-European trade and economic stability in view of the high level of trade integration that had been achieved.

The Snake arrangement did not perform well as some currencies, notably the French franc, would exit when pressures built up and re-enter at a new parity when foreign exchange markets calmed. Often the source of the tension was movements between European currencies as a group and the US dollar which led to pressures within Europe. The presumption among foreign exchange strategists was that when the dollar started to weaken some European currencies (read the Deutsche mark) were a safer bet than others, and as a result the cross rates in Europe came under pressure.

A major reason for the weakness of the Snake arrangement was that it lacked an institutional footing. When the German chancellor, Helmut Schmidt, and French president, Valéry Giscard d'Estaing, agreed in 1978 on the creation of the European Monetary System they set in motion a process that led to the creation of such institutional mechanisms which eventually evolved into full monetary unification. Note that this process lasted over 20 years.

5.2 Will East Asia be next?

There seems little doubt that China in due time will move towards a monetary regime focused on domestic considerations, with a consequently considerable flexibility in its exchange rate. Its greater openness, as measured by exports to GDP and traded goods in the consumption basket, suggest that it may put greater weight on exchange rate stability than other major economies like the United States, Japan, and the euro area, but the broad association of a large country and exchange rate flexibility seems a safe bet. Instead of attempting to set a date for when this will happen, let us instead ask how other countries in the region might react when this time come.

The experience with the floating exchange rate has shown that large changes between the major currencies are to be expected. Fluctuations of twenty% or more in periods as short as two or three years between the US dollar, the Deutsche mark (and later euro), and the Japanese yen have not been uncommon in the post Bretton Woods period. As noted in the previous section, such fluctuations were one of the reasons why European countries attempted to keep intrarregional exchange rates stable, leading eventually to the EMU. When the US dollar weakened relative to the Deutsche mark, it tended to strengthen relative to the French franc and the Italian lira.

It is possible that similar gyrations between the dollar and a more flexible renminbi will lead to similarly unequal pressures on currencies in the smaller countries in East Asia. This would lead to potentially large changes in competitiveness which could be difficult to deal with in these highly open economies. Hence we would likely see a revealed preference for some form of intrarregional exchange rate exchange rate arrangement, as observed in Europe. What form might this take? Is it likely to come about? What are the alternatives?

5.2.1 A full-blown comprehensive monetary union?

The successful introduction of the euro and the success of the ECB in delivering monetary stability have naturally raised the question whether East Asia might be the next candidate for monetary unification. Not surprisingly, academics have had a field-day trying to determine whether on optimum currency area (OCA) considerations such a development would be feasible. Not surprisingly, there is no clear-cut answer, but a number of authors suggest that East Asian economies are no less an OCA than Europe was when it started its process towards unification.[38] In view of the additional real integration that is likely to take place between now and the time the renminbi becomes fully convertible, it is thus likely that East Asia would pass the OCA criteria as well (or badly, depending on one's point of view) as the euro area did in 1998.

But as we noted above, European monetary integration was as much, if not more, a political process as an economic one. Without strong support from the political leadership in France and Germany it is unlikely to have come about at all. Will the two dominant countries in East Asia, China and Japan, be able to play a similar role? At the time of writing this is not obvious, but much water can flow under the bridge in a decade.

Even though current tensions surely will subside, it is difficult to imagine that the political pendulum will swing so far and so rapidly as to bring about a consensus within the current generation of leaders in favour of a supranational monetary authority in East Asia that would be vested with the same independence as the ECB enjoys in the euro area. Independent monetary policies and a floating exchange rate between China and Japan appear to be the more likely outcome for the foreseeable future.

5.2.2 Where does this leave the other economies in the region?

5.2.2.1 Monetary unification in some jurisdictions.
The economies of Hong Kong and Taiwan are likely to integrate more and more comprehensively with the Mainland in the coming years. Economic cycles and price developments will become increasingly similar. On OCA grounds a greater monetary integration would be justified. Indeed, the Hong Kong Monetary Authority has stated publicly that in the long run when the renminbi has become fully convertible, it will make a great deal of sense for the two currencies to become closely linked, perhaps even to the point of one driving the other out of circulation. Using the same time horizon it may be argued that Taiwan and the Mainland will share the same currency.

5.2.2.2 Independent monetary policy with a domestic focus.
For other countries the outcome is less clear. As the third largest, South Korea's economy will have a size of something like a fifth and a third of those of Japan and China respectively. It will increase its trade and financial relations with both of its neighbours. It seems unlikely therefore to link its monetary fortunes completely with either one, especially since it also trades significantly with the United States and Europe. In the absence of a region-wide exchange rate agreement it could well therefore also continue to opt for an independent monetary policy based on a domestic objective such as an inflation target.

Two other countries in the region, Thailand and the Philippines, are also inflation targeters. Arguably, Singapore is also targeting inflation, albeit with a strategy that uses the effective exchange rate rather than the interest rate as the operating target (and thus may not be accepted by purists as 'inflation targeting'). Are these strategies sustainable in an increasingly integrated region? The answer appears to be yes. As Canada, Norway, Sweden and Switzerland are showing, it is quite possible for small countries next to a large currency area successfully to pursue an independent monetary policy based on an inflation target. Such a strategy may, but it need not, lead to much exchange rate volatility, hence satisfying the revealed preference for currency stability in the smaller East Asian countries. Switzerland's experience in the middle of the euro area provides a good example.

5.2.2.3 A common basket peg?

An alternative to the scenario in which several of the smaller countries will focus on domestic inflation would be the BBC (basket, band and crawl) system, in which there would be an agreement on a common basket to which all members of the agreement would peg. While such a system would have the benefit of creating bilateral currency stability, it would require a substantial institutional backing lest it suffer the same fate as the European Snake agreement. There are at least two aspects that are likely to involve difficult choices. If the basket peg arrangement implies a rigidly fixed value of the basket vis-à-vis some external set of currencies, then it will be subject to the usual problems associated with fixed exchange rates, principally the robustness of the system in the context of highly mobile international capital flows. Large amounts of reserves, together with some mutual support mechanism may help, but ultimately the sustainability of the system requires the subordination of domestic monetary conditions to the exchange rate constraint.

If the 'band and crawl' part of the system is meant to imply some degree of monetary autonomy, then a common BBC arrangement requires agreement on who should determine the monetary stance of the group of countries as a whole, and by what criteria. This means some form of monetary cooperation akin to the EMS in Europe. Such cooperation may emerge in due course, but it is currently not actively pursued. Based on the European experience, Latter (2005) argues that if countries do want to go down the road of establishing deeper monetary and exchange rate cooperation in the region, then it is necessary to start regular discussions about the technicalities of such cooperation soon.

For a cooperative BBC system to work smoothly and to be sustainable a strong supranational institutional framework needs to be established. The political exigencies for this are not very different from those needed to establish a common currency. Indeed, participation in such an integration arrangement has been likened to riding a bicycle in that it requires continues forward motion in order to be stable. The BBC model can therefore best be seen as a possible intermediate system on the way towards full monetary unification.

5.2.3 How many currencies in East Asia?

What do these arguments imply for the 'currency map' of East Asia in a 10- to 15-year horizon, assuming the renminbi will then be convertible? The discussion suggests that the renminbi, the won, and the yen will remain independent currencies and the corresponding central banks will gear monetary policy towards achieving internal stability objectives. The Hong Kong and New Taiwanese dollars might become tightly linked to the renminbi. Further south and east there are two main scenarios. One is that countries such as Indonesia, Malaysia, the Philippines,

Singapore and Thailand follow the successful inflation targeting model of many other countries in the world and retain monetary policy independence with exchange rates that adjust (freely or in a managed fashion like Singapore is currently doing) as needed to achieve domestic goals.

The other model is the cooperative solution in which the smaller countries decide to increase monetary cooperation under the auspices of the ASEAN. Ito and Park (2004) argue that five steps would be involved: (1) expanding and consolidating the Chiang Mai Initiative; (2) creating a common basket of currencies as a numeraire; (3) pegging to a common basket; (4) establishing an Asian monetary system; and finally (5) establishing a common currency area. In view of the time it takes to reach agreement in each of these steps, it is safe to say that not all of them would be taken by 15 years from now.

Discussion and Roundtables

The following is a transcript of the discussion that took place during the Geneva Conference on 6 May 2005. On 21 July, 2005, China announced a change in its exchange rate regime. While the text that precedes takes into account the Chinese decision, the remarks that follow could not be adjusted.

Session 1

William R. White
Economic Advisor, Monetary and Economic Department, Bank for International Settlements, Basel
William White agreed with the broad thrust of the report, noting nonetheless a few substantive differences of opinion with those of the authors. His point of departure was to agree that external imbalances represented a serious problem in the current international economic system. The problem might not be an imminent one, he added, but it would eventually surface, with significant potential for disorder in financial markets, recession and increased protectionism.

White agreed with the report's diagnosis that those who argue that Asia is the cause, and the US deficit the passive result, of the (n-1) problem, are wrong. Rather, all countries are contributing to the problem at hand, and consequently, all would have a role to play in its resolution.

White also agreed with the report in re-focusing attention away from the exchange rate and back to the underlying identity, S-I = X-M. A relevant factor, he noted, behind Asia's large current account surplus was the collapse of investment in the region. Even more important was the the collapse of household savings in the United States – clearly a very significant aspect of the imbalances problem.[39] However, he felt that the report went too far in concluding that exchange rate changes were irrelevant to the problem at hand. Clearly, what was needed was absorption in some countries and disabsorption in others, and in this respect, real exchange rate changes could induce a shift from tradables to non-tradables, and vice-versa. Thus, while it was indeed wrong to assert that exchange rates are the problem, and not the savings-investment (S-I) nexus, it was equally wrong to posit that the crux of the problem lies in the savings-investment nexus and not at all in current exchange rates.

As in the report, White emphasized the need to distinguish between the major countries involved, although the point he extracted in so doing was slightly different from that made by the report authors. A significant part of current concerns with respect to China have their roots in the historical trajectory of Japan, he ventured. However, not only do China, Japan and the rest of Asia have different exchange rate regimes, they have different histories, and these must be borne in mind when assessing current problems. Japan experienced a major crisis in the early 1990s, from which it had, to date, not fully emerged. Furthermore, Japan had been running trade surpluses for a very long time - White noted that Japan had shown a mercantilist streak since the days of Bismarck, who advised the then leaders to build up reserves in order to preserve freedom and independence. Other Asian countries, on the other hand, went through a severe crisis in 1997–8, and up until that point, essentially ran deficits. Trade surpluses in Asia were thus a recent phenomenon. China too, was different. China had essentially powered its way through the whole of the latter part of the 1990s until now, and historically, had not really run big trade surpluses.

Nonetheless, trade could certainly become a problem, argued White. While he agreed with the report that much of the reserve accumulation in China was accounted for by capital inflows and not trade surpluses, he raised the concern that, in China at least, a substantial amount of imports into the country were currently used to expand the capacity to produce exports. While this might, for an extended period of time, produce a situation in which a country's trade surplus was tempered, the worry was for the future, when the situation could be reversed. It takes a lot of steel to make a steel mill, White noted; but steel mills eventually make a lot of steel.

Furthermore, noted White, while it was certainly true that China had maintained a fixed exchange rate for ten years, and that most other Asian countries did not consciously choose to abandon their pegs and devalue in 1997 – a situation which hardly justifies the exchange rate manipulation accusation – he also noted that virtually all countries in East Asia have, in the last seven or eight years, fiercely resisted the appreciation of their currencies.

Why are they doing so? White put forward and discussed three possible suggestions. Firstly, he accepted the validity of the argument presented in the report, namely that Asian policy-makers were not motivated by export-led growth strategies. He noted the current efforts being undertaken by some countries, notably Korea and Thailand, to bolster domestic consumption, and agreed that many of these countries were not mercantilist in the traditional sense. However, he argued, the argument was valid only if one was taking a long-term perspective. While an export-led growth strategy might well not constitute a long-term strategy for many Asian countries, White suggested that the short-term growth imperative, particularly important for East Asian countries given the social and political ramifications of slower growth and job creation, made an export-led growth strategy very attractive in the shorter term. Keeping exchange rates down to maintain a high level of exports, and thus to maintain jobs and stability, might well be an internally sensible policy for many Asian countries.

Second, White agreed with the report's authors that the motivation for continuing to accumulate reserves as an insurance policy was today declining. However, he disagreed with the assessment that the current level of reserves in Asia was 'healthy'. By any standard, historical or other, White argued, the current level was wildly excessive. He suggested that Asian policy-makers had in fact drawn the wrong lessons from the Asian crisis. The lessons they seemed to have gleaned is that to deal with a crisis one must accumulate massive levels of reserves; the right lesson was rather that currencies should be allowed to float more. In fact, he explained, the very opposite of this lesson was currently being played out in the region: to accumulate massive levels of reserves, policy-makers were pinning their currencies down.

The third argument outlined in the report drew on the notion that for many emerging economies, particularly those with weak domestic monetary and financial systems, a nominal anchor could be useful and stabilizing. Times change, White countered. While it may certainly have been reasonable for Asian countries to turn to an anchor currency to provide stability in the past, the current problem was rather that the anchor currency had become a source of potential instability. He called on Asian policy-makers to recognize this fact.

In assessing the implications of Asian reserve accumulation, White proposed a simple cost-benefit analysis. The costs of changing policy must be balanced against the costs of maintaining the status quo, he suggested.

On the costs of continuing to accumulate reserves, White argued that there were three reasons to believe that the current policies of holding down exchange rates would lead to problems for Asia itself. His first observation in this respect was that the Chinese have themselves stated that they would like to revalue and possibly float the renminbi – presumably, noted White, this is because there were problems associated with the current accumulation policy – even if there existed various short-term difficulties to prevent them from actually revaluing/floating.

Second, argued White, trying to resist appreciation would result in a looser monetary policy than might otherwise be the case, regardless of the efficacy of sterlization. Real interest rates have been around zero for three years in much of Asia, he noted. In China, if the financial real rate of interest is zero, and if one believes that the natural rate of interest has something to do with the potential rate of growth of the country, then the natural rate of interest in China should be in the order of 10%. A gap between 0% and 10%, argued White, had the potential, at the very least, to cause problems. What might those problems be? One of two things could result: inflation and/or alternatively, a continued build-up of internal imbalances, manifested not only in misallocations on the investment side, but also in prices for property, assets and housing. Should these imbalances unwind, cautioned White, in an environment of low inflation, the outcome would be deflation. In this respect, White joined the report authors in manifesting a concern with possible deflation; his concerns, however, elicited a completely different rationale, namely the build-up of imbalances associated with credit creation and with the maintenance of a depreciated currency. Thus, while the authors compared Asia today with Japan in the early 1990s, and argued that deflation would be aggravated by currency appreciation, White maintained that this comparison did not hold for China. China is Japan, he explained, but not the Japan of the early 1990s. The comparison was rather with Japan in the late 1980s. The key concern, then, lays in the failure to rebalance internal growth in China.

White's third observation was that by holding down their currencies, intervening governments were accumulating a huge long position in US dollars. If and when revaluation were to occur, noted White, a huge hit would be taken by someone, somewhere. In Asia, where reserves were essentially in government hands, this hit would be socialized, and contrary to the opinion of some, White felt that this 'socialization' mattered. If the loss associated with revaluation were to be socialized, he argued, the room for fiscal manoeuvre would be reduced. Furthermore, he noted, if the hit were indeed absorbed by the central bank, which in turn would have to turn to the Ministry of Finance for recapitalization, central bank independence would come into question.

What of the implications of continued Asian intervention for other countries? White agreed with the authors that holding down exchange rates would serve to interfere with the trade adjustment process. Firstly, by holding down their exchange rates, policy-makers were effectively distorting elasticity effects, and by recycling payments into dollars, long bond rates were being held down, thus impeding absorption effects. Secondly, with current Asian policy, real interest rates amongst the G3 as well as amongst many Asian countries, were at zero – not a healthy situation, argued White.

Should the Asian policy-makers change course, ventured White, deflation might well result, as the report's authors conjectured. However, White questioned whether this would be such a bad outcome. In particular, distinguishing between 'good', 'bad' and 'ugly' deflation, White noted that one had to trade off a situation in which deflation was mostly due to positive supply side forces and technological developments with a situation in which deflation was the result of huge imbalances.

In concluding, White noted his agreement with a number of other points made in the report. In particular, he agreed that the public pressure currently being put on Asian policy-makers to change course was not helpful, but was rather making markets somewhat skittish and serving to bolster protectionist voices. He also agreed with the need to go back to basics and focus on the S-I nexus. In that context, Asia was merely a side-show, while the United States was really the main issue at hand. Greater disabsorption in the United States was clearly needed, even if on the other hand, those countries confronted with appreciating currencies should, for their part, find ways to increase their spending. Perhaps, quipped White in a final remark, it was time for another meeting at the Plaza Hotel.

Miranda Goeltom
Senior Deputy Governor, Bank Indonesia, Jakarta
Miranda Goeltom focused her remarks on the sustainability of global imbalances and of continued reserve accumulation. She agreed with the authors that current global imbalances needed to be addressed, but noted that there were many options for dealing with the problem, of which exchange rate changes was just one. The channels through which global imbalances could be resolved, she ventured, were essentially country-specific, particularly in view of the different paths of development across the region.

With respect to the sustainability of continued reserve accumulation by central banks in the region, Goeltom emphasized the significant costs, both direct and indirect, associated with current sterilization efforts. Taking Indonesia as an example, Goeltom spoke of significant costs in terms of fiscal revenue, monetary policy autonomy, and also in terms of real resource costs. On the fiscal side, she noted that the return on foreign reserve assets was much less than the governments' borrowing rate, incurring substantial fiscal costs.

The impossibility of simultaneously maintaining fixed exchange rates and an independent monetary policy in an environment characterized by full capital mobility – the impossible trinity problem – necessarily entailed some degree of loss of monetary policy autonomy. Finally, noted Goeltom, reserve accumulation could also entail real resource costs. Resource misallocation, for example, could result from an undervalued exchange rate, due to the excess investment in the production capacity of tradable goods.

There are costs associated, then, with reserve accumulation, which need to be fully weighted and appreciated against the benefits of such a policy. Any increase, on the cost side, of maintaining the current reserve accumulation policy should manifest itself then in either rising interest rates, increasing fiscal and economic costs, or in excessive monetary expansion and inflationary pressure. To date, noted Goeltom, there is no clear evidence of upward pressure on interest rates in Asia. However, she felt that Asian central banks might find it more difficult in the future to maintain appropriate monetary conditions, suggesting, and here Goeltom agreed with the authors, that the recently observed rates of reserve accumulation in the region cannot be sustained indefinitely. Eventually, as the Asian economies continue to grow, continued sterilization on the scale witnessed to date, would eventually push up interest rates.

Akio Mikuni
President, Mikuni & Co Ltd, Toyko
Akio Mikuni welcomed the report, and following on from Goeltom's analysis, highlighted the significant costs associated with accumulating dollar assets with reference to the Japanese experience. Over the course of the past 30 years, since Japan became a creditor nation in early 1970s, the country has accumulated a current account surplus to the tune of ¥270trn. Currently valued at ¥190trn, some ¥80trn, or US$800bn , has disappeared. Furthermore, there is the very real possibility of further losses, even amounting to some ¥200trn if a potential exchange rate of ¥50-60:US$1 is assumed. Thus, while in this period of the gold standard, deficit countries lost currency and surplus nations gained currency, the situation is reversed under a fiat currency system – surplus countries lose currency and deficit countries gain currency. That explains, noted Mikuni, why the United States, with its attendant current account deficit, is growing much faster than Japan, which, albeit a surplus country, is suffering.

Richard Portes
President, CEPR and Professor of Economics, London Business School
Richard Portes agreed with the basic points made in Chapter 1 of the report. On the issue of exchange rate manipulation, he agreed with the authors that what is currently being observed in this respect in Asia cannot be identified as currency manipulation, certainly not in the sense intended and conveyed by the IMF Articles of Agreement. What matters in this respect, in line with the IMF Articles, is, in the first instance, the intent of the policy, and in the second, whether the policy is creating a fundamental disequilibrium. In both respects, argued Portes, it is difficult to demonstrate clear-cut currency manipulation.

The second point Portes raised concerned the stability of exchange rates, particularly in China. He called for the authors to highlight the very substantial real exchange rate appreciation that has taken place in Asia. With respect to China, noted Portes, it may well be that a real exchange rate appreciation is appropriate, but this is not a hard fact, if only because any attempts to estimate the hot money components of current flows are necessarily very gross approximations. The question that must be addressed in this respect is what would the basic balance be in the absence of capital controls. This is not clear, particularly since in the absence of capital controls, there would be substantial potential for outward Chinese FDI. Portes thus argued that it would be more stable, both internally and externally, to let whatever exchange rate adjustment is required to take place through differential rates of inflation, alongside a gradual liberalization of the capital account. This would certainly, continued Portes, help maintain stability, notably financial stability, in China itself, and those who are calling for a nominal appreciation are advocating a potentially dangerous policy. Finally, noted Portes, even if policymakers were to go down the road of a nominal appreciation, the question would then be how much appreciation should there be. The amount needed to stop the hot money inflow might be well above that which is desirable for the system as a whole in the medium term.

John Williamson
Senior Fellow, Institute for International Economics, Washington, DC
John Williamson expressed his agreement with many of the comments made earlier in the session by White, and raised three key points relating to Chapter 1 of the report. The first point concerned the question of whether China's trade surplus can indeed be characterized as 'large'. Here, Williamson disagreed with the authors and argued that China's trade surplus, even if only 2–3% of GDP as argued

by the report authors, constituted, together with a 2–3% inflow of FDI, a fundamental disequilibrium of possibly 4–6% of GDP – not a small amount by any standards. Furthermore, with something approximating 100m tonnes of new steel capacity coming on stream, with the abolition of the MFA (Multi-Fibre Arrangement) at the beginning of 2005, the Chinese current account surplus was looking set to reach around 8% of GDP for 2005.

In a second point, Williamson challenged the references made by speakers as well as by the report authors, that there are some in Congress, who are calling for an RMB appreciation as the solution to current global imbalances, but this is not a view that is widely held elsewhere, for instance by Fred Bergsten, by the US Treasury, or by the Fed.

Sushil Wadhwani
Chief Executive Officer, Wadhwani Asset Management LLP, London
Sushil Wadhwani expressed his support for the report, but called for greater analysis in Chapter 1 of some of the key issues raised and arguments presented. In particular, he urged the authors to provide more substance and detail to support their conclusion that exchange rates in Asia are not hugely undervalued, as their assertion seemed to be at variance with the message from PPP-style measures, which still implied significant undervaluation. In a second point, Wadhwani urged participants and the authors to give greater credence to market players and the instigators of hot money speculative flows. Noting that there are certainly many cases in which the market has misjudged the situation, he nonetheless felt that, in this particular case, market players may have spotted the fact that trade surpluses in China are going to balloon, which had already started to occur during 2005.

In a final point, Wadhwani called for more attention to be given to the potential for instability ahead. In particular, he noted that to date, only the smaller central banks had begun to diversify their holdings away from US dollars, while the larger central banks had stayed the course. Wadhwani argued that any diversification away from US dollar holdings on the part of large players in the region could herald significant instability.

Ignazio Visco
Central Manager for International Affairs, Banca d'Italia, Roma
Ignazio Visco reminded participants that Asia does not constitute a single entity and should not be treated as such. Substantial differences exist between Japan, China – the newcomer – and South East Asia, he stated. In this respect, then, while most would agree that the United States has to save more and that Europe has to invest more, it was not clear whether Asia, as a whole, needed more investment or less saving.

Visco also outlined a number of additional domestic reasons for China to revalue its currency. Indeed, he noted, several economic and political constituencies were also rooting for a revaluation. On the political side, one argument for revaluation refers to the mismatch in returns, namely that a lot of money is coming in from abroad because returns, at 15%, are high, whereas the money is then invested by the authorities in US bonds, with returns of 3-4%. Others, still on the political element, argue that many jobs are being created in the export-oriented industries, at the expense of domestic demand. Then, noted Visco, there is the monetary policy argument. With the substantial capital inflows into China, any rise in interest rates would attract further capital inflows. To allow for more policy space in terms of interest rate policy, some argue then that an appreciation would help.

In a final comment, Visco asked the question of what would happen if interest rates were to be raised, referring to White's earlier comments on this. If the authorities really did raise interest rates, Visco threw doubt on the notion that this would inevitably lead to an increase in capital flows. He noted that there is a great deal of circularity in capital flows, whereby the Chinese themselves are able to borrow at low rates from the monetary authorities, go out and re-import the capital to then invest it in other assets, such as real estate. Tying in to his earlier comments, Visco ended by calling for more analysis and understanding of the difference between the rate of borrowing and the rate of return on investments; this woud help explain current asset price bubbles in the country and hence some of the pressures for change in the exchange rate regime.

Gilles Moec
Head, International Economy Division, Research, Banque de France, Paris
Gilles Moec asked the panelists to comment on the relationship between renminbi appreciation on the one hand, and the state of the banking sector in China on the other. He cited the oft-heard argument that an renminbi appreciation would precipitate huge capital losses in the commercial banking sector, suggesting instead that, given that sterilization costs in the Chinese economic system are essentially passed on from the Central Bank to the commercial banking system – in turn constrained to buy virtually non-interest-bearing paper from the Central Bank, clearly aggravating an already dire profitability situation – it is not so clear that an renminbi appreciation would be quite so negative from the commercial banking sector's point of view.

Benoît Coeuré
Deputy Chief Executive, Agence France Trésor, Ministry of Economy, Finance and Industry, Paris
Benoît Coeuré raised two questions for the authors and panelists concerning hot money inflows into China. Where did the money come from, asked Coeuré, and would it be outlandish to argue that part of the explanation for reserve accumulation in Asia lies in the current low interest rates in both Europe and the United States? Second, where does the money go, and why? In particular, are capital inflows into China essentially speculative and self-fulfilling, or are they anticipating future capital surpluses? In both cases, they are rational, but the prescription is very different.

Chen Pochih
Chairman, Taiwan Thinktank, Taipei
Pochih Chen provided some insights from the Taiwan experience with current account surpluses. Noting that the surpluses may not necessarily stem from a higher degree of competitiveness, he suggested that a freely floating exchange rate might well not be the best system for the region. He noted that in the case of Taiwan the trade surplus actually increased when competitiveness declined. The reason was that while reduced competitiveness did lead to less exports, imports of investment goods declined even more due to the lower level of investment in the economy.

In another point, Chen agreed with the authors on the importance of increasing domestic demand in surplus countries. He proposed trade liberalization as an important tool to do this. Recent suggestions by Larry Lau and Joseph Stiglitz (Lau and Stiglitz, 2005) were therefore leading policy-makers in the wrong direction, argued Chen. An export tax is the equivalent of an appreciation plus an import tax, he noted, and should therefore not be used in surplus countries.

Edmond Alphandéry
Chairman, Supervisory Board, CNP-Assurances, Paris
Edmond Alphandéry felt it was necessary to draw a distinction between a global dimension and a domestic Chinese dimension when addressing the question of revaluation. With respect to the global dimension, what was crucial, and here he agreed with the report authors, was the need to dampen global investment-saving imbalances around the world. This could only be made possible, he argued, through international cooperation, and in this respect, he questioned the lack of effort made to date to integrate China into the G7.

On the domestic Chinese dimension, Alphandéry agreed that a renminbi appreciation would have serious drawbacks for the Chinese economy, particularly through export and balance sheet effects, but he sided with Visco in noting the potential positive effects of such a revaluation, notably an improved allocation of aggregate demand. Noting that the domestic dimension was likely to be the crucial element in any Chinese decision to revalue, Alphandéry called for greater attention to be given to domestic Chinese perceptions of a renminbi revaluation.

Concluding Remarks, Panel

Avinash Persaud
Chairman, Intelligence Capital Limited & Investment; Director, GAM London Limited, London
In concluding remarks, Avinash Persaud raised four points. On the revaluation issue, he urged caution when talking about the current account, particularly in China and East Asia, where capital accounts are not open, where capital flows are often unrelated to price and where if there were to be capital account liberalization, one might easily see a scenario dominated by large and offsetting capital outflows from China. Indeed, noted Persaud, evidence of this phenomenon is already visible, particularly amongst Chinese corporates. A revaluation, then, would have limited benefits, he suggested, and furthermore, could possibly lead to deflation. Taking a cue from the private sector, Persaud concluded that revaluation could only be a low-return, high-risk venture.

Regarding the criticism of some conference participants that the authors had presented a 'straw man', Persaud replied that market expectations today are clearly leaning towards a revaluation on the part of China and a lack of action to curb excess spending on the part of the United States. These expectations are embedded in equity sector prices and in the forward renminbi rate. Thus, whether a revaluation is a solution or not, the view that it just might be is out there, in the markets. It is something that could well happen, and it therefore behoves policymakers to address some of the implications of such an event.

Persaud agreed with White that China and other East Asian countries may well have pursued a peg as a stability-oriented policy, and that the world has since changed. Floating might not be the best option, however. There are other options, he ventured, such as trade-weighted pegs, and he suggested that there was a tendency within Asia to move towards a non-one-dimensional approach to exchange rate stability, including possibly a greater role for the yen in trade weights.

A final point made by Persaud touched on the allocation of assets in Asia. Imagine, he said, that the private sector is saving a large amount because of the lack of welfare. In such a situation, then the private sector is making a private decision, based on fear stemming from the lack of insurance and security available in the region, particularly acute in the aftermath of the Asian financial crisis of 1997. Equally, the private sector makes a decision that it does not want to invest these savings entirely in Asia. Perhaps the return is not high enough, or perhaps there is an overhang of investment. This would then be an entirely private sector decision, with absolutely no state intervention. Would there be any objection to that? Persaud suggested that, in fact, there would probably be little objection. One of the problems, then, he noted, is that because Asia has underdeveloped financial markets, the public sector becomes the key agent to recycle excess savings, and the public sector itself has a very narrow universe of assets in which it invests those savings, namely US government securities. If an institution, such as an Asian Investment Corporation, were to be established, which were to take Asia's savings and invest them in ways that would ensure high long-term returns – clearly not the way typical reserves are managed – a key problem today might well be solved.

William R. White
Economic Advisor, Monetary and Economic Department, Bank for International Settlements, Basel
White reiterated his conviction that we are today in a dangerous place. Let's ask ourselves a question, he ventured. Suppose the Chinese do change the peg, and other countries follow; perhaps even Japan. Would that be a good thing? In principle, suggested White, that would be a good thing. It would give others lower effective exchange rates, notably the United States, and in turn there would be a reasonable chance that with a slower pace of intervention, long bond rates would rise. In terms of inducing dis-absorption, particularly in the United States, such a move would also be a good thing. Having said that, however, White noted that on both fronts, things could also go seriously wrong. Once the Chinese start to change the peg, there could well be a collapse in support for the US dollar and the beginning of a generalized depreciation against everybody – a form of contagion in which things get out of hand. In terms of long bond rates, if these were to rise, there is some potential that they would take a number of other assets with them. At the moment, credit spreads are historically low, mortgage rates are very low in most countries, house prices very high, and these are some of the asset prices that could well become unstuck.

White concluded that, yes the Asians should revalue, as well as take appropriate policies at home. While this move could be dangerous, he cautioned that to do nothing could well be more dangerous. As the old phrase has it, 'be careful what you wish for'.

Session 2

Hélène Rey
Professor, Princeton University, Princeton, NJ
Hélène Rey organized her comments around three main points raised in Chapter 3 of the report. First, she discussed whether the share of dollars in the reserves of Asian Central Banks was appropriate, as claimed in the report. Second, she asked whether official purchases of US securities had held down the US long-term interest rate. Finally, Rey claimed that it was possible to use portfolio balance models to gain some quantitative insights on the effect of reserve diversification on the dollar exchange rate. She concluded that a shift out of the dollar by the official sector would have a significant but not dramatic effect on the exchange rate unless it were accompanied by a private sector sell-off of dollar assets.

First, Rey discussed the assertion of the authors that the share of dollars in Central Banks reserves was currently appropriate. The authors justified this statement, she noted, by taking account of the size of the dollar zone, which they measured by the share of countries, which are in some way fixing their exchange rates to the dollar. However, she countered, there is no underlying theory to explain this measure and there are certainly other potential definitions for a dollar zone. Furthermore, she added, the report does not provide any theory to determine the optimal composition of reserves.

Does the proposed measure at least provide a good positive description of the share of dollars in reserves? Table 3 in the report provides a time series of the dollar zone. Whereas today the dollar zone is almost equal to the share of dollars in world reserves, in 1995 the dollar zone was much bigger, meaning that the share of dollars in official reserves was seriously underweighted at that time, if the authors' measure were right. Also, according to this measure the share of euros in reserves should have doubled since 1995. Therefore, argued Rey, the measure proposed by the report does not fit the time series evidence.

Rey observed that the report authors did not tackle the difficult question of why Asian Central Banks – particularly Japan – seem not to care about past, current and expected capital losses that would be triggered by a dollar depreciation. Indeed, the objective function of reserve managers is not spelt out. Expectations about the extent of a dollar depreciation vary across forecasters but there seems to be an agreement that a depreciation will take place. The puzzle is thus that Asian Central Banks do not seem to take that into account and that there is no public debate about the large capital losses that Asian Central Banks make or will make on their reserves. Interestingly, noted Rey, the Korean Central Bank – which may be one of the most accountable in the region – has actually been the first one to hint at a diversification. An alternative explanation to the lack of reaction of Asian Central Banks is worrying and was also mentioned by White: reserves might just be too big – especially for Japan and China – and Central Banks prefer to keep accumulating them rather than precipitate a fall in the dollar which would mechanically generate large capital losses.

Rey's second point was about long term interest rates in the United States. While the current account in percent of world GDP of Japan is largely positive and is mildly positive or midly negative for other regions of the world economy, the United States stands out as having a substantial negative deficit. Yet the yield on inflation indexed US 10 year Treasury securities is very low and has been going down as the US current account deficit deepened. This puzzle should be explained in the report, suggested Rey.

One potential explanation for the puzzle could be that the official purchases of US Treasury securities, notably by Asian Central Banks, are holding these yields down. However, in searching for any explanation, one should not forget the role of the private sector. The 2004 BEA numbers regarding US net financial flows show that net private inflows into the United States are roughly equal to net official flows ($323bn and $358bn respectively). All the econometric studies conducted on the issue focus on official transactions and therefore omit a key component of the issue. Still, noted Rey, most of these studies do find an effect of official flows on the long term US yield, and sometimes a relatively big effect. Thus, for Rey the review of the literature in the chapter should be more careful.

The third point raised by Rey concerned the diversification of reserves out of the dollar. According to the report, from a balance sheet point-of-view, reserve diversification is equivalent to sterilized interventions. However the report also mentions the following paradox: those who usually think that reserves diversification would lead potentially to a big impact on the exchange rate are also arguing that sterilized interventions may not work. The report stops there and fails to try to assess quantitatively the exchange rate effects of portfolio shifts. Rey reminded the audience that sterilized intervention seems to have worked pretty well so far in China, India and East Asia. Rey thus addressed the difficult question of what reserves diversification could mean for exchange rates.

The appropriate models to think about these issues have valuation effects (the dollar value of the net foreign asset position of the US changes as the exchange rate fluctuates) and feature assets which are imperfect substitutes, in short, portfolio balance models. Gourinchas and Rey (2005) find very strong evidence of imperfect asset substitutability and wealth effects across countries. In particular they find that, historically, around 30% of the process of international adjustment for the United States comes through the valuation channel while the rest comes through the trade channel. As the dollar depreciates, the value of US external liabilities, which are in dollars, do not change whereas the value of US external assets, which are in foreign currencies, increases. One would thus like to write down a portfolio model in which these effects feature prominently. Such models were developed in the 1980s by Black, Henderson and Rogoff, Kouri, etc. and recently revisited by Blanchard, Giavazzi and Sa (2005). In this model, the asset market equilibrium is:

$$X = B + \alpha W + (1 - \alpha^*)W^*/E$$

where X is the supply of US securities which is fixed in the short run.
α is the share of the US invested in US securities (it depends on relative returns).
W is the wealth of the United States.
E is the exchange rate (in foreign currency units per dollar: if E goes up the dollar appreciates)
* denotes the rest of the world
B is the purchase of US securities linked to official interventions (i.e. the Chinese pegging or Japanese interventions in the foreign exchange market).

The net debt accumulation (the current account) is defined by the following equation:

$$\begin{aligned}\Delta \text{ Net Debt} = {} & (1 - \alpha^*)(1 + r)W^*/E \text{ (payments to foreigners)} \\ & - (1 - \alpha)(1 + r^*)W\ E/E + 1 \text{ (payments from abroad)} \\ & + \text{trade deficit}\end{aligned}$$

As the dollar depreciates, the payment to foreigners is constant in dollar terms while the payments from abroad in dollars increase.

The trade deficit depends on wealth both at home and abroad, and on relative prices. The report and McCauley (2005) suggest that the negative effects of a dollar depreciation on wealth in the rest of the world could dwarf its effects on relative prices hence aggravating the US trade deficits. If that were the case, then, whether a depreciation of the dollar would have a stabilizing effect is questionable. While this is an interesting theoretical argument, it is rejected by the data, at least from 1952 until now, as shown in Gourinchas and Rey (2005). Historically, dollar depreciations have contributed to alleviate the net external debt of the US both via an increase in net exports and via valuation effects.

As is well known, there is a significant home-bias effect and the share that the United States invests in US securities is high (85% or more). Conversely, there is also a strong home bias in the rest of the world. This means that, as the United States' net debt is increasing (US wealth is falling and the wealth of the rest of the world is increasing) less world wealth is invested in US assets by the private sector. Hence, as time goes by, B – the amount that the Central banks have to invest in order to make up for the shortfall in private demand for US securities – is actually increasing. Therefore, if the home bias effect is strong, and net debt is increasing in the United States, the shortfall for US assets is growing. To stabilize the exchange rate, B has to necessarily go up (reserves accumulation by Asian Central Banks has to go up).

What would happen to exchange rates if China were to abandon its peg? The model predicts that, in the short run, there would be a depreciation of the dollar and valuation effects ensure that there is a decrease in the net US debt in dollar terms. But along the path to the steady state, the dollar keeps depreciating and US net debt keeps on accumulating again. The longer the peg is kept, the larger is the depreciation needed in the end.

The model can be used to make quantitative predictions. Rey provided estimates of the model predictions of the consequences of China and Japan halving their dollar reserves (2003 reserves, going from US$bn to half) as has been done by Blanchard, Giavazzi and Sa (2005). The effect on the total world portfolio is rather small since, overall, the share of US assets in total foreign portfolios declines only from 30% to 28%. The model would thus imply at most a depreciation of the dollar of 9%. This is not negligible but this is not a huge effect either. However, if the private sector were also to diversify out of the dollar, the numbers could be much more sizeable. Rey suggested that the report should perform similar quantitative exercises.

To conclude, Rey mentioned that abandoing the Chinese peg would push the dollar down against the euro quite significantly. This contradicts the common wisdom that Asian pegs contribute to the appreciation of the euro by putting all the burden of adjustment on that currency and that, were China to abandon its peg, the appreciation pressure on the euro would fade. This argument is misguided in the context of portfolio models because if China abandoned its peg then the agent – the Chinese Central Bank – whose preferences are the most skewed towards the dollar would start buying currencies other than the dollar. This would lead to a dollar depreciation against the other main currencies, in particular the euro. This depreciation could be sizable if the private sector were to follow suit. The US Congress drive to push China to abandon its peg could hence backfire and trigger an unwanted plunge in the dollar as well as undesirable interest rate increases in the United States.

Neal Soss
Chief Economist, Credit Suisse First Boston Ltd., New York
Neal Soss commented on three questions arising from Chapter 3 of the report: 'why the dollar?'; 'how do we link the evolution of the composition of dollar assets abroad with the valuation of assets in the US markets?'; and finally 'what is the role of financial innovation in the United States in creating the macro environment of recent decades?'

First, 'why the dollar?' The authors, noted Soss, reported that some 64% of all official foreign exchange reserves were held in the form of US dollars as of mid-2004. They try to rationalize this figure, given that it is much larger than the scale of US GDP in the world economy or the scale of US dollar financial instruments in the world's financial array. Soss himself was however more surprised that the share of the dollar 'only' amounted to 64%. One could certainly provide reasons for it to be much larger.

What makes for a good reserve currency?, he asked. Soss provided a 'laundry list' of factors that might be important, noting that no single factor alone is sufficient, but that the higher a country ranks on each factor, the better suited its currency is to being held as a reserve currency. The conclusion would be that good seignorage is valuable and paid for in an international context just as it is in a domestic economy.

Pride of place on the laundry list goes to a legal culture that does not unduly discriminate against foreigners, suggested Soss. In a commercial dispute involving a domestic citizen and a foreigner, can the foreigner expect a fair hearing and an unbiased adjudication? It is widely believed that the Anglo-Saxon legal tradition offers a greater likelihood of a fair shake for a foreign litigant than most other legal systems around the world. This is consistent with the revealed preference in financial markets that private contract disputes are by prior agreement of the parties more often to be adjudicated under New York or other Anglo-Saxon law than other competing alternatives. No country is perfect in this regard, but the Anglo-Saxon legal culture starts from the premise that justice is blind.

Another characteristic of a good reserve currency is the backbone of the central bank that issues the money. That was certainly true of the Bank of England in its heyday and (with some debatable lapses in the 1970s) of the Federal Reserve in the last half-century. Of particular value in this regard is that the Federal Reserve is barred from direct financing of the central government's budget deficit. This does not ensure that fiscal policy will always be good; only that any resultant budget deficit must pass a market test for financing.

Furthermore, a good reserve currency should be available in magnitudes roughly commensurate with the needs of the world economy and especially international trade. This requirement can be met with capital exports, as in Edwardian England or Marshall Plan America, or by a trade deficit, as in the American case in the last quarter-century. In this regard, Soss thought it fair to say that the most enduring tenet of US foreign policy since the end of World War II has been free trade. As in the case of the administration of justice, the record was not perfect, but on the whole the United States have championed free trade on the global stage for more than a half-century. The motives may well have included the desire to win friends and influence individuals during the Cold War and the War on Terror, but the objective result has been the progressive liberalization of international trade that we have come to label 'globalization.' It is fair to consider that the US trade deficit is the most effective foreign aid program ever devised, helping to lift tens of millions out of poverty, particularly in Asia in recent decades. This is another way of saying that foreigners hold dollars because they come into possession of them in foreign trade transactions on a scale that is not paralleled for, say, the yen or the euro. If Japan or Europe ran a sizable trade deficit, then their currencies would naturally loom larger in foreigners' portfolios, whether private or official. The global economy would also be viewed as better balanced.

A final characteristic of a good reserve currency is that the country that issues it be known to possess the power to enforce the decisions of its courts of law. Until the lion truly does lie down with the lamb – instead of taking it out for supper – the world system will need a policeman. The liabilities of an efficient cop will be more eagerly held than otherwise. This was the case of Great Britain at the height of its gunboat diplomacy and of the United States in turn. Ironically, a universally respected neutrality may convey some of the same benefits as a muscular geopolitical posture. This may help account for the interest in Swiss francs, which is out of all proportion to Switzerland's role in the world economy over the last few centuries.

So, in answering the question 'why the dollar?', one can ask another question, namely, 'what's the alternative?' What other currency offers the same combination of judicial transparency, stable monetary institutions, availability, and clout? In a sense, this fleshes out the idea that good seignorage is valuable and therefore paid for on an international basis just as it is in each domestic setting.

Soss's second point was about the asset composition of dollar holdings. According to him, the authors were quite right to note the revealed difference in risk appetite between foreign private holders of dollar assets and public sector holders. The political scrutiny to which official institutions may be subjected will naturally encourage them to hold 'safer' instruments and deter them from holding 'riskier' ones. Cash substitutes such as US Treasury bills will naturally comprise a larger fraction of the portfolio. Coupon instruments with greater duration will carry market risk as interest rates fluctuate, but if held to maturity, the central bank or finance ministry will at least get its money back. Banks that are 'too big to fail' or government-sponsored agencies, which enjoy the same market perception no matter what the occasional protestations of US government officials, are a natural extension. Not so with equities or riskier private sector bonds, or at least not necessarily, for companies do default and go bankrupt. This continuum is evident also in the investing behaviour of the private sector.

The progression seems to get attenuated for official institutions at the threshold between duration and credit risk and nearly completely truncated at the threshold between credit risk and FDI. In the case of Asian official institutions, there may be an additional motive for overweighting 'safe' dollar-denominated assets, stemming from rather more narrow, traditional economic motivation. The government is ultimately responsible for the safety and soundness of the banking system and the smooth functioning of the financial system. Many Asian countries are viewed as having weak banking systems and immature financial systems. This certainly played a role in the 1997–8 crisis, in Japan's decade-long downturn, and in the current understanding of China's macroeconomic context. Central banks and finance ministries in emerging countries never know when they will have to bail out a banking system that is submerged by bad loans. Consolidating a horde of always-liquid and default-proof US Treasuries held by official institutions into a national balance sheet already laden with (domestic) credit risk held by 'private' banks may be nothing more than prudent portfolio management. This is a different dimension of the insurance motivation for reserve accumulation than the one noted in the report.

Finally Soss concluded by talking about the irrelevance to the United States of what foreigners buy. What the customer wants to buy is a necessary consideration for a securities salesman. Indeed, Soss performed some simple calculations suggesting that some $39trn of gross transactions – the bread and butter of financial life – are required to fund a net inflow to the United States of some $650bn – the jam of macroeconomic analysis. This is what Mikuni was stressing so perceptively when he noted that the dollars are recycled by the purchase from an American of a dollar-denominated asset. (this is also the point about high-powered money in the earlier session.) And what the American does with the funds is the key to macroeconomic and sectoral developments in the United States.

The one constant in this quarter-century of foreign funding of the US is the fall in the personal savings rate. White noted this point earlier, and Soss elaborated on it. Foreign investors, private and especially official, have been over-represented in government and similar securities and hence under-represented in asset-backed securities based in car loans, credit cards, home equity and other household activities. But by putting the American financial system constantly back into funds, foreign capital inflows may have played the critical role in the financial innovation of this generation.

General Discussion

Charles Wyplosz
Professor, International Economics, Graduate Institute of International Studies, Geneva
Charles Wyplosz reacted to Soss's provocative assessment that the world, especially the poor, should be grateful for the US trade deficit. It is true that the United States has continuously served as the locomotive for world growth over the last few years. The question is, he argued: how long can that go on? Can it last forever or is it unsustainable?

Assuming that it can last forever, then the gift is of a strange nature because it means that the United States borrows from the rest of the world and never pays back the borrowing. Put differently it means that the rest of the world, and the poor of the world, work hard to provide goods free of charge to US citizens.

If the situation is not sustainable, then the question becomes – and this is the theme of this conference – how to un-stick the current imbalances? The worry, stated Wyplosz, is that dealing with these unsustainable imbalances could be a nasty affair and that the gift might have a bitter after-taste.

Sushil Wadhwani
Chief Executive Officer, Wadhwani Asset Management LLP, London
The report gives the impression that the authors believe that on the one hand the share of dollars in reserves is close to an equilibrium and that, on the other hand, even if the share of dollars was reduced, it would not have significant market consequences. Wadhwani had difficulties with both notions. In terms of the equilibrium phenomenon, one has just to talk to the central bankers in the region, especially those from the smaller banks which do not have large holdings as both China and Japan have, to find out that there is certainly a very significant discomfort. It comes from the very simple notion that many central bankers fear that the dollar will depreciate by a large amount over the next years. They do not want the political problems associated with having held on to that asset and having to face a parliamentary inquiry to explain the losses. The notion, then, that the accumulation of reserves in dollars is an equilibrium phenomenon was not accurate, he argued. Wadhwani suggested rather that Japan and China are somehow 'locked in'. The authorities in both countries think that they are basically too large to move, because the price impact of any hint of such a move would be too large. It is thus far from a long-term equilibrium phenomenon for them as well.

In terms of market impact, if one accepts that very large sterilized interventions work and that if all central banks were to move their dollar reserves significantly it is very hard to believe that there would not be a huge market impact. The key point to remember is that the potential catalytic effect of it being known that these central banks were moving on all other agents who have too many dollars in their portfolio would just be enormous.

Angel Ubide
Director of Global Economics, Tudor Investment Corporation, Washington, D.C.
Angel Ubide raised two issues. First, he felt that depreciation was not the only likely evolution for the dollar, and thus agreed with Rey that there should be more discussion about the reaction function of reserve managers. There should always be savings for a rainy day. Given the strange dynamics of the US current account deficit, it would not be outlandish to see a solution to this problem in the United States experiencing a significant slowdown. During slowdowns, there is a flight to quality which triggers a widening of the spread on emerging markets and in many

cases a decline of their currencies.

Ubide thus suggested adding the following alternative scenario in the report to make the discussion more complete and more balanced: namely, if there is an outflow of capital from emerging markets, they would make money out of their reserves and their strategies would seem reasonable. The likelihood of the two scenarios would also merit further discussion.

Ubide made a second brief point about the impact on interest rates. This impact has to be found in the expectations effects, he argued, not only in flows or stocks. Markets are trend-following at the moment – there is a big influence from hedge funds and other institutions which are basically trend-followers. When there is an embedded expectation in the market that the Asian central banks and official actors will continue to buy fixed income securities, the markets follow that trend. For Ubide, this explained why the evidence is inconclusive.

Alexander Swoboda
Professor, International Economics, Graduate Institute of International Studies, Geneva

Alexander Swoboda elaborated on the expectations effect and made three points. First, it is not true, he argued, that sterilized interventions and portfolio diversification have the same effects. It is true that both leave the monetary base unchanged, but the substitution margin on sterilized interventions is between domestic assets and foreign assets while that on reserve diversification is between two types of foreign reserve assets. This should have an influence on the euro:dollar exchange rate in addition to the domestic currency's foreign exchange value.

Second, Swoboda agreed with most of what Soss had said concerning the reasons for the use of the dollar as a reserve asset. However, he added that one of the main reasons for this was also that there are deep, broad and resilient markets for US dollar assets and, at least until recently, there have not been many alternatives. Today, however, there exists another category of assets that may compete with US assets in the fixed income field, and one would certainly expect some diversification into euro assets of this type.

Finally, Swoboda wondered what would happen to interest rates if there were to be an abrupt and large change in expectations. He noted that when expectations about the value of the dollar and relative yields – and this is where the signalling effect is important – change, then a very large and probably very harmful change in exchange rates could occur, unrelated to the long term characteristics of the types of models that Rey mentioned.

Benoît Coeuré
Deputy Chief Executive, Agence France Trésor, Ministry of Economy, Finance and Industry, Paris

Benoît Coeuré made two comments on the issue of duration, which he felt was often overlooked. He concurred with the authors that there is a duration issue in the asset allocation of Asian central banks in the sense that they are acting as agents to allocate the country's savings. They are thus indeed managing an investment portfolio, not a liquidity portfolio. Being central bankers they are managing it with a short duration and high standards in terms of the security of the assets. This is all right for a central bank but not for an investment portfolio. Coeuré thus agreed with the recommendation to create an investment corporation but did not understand why there should be a single one for all Asian countries and rather advocated one such vehicle for each individual country.

In addition, he noted, the interaction between duration and currency allocation was not discussed in the report but would be an interesting topic for inclusion. At first sight, there seems to be no relation between the two, but having a very liquid (short duration) portfolio makes it easy for Central Banks to have their currency allocation conditional on the current monetary regime without having to think about what is likely to happen in the next 10 to 15 years. If Central Banks continue to lengthen the duration of their portfolios they will also have to take into account future monetary regimes. This may change the nature of the monetary equilibrium. The fact that the reserves are currently very liquid is reinforcing or stabilizing the equilibrium because nobody has an incentive to depart from the equilibrium. If however central banks invest at a 10 or 15 years horizon, they will have to think about the future regime and in turn this may lead to another kind of currency allocation.

Jose-Antonio Ocampo
Under Secretary-General for Economic and Social Affairs, United Nations Economic and Social Council, Geneva
Jose-Antonio Ocampo made two remarks. First, he noted, central banks are very conservative creatures. They do not change their portfolio allocation frequently, partly because they are subject to political criticism. Rules are long term and central banks try to deviate as little as possible from them. Benchmarks for asset allocation are typically based on the structure of the bank's liabilities; if debts or current transactions are in dollars, the central bank is likely to remain in dollars. Ocampo thus argued that the shift of currency was not very relevant for central banks but rather for private agents.

Second, Ocampo doubted that political considerations were completely absent from some of the decisions involved. China must be afraid of retaliation from the United States if it were to shift massively against the dollar, while in the case of Japan, Taiwan or Korea, Ocampo doubted that being allies of the United States did not matter for their portfolio allocation.

Ric Battellino
Assistant Governor, Financial Markets, Reserve Bank of Australia, Sydney
Ric Battellino reacted to the comments made by Wadhwani earlier in the session, and felt that he might have been too pessimistic in his assessment. The points made by Soss were very important, he argued, because the US financial market does offer very strong advantages to international investors and that should not be underestimated. In addition, many of the countries which are running up their reserves at the moment are de facto dollar-based economies. They have a very natural link to the US dollar. There was plentiful opportunity to diversify a few years ago when the euro was weak, but, he noted, most central banks that did start to diversify stopped doing so because for them a move from dollars to euros was taking on additional risk. Battellino thus argued that the US dollar would remain a very important element of the reserves management system.

William R. White
Economic Advisor, Monetary and Economic Department, Bank for International Settlements, Basel
Building on what Soss said about the availability of dollars provided through trade, William White argued that the euro did provide an alternative to the dollar, since euros are available through the capital market.

White also talked about optimal currency allocation. Here uncovered interest parity was interesting. Over time the currency allocation does not matter because one will take capital losses which will be just equal to the differential in interest rates. However, for countries thinking in terms of linking their own currencies to an effective exchange rate, it can be shown that the minimum variance portfolio measured in domestic currency is going to have the same weights as the trade weights.

Karen Johnson
Director, International Finance Division, Federal Reserve Board, Washington, D.C.
For Karen Johnson, the report did not spell out clearly enough the links between reserves diversification and intervention on the one hand, and the studies of whether or not Asian Central Banks purchases of US dollars securities affected US interest rates on the other. These are really one issue, she argued. The intervention literature is predicated on the assumption that euro and dollar assets are perfect substitutes. Therefore, behaviour on the part of any entity to change for any given quantity the mix of dollar and euro denominated assets in the interest bearing securities held in the private sector will have no effect.

It is intervention by the United States or by the ECB, not by the Chinese, which is being alluded to here. If one believes that those assets are perfect substitutes, then the decision on the part of some other official entity to buy one or the other would simply affect the collective total and the interest rate of euro assets and US assets. The logic of this perfect substitute assumption needed to be drawn out better to clarify the question about reserves diversification, which only affects the mix of dollar and euro assets, as well as the question of whether this would have an effect on US interest rates. Johnson was inclined to think that maybe the intervention literature got it right for small quantities but that the empirics might change when the scale of intervention got very large.

Second, Johnson was puzzled by the conversation about portfolio management by the authorities and how that drives their decision making. One cannot have two separate objectives of using the reserves to obtain a given exchange rate on the one hand and maximizing the returns on your portfolio on the other. Johnson was sure that there are many central banks that do not have an explicit exchange rate objective and that therefore want to use their portfolio in a way that best serves their national wealth. If there were an explicit exchange rate objective, the portfolio objective should be given up.

Ulrich Kohli
Alternate Member of the Governing Board, Swiss National Bank, Zurich
For Ulrich Kohli the report seemed to argue that the share of dollars in reserves was adequate simply because it corresponds more or less to the relative size of the dollar zone, although there seems to be no theory to justify such a correspondence. Soss gave arguments for the dollar to be a reserve currency and indeed according to his criteria, the dollar is the only candidate. However, as noted by Soss, the argument about diversification should also be taken into account.

The report looks at three regions and three currencies: the dollar, the yen and the euro. What about gold, though? Gold is also an important reserve asset. In addition, it has the advantage of not being related to any particular country. Gold can be held anywhere and hence the likelihood that it might be frozen by a foreign power is very small.

Kohli's last point was to share the authors' skepticism about the impact of Asian central banks on US interest rates. The impact might be significant if it turned out that central banks buy US assets in lieu of the private sector, and that this leads to a bias in favour of government bonds. In that case, the price of US Treasuries would be driven up, thereby leading to lower interest rates in the United States. Why would central banks invest in lieu of the private sector? It might be because capital flows are not free and private investors in Asia might thus not be able to buy US assets themselves. However, this should also lead to an increase in interest rates on corporate bonds, but the evidence does not support this hypothesis.

Gilles Moec
Head of the International Economy Division, Research, Banque de France, Paris
Giles Moec discussed the impact on interest rates of the purchase of public bonds by Asian Central Banks in the United States. Rey pointed out that most studies quoted in the report do conclude that there is some positive impact. Moec suggested that poor data accounted for the difficulty of demonstrating such an effect. Analysts talk about official reserves but broken-down data are desperately lacking. Second, he noted that, at the same time as Asian Central Banks started increasing their purchases, many non-quantifiable factors – such as talk about debt buybacks by the Treasury – had an influence on the US yield curve

Charles Wyplosz
Professor, International Economics, Graduate Institute of International Studies, Geneva
Charles Wyplosz worried that one message of the report might not have been made clear. The report worries about excess reserves. Obviously, central banks need adequate reserves for future interventions and these have to be liquid. If reserves are too large because of ongoing intervention due to imbalances, the question of what to do arises. The proposal to set up an investment corporation is precisely designed to absorb the excess reserves as long as the imbalances continue.

Wyplosz also reacted to what Coeuré and Johnson said about the two conflicting goals of an exchange rate target and portfolio maximization. Their views clash with the perfect asset substitutability assumption, he argued. If there is perfect asset substitutability then reserves are needed, in whichever denomination. The same is true about duration. Could central banks hold most of their reserves long term and use them as collateral for borrowing for short term intervention, instead of Central Banks holding their reserves entirely short term?

Hugo Frey Jensen
Head of Financial Markets, Danmarks Nationalbank, Copenhagen
For Hugo Jensen, a useful way of looking at Central Bank functions is to separate the monetary policy functions and the portfolio management functions. The crucial issue is monetary policy functions. If the exchange rate is fixed, the level of foreign exchange reserves is an endogenous variable. Normally, all portfolio decisions will be subject to the restrictions generated by the monetary policy functions. The savings-investment imbalances are probably what lead to changes in monetary policy decisions. Jensen did not see that the portfolio decisions in themselves would lead to major changes in monetary policy. Most Central Banks can explain why they lose money on dollar assets, but it is very difficult to justify losing money on investment in stocks.

Benoît Coeuré
Deputy Chief Executive, Agence France Trésor, Ministry of Economy, Finance and Industry, Paris
Benoît Coeuré noted that Singapore was already doing what Jensen proposed. The monetary authority was managing the reserves portfolio while the government-led Singapore Investment Corporation was managing long term reserves.

Session 3

David Mayes
Advisor to the Board, Bank of Finland, Helsinki

David Mayes commented on what he perceived as a gap in the report, namely the role of Europe in helping to resolve global imbalances in the world economy. He emphasized, however, that his comments should not be interpreted as a disagreement with the report's analysis and conclusions.

The underlying assumption of the report, he noted, was that, because the United States has major fiscal and current account deficits and the Asian countries a substantial trade surplus and a rapid build-up of reserves, the problem of adjustment should largely be addressed by the two countries, and not particularly by Europe, which, in contrast, has a moderate fiscal deficit and is close to current account balance. However, he asserted, Europe's share of world GDP, trade and investment is on a par with, and sometimes greater than, that of the United States. Hence one could expect Europe to contribute as much to the orderly reduction in imbalances as the other regions.

The question then, pursued Mayes, is why does Europe feature so little in the discussion? The first point is obvious. If Europe is starting near balance, then it would probably have to move away from balance to assist in global rebalancing. Prima facie there is no reason why this should not occur. Indeed in the OECD's simulations of the adjustment process, Europe plays the main role outside the US (Brook et al, 2004). The second point is also obvious: Europe seems to have its own problems and with slow growth, a low inflation strategy and some fiscal difficulties, it does not present a strong candidacy for absorbing further shocks. However, in some respects Europe is far from being in balance since it has a major unemployment problem and hence slack resources that could be brought to bear. Indeed it might make more sense that Europe shows other signs of imbalance as it responds to the shifts in global production and alters the structure of its wealth creation.

Following these preliminary comments, Mayes considered how Europe's role might play out. He tackled three issues in particular: the contribution of failures in demand management; the extent of the misalignment of exchange rates; and the degree of sustainability of the current position.

First, he looked at demand management performance in Europe. Despite the fact that fiscal deficits were well below that of the United States, he noted that these could not be expanded further and relied upon to stimulate growth in Europe, notably under the framework of the Growth and Stability Pact. In addition, increasing the fiscal deficit would be unlikely to do much simply because monetary policy would react to prevent the fiscal expansion from being inflationary.

Mayes used simulation results from the US-EDGE model of the Bank of Finland to illustrate the effect of fiscal policy in the United States and in Europe. This is a dynamic general equilibrium calibrated model of the US and euro area economies. Essentially Mayes found that fiscal policy is unable to affect the US current account deficit significantly. Achieving a reduction of two percentage points of GDP within two years requires an implausibly large switch in public expenditure, even with fairly strong Ricardian equivalence in the model. Mayes found further that increasing the saving rate in the United States would be the most efficient way to reduce the current account deficit; adding three GDP percentage points to the savings rate would reduce the deficit by 2% of GDP in a couple of years. This finding is consistent with the literature

To generate a matching effect from Europe the opposite should be done, i.e. decreasing the savings rate by boosting consumption, which in the model is achieved by altering the rate of time preference. A substantial proportion of the increase in European consumption would go into imports, but only some of these would be from the United States. The rest would go elsewhere in the world, no doubt with a sizeable proportion falling on Asia. In addition, such a surge in demand would be inflationary, so interest rates would rise. This would in turn drive up the euro, which is part of the reason why there would be a substantial impact on trade.

However, altering the rate of time preference, while fairly effective, is not necessarily the most plausible shock that could be imagined for Europe, although it might possibly represent a lasting improvement in consumer confidence. One way of doing this could be to make people more confident about their pensions. The easiest solution, however, would simply be to assume some degree of success in achieving the goals laid out in the Lisbon Strategy, and an increase in the sustainable rate of productivity growth. This strategy is aiming for 1% improvement.

This positive shock would have several consequences. First of all, since it is known and assumed permanent, it would increase the expected rate of return in Europe, which would stimulate investment both domestically and from foreign countries. The inflow would appreciate the European currencies. The greater expected returns would also increase future expected incomes and hence wealth, which would result in an increase in consumption. Both of the last two would be to the benefit of the United States. The simulations thus show that if Europe were to return to its earlier trends it would help reduce the US trade deficit and could have quite a strong effect, possibly large enough to remove the deficit. However, by the same token it would make the position of the Asian countries more imbalanced unless Europe looks like a better place to invest and the rate at which the euro is substituting for the dollar as a reserve currency increases.

Mayes's second point was about the possible misalignment of exchange rates. The current level of the euro is not outside historical experience, he affirmed, and a 10–15% increase would still not take it beyond its historical limits. Much in the same way, the current level of the real exchange rate is still within the limits of previous experience, and raising it by 10–15% would just place it above all but the 1980 numbers. The European current account remains in surplus and the increase in the exchange rate during 2004 helped reduce the impact of rapidly rising oil prices in US dollar terms. However, while this might imply that some further appreciation could be absorbed, it is clear from the remarks by governments and the president of the ECB that such moves would not be welcome, particularly if they were to take place rapidly.

The euro area provides an additional conundrum. Part of the reason that it is not growing as fast as expected may be that it has had difficulty adjusting to fixed nominal exchange rates, not externally but internally. The euro area is not an optimal currency area in the strict sense of the term, even though it may offer a net benefit to all members. At present there is an obvious discontinuity between the needs of Germany, the largest member, and many of the other countries. Germany still appears to be having difficulties accommodating the full costs of unification, and productivity has not caught up in the former East Germany. In effect, Germany needs to lower its costs relative to the rest of the euro area. However this process is asymmetric and it is easier to achieve through higher inflation in the more rapidly growing parts of the area. Since the overall inflation target is a little below 2%, this can push Germany close to deflation which make the adjustment rather costly.

Real interest rates are clearly lower in Spain, which is one of the more rapidly growing countries in the euro area, than they are in Germany. The process is thus reinforcing to an extent. Saving is encouraged, relatively speaking, in Germany while investment is encouraged in Spain. It is only when Spanish production reaches the point of being uncompetitive that the process ends. At present several other countries have such a competitive advantage: Portugal, Greece and Finland, for example. As new countries with even greater advantages, such as Estonia, Lithuania and Slovenia, also join the euro area so the problem is perpetuated. However these countries are very small by comparison. Nevertheless, since EU integration requires countries to join the euro area at some stage, all of the new members will tend to be following strategies that link their exchange rates quite closely to the euro, even if they are inflation targeting.

These remarks help to explain why Europe may not be making as large a contribution to rectifying world imbalances as it could, but they also illustrate that there is a rather greater problem for those who need to adjust downwards than for those who need to inflate (achieve a real depreciation). This reflects the odds that the major adjustment will need to come from the United States rather than from Asia, which would have higher costs from symmetric adjustment and less urgency to make any changes.

Finally, Mayes looked at the sustainability of the situation. One of the fears in Europe is that the current circumstances of low inflation, low growth, high unemployment and slowly worsening public finances are indeed sustainable. This would imply that Europe has got itself into an adverse equilibrium, with short interest rates already at only 2% for over 18 months, and implies that scope for further non-inflationary stimulation might be rather limited. Furthermore, Europe faces difficulties stemming from its ageing population and other contingent liabilities that have yet to be fully incorporated into fiscal projections. Markets are of course aware of this and draw their own conclusions but nevertheless it implies that there are substantial adjustments that need to occur fairly soon if the problem is not to become very serious. It is not clear whether the continuing labour market disequilibrium will actually be solved by the problem of ageing. What is clear is that Europe needs to undertake an extended period of real adjustment rather than the shorter-term nominal adjustment that is often the focus of discussions on current account imbalances. That in itself will help address the wider problems of international imbalance.

John Williamson
Senior Fellow, Institute for International Economics, Washington, DC
John Williamson acknowledged that Chapter 4 of the report had a number of important insights but regretted that these were obscured by a number of errors and misconceptions. He felt, for example, that the title of the chapter was misleading since it deals with global imbalances and not just the trans-Pacific imbalance. Second, he noted, there is a sentence that implies that because politicians fret about bilateral imbalances, economists ought to fret as well. For Williamson this was not acceptable because, he maintained, the duty of economists is to 'educate' politicians and explain that bilateral imbalances do not matter.

In a third point, Williamson noted that the chapter mentions that partial equilibrium models ignore the savings-investment constraints. This is not quite correct, he felt, since partial equilibrium models are explicit in assuming that expenditure policies will be adjusted in such a way as to keep aggregate demand constant in the two regions.

Fourth, Williamson referred to the assumption that there is no demand for the yen to participate in the adjustment process. Various reasons for why this might be are advanced in the report, including the fact that the yen floats, that it might be disruptive for the international financial system and that there is no relationship between the value of the yen and the Japanese current account. However, for Williamson, the major explanation was that in recent years Japan has been unable to expand demand through various internal policies. When Japan comes out of its economic doldrums, one may perhaps be able to ask legitimately for a Japanese contribution to the adjustment process, at least up to the point of not resisting a yen appreciation

Williamson also disagreed with the view that exchange rates follow changes in expenditure. If this were true, how could one explain the performance of the euro over 1999–2003? What great changes were there in relative expenditure in Europe and the United States that could help to explain why the euro depreciated to 80 cents at one stage?

Finally Williamson noted the assertion that it is uncertain that an increase in east Asian imports would significantly reduce the US current account deficit because it would not trigger savings and investment changes. One mechanism that can lead to such changes is higher output which would mechanically generate an increase in savings as a consequence of a rise in East Asian demand, but Williamson did not see much scope for this in the United States given that there is close to full employment. The second mechanism comes through interest rates. An increase by the Fed or in bonds rates – which would rise in response to an increase in activity – would contract US spending and in turn create an opening to finance an increase in exports. Williamson acknowledged that one does not want to completely rely on those channels but ignoring them is misleading and devalues the chapter, he argued.

Turning to the major insights of the chapter, Williamson discussed first the notion of export-led growth. Export-led growth arose as a reaction to the doctrine of import-substituting industrialization which was taken much too far in many countries. Microeconomic explanations are not particularly convincing, he noted, in explaining the success of export oriented strategies. The one mechanism that does convince is that of increased competition, since to export one has to produce goods which are wanted on the world market. This incentive is lacking when one has complete protection against imports. According to Williamson, the key feature of export-led growth is that it is more likely to solve the macro issue of the external constraint than ISI (import substituting industrialization). This is perfectly consistent with what happened in East Asian countries prior to 1997. Export-led growth actually generated current account deficits since the capital markets saw these countries as attractive places for investment. East Asian countries thus imported capital and built up their capital stocks while running current account deficits.

Growth is often, quite normally, constrained by the supply side rather than the demand side. However, the biggest error made by the new proponents of export-led growth is the notion that the supply side did not matter. To increase growth, it is valuable to be able to import additional resources by running a current account deficit. For Williamson East Asia would benefit from the policy which is advocated in Chapter 4 of the report, namely moving away from export-led growth towards domestic demand-led growth. Williamson had difficulties in believing that any country, except conceivably Japan, is constrained from expanding domestic demand.

The second major insight of the report, noted Williamson. is that the problem requires a global response such as a new Plaza Agreement, i.e. a global cooperative solution in which all the major parties contribute. The chapter emphasizes well that if only exchange rates change, balance of payments problems will not be resolved. For Williamson the point made by Mayes is equally true: if one changes aggregate demand but not exchange rates, then internal demand would be excessive in the surplus region and deficient in the deficit region. Therefore a joint switch – a combination of expenditure switching and expenditure changing policies – is needed.

The early part of the chapter presented three contrasting views but Williamson thought that these were complementary rather than contrasting. The first was that East Asia needed to address the over-savings problem. Intertemporal utility would be maximized by increasing consumption rather than investment. The reason why people over-save is diagnosed quite correctly in the chapter, namely self-insurance, itself the result of the absence of any social insurance system. The solution hence consists in providing some social insurance mechanism which could be a rather modest fiscal expenditure but would encourage people to increase their consumption. China is still a country where over 100m people are absolutely poor on the World Bank's dollar-a-day standard. To have such a country invest $200bn a year in US Treasury bills seems not only absurd but somewhat immoral.

In a second point, noted Williamson, the report is right in pointing out that there is a collective action problem with respect to the issue of East Asian exchange rates and that the yen should be part of the solution. The problem should be dealt with globally rather than being left to each country individually. And finally, a third element in the report calls for a tighter US fiscal policy, essentially a tax increase. A fourth element, added Williamson, could be European growth and here one could think of a limited traditional monetary expansion. In addition, the point made by Soss is right, agreed Williamson. The major increase in consumption in the United States was triggered by US financial innovation and, he noted, other rich countries ought to be emulating such an evolution rather than running away from it. The United States has gone too far, but the approach is nonetheless basically right.

Williamson concluded that the likeliness of these measures being adopted was very low. He also regretted that it was unlikely to happen in the absence of crises which unfortunately seems to be necessary to spur on action. The main victims of that crisis would not be the United States but the rest of the world. When the value of the dollar collapses, it produces recessionary effects on domestic demand in the United States but this is offset by an increase in demand from the rest of the world. Politicians and officials who resist the adjustment will not be looked on kindly by history.

He Liping
Professor, Economics, Beijing Normal University
He Lipping focused his comments on the links between the trade balance and the accumulation of foreign exchange reserves in China. The Chinese trade balance has moved upwards and downwards before 1994 and has remained in surplus since then. In the meantime there has been a persistent increase in China's official foreign exchange reserves. In 1994 China undertook a major reform of its reserve management system and changed the value of the peg of the renminbi to the US dollar.

He Liping tried to determine how much the recent increase in China's reserves could be attributed to hot-money inflows and how much was related to capital account changes. To do so, he first looked at the relation between the trade balance and the current account balance. Between 1995 and 2001, i.e. after the currency reform of 1994, the trade balance was greater than the current account balance. This essentially reflected fundamentals, because there were enormous FDI inflows in China during the period – currently, he noted, there is over $600bn of FDI stock. Because the FDI firms are expected to make a yearly profit of 5–10% it has contributed to the current account situation. Thus up to 2002 the trade balance was larger than the current account balance as expected. Between 2002 and 2004 the current account balance was greater than the trade balance. Liping interpreted this as evidence of the existence of speculative flows.

He Liping made three observations about the relation between FDI inflows and the capital account balance. First, between 1993 and 1996, FDI inflows were equivalent to the current account balance, evidence, he argued, that FDI inflows contributed to China's capital account balance. However, between 1997 and 2002 FDI inflows were usually greater than the capital account balance. This period corresponds to the Asian crisis when capital left China – although the situation was moderate, it still had an impact. Between 2003 and 2004 the capital account balance exceeded FDI inflows. This points to a big non-FDI capital inflow to China and could be considered as short term or speculative moves.

What does this evolution mean? Liping concluded that hot money and speculative capital movements are a recent feature of China's balance of payments. Capital account movements are not the cause of foreign exchange reserves accumulation – this is rather due to the trade balance and FDI movements – but merely an accelerating factor.

The structure of the Chinese economy and its external relations is significantly affected by the currency regime and the extent of its flexibility. China should tackle its restructuring with appropriate consideration. He Liping noted that this view is shared by many economists in China as well as by the government. The problem is how to conduct the policy change. Given the size of the Chinese economy, any policy change carries large risks to the domestic economy as well as neighbouring countries and the world economy.

General Discussion

Ignazio Visco
Central Manager for International Affairs, Banca d'Italia, Roma
Three scenarios were presented in the chapter. However, a fourth, the 'malignant neglect' scenario, was only outlined in a presentation. For Ignazio Visco, however, this fourth scenario was the most interesting one, mainly because it is the Nash solution and the most likely to occur. He thus asked the authors to elaborate this. Visco also requested further clarifications about the effects of an adjustment coming through a recession in the United States. That would bring up the savings rate and re-equilibrate the import-export imbalance, he noted.

Alexander Swoboda
Professor, International Economics, Graduate Institute of International Studies, Geneva
Alexander Swoboda was struck that in the fourth scenario presented, one seemed to be going back in the direction of a 'new Washington consensus' whereby the United States would get its fiscal house in order; Europe would endeavour to get growth going through structural reform and a looser monetary policy; and Asia – with some difference between Japan, China and the rest of the region – would somehow, at least in the case of China, stimulate consumption spending, while at the same time allow for some degree of joint appreciation of currencies.

Swoboda offered two comments about this situation. The first was that, in such a scenario, not much international cooperation would (or should) in fact be needed. The policies called for would seem to be those that are in the best interests of each individual country acting on its own. It would thus seem to be a low risk policy venture, and yet, after hearing the panel, Swoboda was very much afraid that the 'malignant neglect' scenario would prevail. Second, for him this scenario was in fact worse than the Nash solution because Nash at least assumes that each country does what is best in its own interest on the hypothesis that there is no coordination. Here we have a situation in which a lot could be gained from just moving towards the Nash solution – which would itself not be so very far from the cooperative solution.

Jean-Jacques Rey
Honorary Executive Director, National Bank of Belgium, Brussels
Jean-Jacques Rey remarked that the solutions proposed were essentially optimal solutions. From any individual part of the world – or all of them – these seemed rather remote outcomes. How would the panel react to 'second best', which would ECB and the Asian central banks? This would leave the United States completely outside and allow the Asian central banks to diversify their reserves by buying huge amounts of euros which would be created by the ECB. While Rey would not advocate such a solution, he was interested in hearing the views of the authors, particularly as such a step had been advocated by others.

William R. White
Economic Advisor, Monetary and Economic Department, Bank for International Settlements, Basel
William White made three comments, mostly relevant to Europe but also to Japan, albeit to a lesser extent. In the first instance, he proposed a solution in which countries would liberalize their financial markets to increase the extraction of equity from housing and allow more spending. However, if this facility was indeed a way to allow intertemporal smoothing, then by definition there must be a pay-back. In the United States, there could be a problem if the payback is still to come in the context of very high household debt levels. In contrast, in Europe it could still be a good idea to move some of the spending upfront, since household debt levels are lower than in the United States.

Second, if one solution is to generate a transfer of resources and production capacities in Europe and in Japan from the tradable goods sector into the non tradable sector, then strong emphasis should be put on the necessary structural reforms to achieve these goals. However White failed to see how generalized increases in aggregate supply, in Europe and Japan were going to help the US current account deficit problem.

White's last point was about cooperation. If a crisis occurs as the outcome of the 'malignant neglect' scenario, the impact of that crisis due to the depreciation of the dollar is likely to be greatest outside of the United States, namely in Japan and particularly in Europe.

Jose-Antonio Ocampo
Under Secretary-General for Economic and Social Affairs, United Nations Economic and Social Council, Geneva
For Jose-Antonio Ocampo, the key issue was what kind of expansionary policies should be put in place in China should the investment rate come down. The major risk was that China would become a deflationary force in the world economy.

The report concentrates on East Asia, Europe and the United States, he noted, but there are of courses other parts of the world economy. One of the very important effects of Chinese-led growth is the commodity price effect that it triggers.

This explains why all the developing countries are currently doing well. Events in the United States or Europe will not be able to replicate the magnitude of the Chinese effect on commodity prices and the continuation of the Chinese boom is thus important for the balance of the world's economic growth. At the same time, Ocampo noted, a large part of the commodity boom effects is being put aside in the form of savings. Indeed, part of the reserve accumulation that we have seen in oil-producing countries and also in other countries, such as those in Latin America, is currently being put aside for self-insurance purposes.

Session 4

Ulrich Kohli
Alternate Member of the Governing Board, Swiss National Bank, Zurich
Ulrich Kohli introduced the session, raising a number of questions for the panelists, and touching notably on the relevance and usefulness of lessons learnt from European monetary integration, as well as on the feasibility and usefulness of an Asian Investment Corporation, as suggested by the authors in the report.

Pochih Chen
Chairman, Taiwan Thinktank, Taipei
To discuss the future, and in particular the future exchange rate system in Asia, Pochih Chen reasoned that one must first examine the basic environment in which any exchange rate system decision might be taken. In the case of East Asia, the choice of exchange rate arrangement for any country would thus necessarily have to take into account not only the arrangements of closely related countries but also the arrangements prevailing in large countries. With this a priori, stated Chen, the best arrangement for East Asia might well not be possible without a better world arrangement, while the scope for East Asian countries to, in turn, influence global arrangements might itself not be that great either.

The major deficiency in the current international system, continued Chen, was the wide fluctuation in exchange rates between the three major currencies, in large part caused by speculative capital flows. Small countries might not be able to find policies to enable them to avoid related disturbances. For example, when the Japanese yen appreciated sharply against the US dollar, many of the smaller East Asian economies importing Japanese components for re-export to the United States, such as Taiwan, were affected either by the rise of import costs in terms of US dollars or by the fall in exports in terms of domestic currency. In addition, noted Chen, smaller countries might find it more difficult to control speculative activities. If a small country were to adopt a freely floating exchange rate system without any intervention, the exchange rate might fluctuate wildly and possibly move away from the equilibrium rate optimal for trade.

Notwithstanding the above, continued Chen, let us assume then that the three major currencies will continue to float as is the case currently. The first question to be answered is whether China would, in such a system, choose a freely floating exchange rate system or some other policy. Using the Japanese yen as an example of what would happen if China were to allow the degree of freedom currently accorded to the yen, Chen noted several considerations. First, China might well have the ability to stabilize the market. As a country less open to market forces than Japan, China could potentially control its capital flows and other transactions more successfully and consequently limit the possibility for speculative attack on the renminbi. However, noted Chen, the production side of China's economy could well be significantly adversely affected by a freely floating exchange rate system, and more so than in the Japanese case. On the one hand, the share of exports and imports in China's economy is much greater than that in Japan, he argued. But even 20 years down the road, most parts of the Chinese economy will be significantly less developed than the economy of Japan and even Taiwan today. Most industries will have many competitors in other countries, so that profit margins will remain fairly low and firms will not have the power to determine the price of their products. As a result, much of Chinese industry would be adversely hit if the renminbi were to fluctuate as the Japanese yen does in today's system. The Taiwanese experience shows that a high-tech industry is less sensitive to exchange rate fluctuations, yet, even in Taiwan, most labour intensive industries do not easily weather currency fluctuations. Given then, that a large part of Chinese industry would still be labour intensive and face intense competition from other countries, China would not be in a position to accept the kinds of fluctuations experienced by the Japanese yen.

Secondly, suggested Chen in a personal judgement of the political priorities in China, nationalism and China's desire to be a major power on the world stage would clearly work against the continuation of a 'public' renminbi peg to the US dollar.

Thus, with these two premises in mind, Chen argued that if the major currencies were to continue fluctuating as today, the renminbi would most likely to be allowed to float, albeit strongly managed. Thirty years ago, added Chen, when the New Taiwan dollar switched to a floating exchange rate system, the then Minister of Finance stated clearly that Taiwan would practise a very dirty float. Similarly, conjectured Chen, the renminbi would constitute a very dirty float.

If the renminbi were to be virtually fixed to the US dollar or to any other basket of currencies, the arrangement then to be practiced by other East Asian countries would be similar to that in place today. While the choice of renminbi might well influence the weight of the US dollar in the choice of basket, the US dollar would nonetheless remain the most important standard for these economies.

China and Hong Kong, on the other hand, might have the political intention to use the RMB in Hong Kong or to peg the HK dollar to the renminbi instead of the US dollar. From an economic point of view, however, Chen did not think this was likely to happen, mainly because using the renminbi in Hong Kong would undermine the city state's legal system and standing as an international financial centre. The probable outcome then, argued Chen, was for Hong Kong to continue pegging its currency to the US dollar, but possibly to allow the renminbi to circulate in the territory, as is indeed currently the case.

If the renminbi were to be allowed to float freely, like the Japanese yen, the choice of other East Asian countries would depend on the relative stability of the major currencies, their trade and production linkages with the major currencies, and of course, political considerations. Trade and production considerations would include market power, profit margin, competition and other production cooperation characteristics amongst the countries.

Japan's history of exchange rate fluctuations and Japanese firms ability to survive under the wide fluctuations, would however continue to preclude other currencies from pegging to the Japanese yen. The yen can appreciate by 100% and depreciate by 50% within a very short period, noted Chen, and few countries would accept such a situation. But close economic ties to China might not, in itself, indicate any necessity for currencies to peg to the renminbi or to have a high weight on the renminbi in any basket peg. Indeed, if exports to China were to remain mainly intermediate or capital goods for re-export, pegging to the US dollar might continue to be a better option than pegging to the renminbi.

Several higher income countries in Asia, such as Korea and Taiwan are increasingly in a process of transition to high-tech or knowledge-based economies, in which firms retain a degree of price setting power and higher profit margins. In this environment, fluctuations in the exchange rate of their currency with the renminbi might not affect them significantly. Markets in other countries will be more important than the Chinese market, particularly as high-tech products tend to view the global marketplace as their primary market. Furthermore, competition tends to be greater with high income countries than with China. Thus even if China were to become Taiwan's and Korea's biggest market, the renminbi weighting in their foreign exchange rate policy would continue to be smaller than their share in China's trade. As Chen noted, who is competing with you is more important than who is buying your products.

Another factor to note, added Chen, was that China will still have many low-wage workers, even ten years from now. Trade cooperation between China and East Asia will thus continue to be dominated by production chain cooperation, such that the share of labour intensive consumer goods competing with Chinese products in the Chinese market will remain low. Unless, then competing countries were to decide to peg to the renminbi, the likelihood of individual East Asian countries pegging to the renminbi would be small. This would certainly be the case for the New Taiwan dollar – in addition, of course, to political considerations in that particular case.

In a brief comment on the likelihood of an Asian monetary union, Chen argued that given the diversified income and stages of development characterising the region, it would be inappropriate and even almost impossible to establish a common currency. The environment in East Asia, he emphasised, is quite different from that of Europe.

Chen concluded by reiterating his conviction that in the foreseeable future, East Asian countries would be better off if the exchange rates between major currencies were to stabilize. It might, however, not be in the interests of major countries, notably the United States, to strive for such stability. Still, suggested Chen, the United States should, in its own interests and to preserve a role for the US dollar in the long run, aim to encourage countries to establish closer ties with the US dollar, particularly at this time when individual preferences are still largely in favour of the US dollar.

Karen Johnson
Director, International Finance Division, Federal Reserve Board, Washington, DC
The challenge in thinking about long-run monetary and exchange rate arrangements in East Asia, began Karen Johnson in her remarks, is that we know very little about the relevant circumstances ten or more years from now, and we need to speculate so much. The only thing that we can say with some degree of certainty is that the region is changing at a rapid rate today, and that change is likely to continue.

With this in mind, Johnson outlined a few thoughts about the possible trends and scenarios for Asia's exchange rate arrangements.

The economic literature suggests that issues of monetary union depend on a few key variables. The degree of trade integration is of primary importance. Much is being said, including in the report, about the evolving trade relationships amongst the East Asian countries, as well as the production location decisions that are driving trade in the region. Johnson doubted that in ten years time, this process of change would be at an end. Rather trade patterns would continue to evolve and change. A second, frequently cited issue is whether the preponderance of shocks within a region are common to or are largely idiosyncratic across members. Give the huge size of the overall East Asian economy, Johnson argued that it would be hard to make the case that most shocks are common across the region. A third factor often cited in the literature is factor mobility, particularly labour. Johnson estimated that labour mobility in the region would continue to be high in the medium to long term.

Beyond the traditional literature, other factors are today emphasized in assessing the choice of exchange rate. One such factor is that of financial linkages – of crucial importance given that capital flows are often the channel of exchange rate pressures. The strength of banking systems, the differences in banking system development, and the scope of cross-border banking activities or branching contribute to determining how the non-financial sector can manage its exchange rate exposure. Capital market developments, cross-border flows in particular, influence the type of investments and the nature of instruments being used. More developed markets are better able to handle the flows of capital in a world of potential exchange rate risk. Clear property rights, good governance in the private sector, and adequate bankruptcy mechanisms are also important, in that they provide protection for investors and so facilitate the efficient allocation of capital across countries and more broadly. These factors clearly matter.

The range of options for exchange rate regimes start at one extreme, with a currency union similar to that in place in Europe. An Asian monetary union (AMU), argued Johnson, would, however, not be in the picture in the time frame under consideration. Indeed, noted Johnson, East Asia is not, at present and at least into the foreseeable future (10 years), a good candidate for monetary union. The reasons for and the energy behind monetary union in Europe were as much political as economic, she reasoned, and no such political agenda currently exists in East Asia. Until one emerges, AMU does not represent a good option.

A system in which many of the East Asian currencies stabilize currency baskets, perhaps on the model provided by Singapore, is more plausible, Johnson suggested. This system would enable the participating countries to design baskets that are similar, owing to the highly developed trading relationships amongst themselves, but that are different enough to reflect existing differences across the countries. These baskets could furthermore be adjusted over time. Thus, such a system would provide relative stability of nominal exchange rates in the medium term, while allowing for real exchange rate adjustment over longer horizons.

In Johnson's view, however, a system of less-managed, essentially floating exchange rates, was the preferable option. East Asia is arguably the most dynamic region in the global economy, she posited. Its rapid pace of growth, development and change implies that real exchange rate adjustment will be essential. Allowing the nominal exchange rate to serve as a buffer for some of the shocks hitting the region would likely smooth and facilitate that process of change and development. Some might argue that certain features of the East Asian economy argue against floating rates. Notably, trade within the region is expanding rapidly and manufacturing production is being organized such that trade in primary and semi-processed goods is growing rapidly. Furthermore, there are huge imbalances in such trade in the region, and the member countries differ substantially in size, with two large countries and several smaller countries, all at different stages of economic development and with different resource endowments.

Johnson suggested, however, that some of these characteristics provided an accurate description of the current trading picture of the North American Free Trade Area (NAFTA). The members are each others' major trading partners, but one is much larger than the other two. Two countries are much more industrialized than the third. Trading amongst the partners for further processing and assembly has grown robustly. Notwithstanding these elements, the United States, Canada

Figure D.1 Mexico

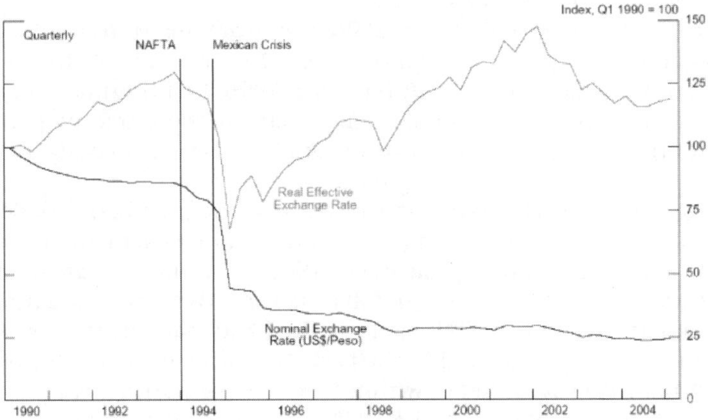

Figure D.2 Mexico

Figure D.3 Canada

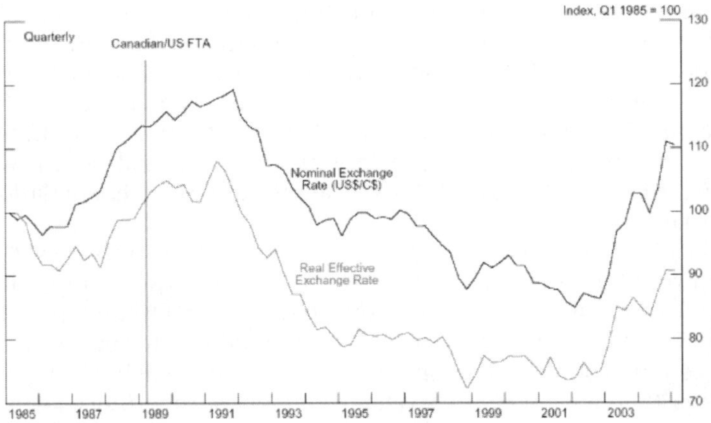

and Mexico have retained floating exchange rates and trade amongst them has flourished, with, for example, US trade of goods within NAFTA growing on average 1% faster than the total US goods trade.

Johnson noted that Mexico's move to a floating exchange rate in the 1994 financial crisis occurred just after the signing of NAFTA. The value of the peso in terms of the dollar dropped sharply then, but since 1996, had been rather stable. This, offered Johnson, constituted some evidence that two close trading partners, each pursuing sound monetary policy, can experience relative stability in their bilateral exchange rates under floating regimes.

Referring to Figures D.1 to D.3, Johnson showed that the peso had experienced some movement against the dollar, but not on a scale that was actually damaging trade[40]. In a similar figure for Canada, starting in 1989 when the US-Canadian free trade agreement was signed, the Canadian dollar had shown some fluctuations in terms of the US dollar, but both the bilateral nominal and real effective exchange rate of the Canadian dollar had moved in the past ten years within a range of plus or minus 20% and had now returned to within 10% of their starting values. In the ten years since NAFTA was signed, the US dollar, the dominant currency in the region, had trended up strongly in terms of other currencies and was now retracing its steps. Nevertheless, within NAFTA, floating rates served the members well and was not the source of any problems.

Johnson concluded that, given the likelihood that much will change in East Asia over the next ten years, coupled with the substantial differences across the countries in the region, flexible exchange rates were needed to permit real exchange rate adjustment along the way, to allow monetary policy independence among the countries, and finally to accommodate the rapid economic development currently under way in several key economies in the region.

Jose Antonio Ocampo
Under Secretary-General for Economic and Social Affairs, United Nations Economic and Social Council, Geneva

Jose-Antonio Ocampo wholeheartedly welcomed the report. He prefaced his remarks on future scenarios for monetary and exchange rate arrangements in East Asia by noting three important implications for the international monetary system that emerged from the report.

The first implication drew on the case made in the report that exchange rate variations amongst major currencies constituted a relatively inefficient system of adjustment within the international economy. Aside from the need for international coordination, while the current system, in which the major currencies were likely to fluctuate widely, might not have many implications for global stability, it was likely to generate many risks for emerging, developing economies.

A second implication was that the perceived need for self-insurance in emerging economies and in the developing world in general, generated a significant deflationary bias in the international system. This implied that, as outlined in Chapter 4 of the report, issues relating to international financial reform would need to be addressed in order to avoid the appearance of just such a deflationary bias in the international system.

A third implication, ventured Ocampo, was that, for very open developing economies, following the capital account rather than other criteria for exchange rate determination might well be the wrong direction to take. Ocampo noted that this implied that inflation targetting was not the optimal rule for monetary policy. This was to be rather some type of intermediary regime, which, he suggested, was nothing other than a form of real exchange rate targetting. Indeed, this was an inevitable feature of an optimal exchange rate policy for an open, developing economy. In turn, the implication of this, stressed Ocampo, was that without coordination mechanisms in place between competing economies, the incentives for real exchange rate targeting vis-à-vis competitors would necessarily be very strong.

Real exchange rate targeting, continued Ocampo, would render certain capital controls useful so as not to place the entire burden of adjustment on, for example, monetary sterilization, in whatever form, which would prove costly in the longer run. This conclusion, he suggested, had important implications in any discussion of the future of Asian monetary and exchange rate systems.

Turning to his main points, Ocampo noted that his initial reflection when thinking about the future Asian monetary system had been to think back to the argument presented some years ago by several economists that a reduction in the number of world currencies was an inevitable side-effect of globalization. Agreed, that period had seen the birth of the euro, and several countries in Latin America had been – wrongly, he pointed out – convinced to dollarize their economies. However, argued Ocampo, it does not make any sense to reduce the number of currencies in the world as long as there are so many unstable features in the global economic system. Indeed, from the point of view of any individual developing or emerging economy, retaining an individual currency still has a lot to offer. Ocampo thus agreed with previous speakers that the likelihood of the emergence of an AMU was very small.

However, in this regard, Ocampo noted a few additional points. First, the choice of exchange rate regime by China would clearly be crucial. Whatever China would do in terms of its own exchange rate system would have important implications for other countries in the region, which would be fairly likely to follow China's decision in some way. Second, there might well be some intermediate forms of monetary cooperation in the region. The Chiang Mai Initiative was one step in that cooperation. The key issue in thinking about forms of cooperation, as pointed out in the report, was of course how Japan and China worked together within the system. To date, little positive movement in the direction of cooperation had been registered, and as a result, any deepening of monetary or other form of cooperation would clearly require significant institution-building.

What we will probably witness in the medium term in the region, suggested Ocampo then, is the continuation of national currencies, possibly following some form of exchange rate targeting, for macroeconomic reasons as well as because of competition between countries. Any decision, furthermore, on the degree of exchange rate flexibility would be closely related to decisions about capital account liberalization.

Finally, Ocampo reminded participants not to leave out considerations about India in their analyses of the future of Asian monetary and exchange rate arrangements. India would clearly not resign its own currency, and for that reason, would play an important role in any future East Asian arrangement, alongside both China and Japan. What role, then, would India play in the region and how would India interact with the other key players in the East Asian region?

Mikio Wakatsuki
Chairman, Axa Japan Holding Co., Ltd., Tokyo

China has three major resources, began Mikio Wakatsuki: a large population, a huge land space and, perhaps most importantly, a very long time horizon. Consequently, when China says that a change in its exchange rate regime will come in due course, that could well mean something quite different from the average interpretation. Wakatsuki suggested to participants that they would do well to remember this in their analyses of China.

Wakatsuki focused his remarks on East Asian regionalism and possible monetary cooperation, and began by providing some background information and analysis. A key factor behind the movement towards monetary cooperation and integration in the region lay in the advancement of economic regionalism in other parts of the world, notably in North America (NAFTA) and Europe. Against the development of these regional economic blocs, Asia was very conscious of being left in a vacuum. Indeed, there is a latent fear, suggested Wakastuki, amongst Asian countries that they might be increasingly isolated and discriminated against in the global economy. Thus, while most Asian countries have to date been inclined to advocate a multilateral rather than regional approach to trade and cooperation, they have increasingly been faced by the reality of regionalism and have consequently felt the need to counter other regional entities by stepping up cooperation among themselves.

Indeed, the evidence is clear: throughout the 1990s, Japan, China and South of Korea did not enter into any form of free trade arrangement with their neighbours. Since the turn of the century however, as free trade arrangements have become predominant and multilateral principles rather nominal in nature, these three countries have started to explore the potential of free trade arrangements with countries, both within and outside the region.

A second factor in East Asian cooperation was clearly the Asian financial crisis of 1997–8. In the aftermath of the crisis, Asian countries came to the conclusion that the financial support extended by the IMF and the policy prescriptions attached were not necessarily appropriate and adequate to cope with the effects of the crisis. This was not to say that the Asian countries denied the benefits that IMF support provided, but the crisis instilled a feeling among them of insecurity. Increasingly then, Asian countries have felt the need to build some form of regional assistance to provide help, prevent crises, and complement the multilateral safety net.

These factors, pointed out Wakatsuki, suggest that the movement towards monetary cooperation and regionalism in East Asia is essentially of a defensive, rather than offensive, nature. This helps to explain why the move towards financial integration in the region has not to date gathered much momentum. This defensive or passive nature can also be detected in the relationship with the dollar. In the case of Europe, one of the major motives to form a currency union was a wish to be independent from the dollar and from US monetary policy. In contrast, many Asian countries consider the link with the US dollar to be beneficial to their trade and capital flows.

In terms of political integration in the region, the principle of non-interventionism clearly continues to be the dominant thread. This is clearly seen in the cooperation undertaken under ASEAN auspices. ASEAN is, through deliberate choice, an association, rather than a community, union or alliance. Though this attitude has been changing in recent years, noted Wakatsuki, there continues to be considerable reservations amongst members to commit themselves to each other. Moving beyond technical financial arrangements would involve a stronger political commitment and in turn imply a loss of sovereignty which most countries in the region are not ready to accept at this juncture.

Political leadership represents another obstacle to closer cooperation. Forming a regional bloc or currency union clearly requires strong political leadership - this was evident in the case of the European monetary union. In the case of Asia, there is a strong rivalry between China and Japan when it comes to taking initiatives in the region, as seen notably in recent incidents. Historical memories take a long time to fade and certainly do not make the task easier. Moreover, US geopolitical interests in the region also create a delicate political relationship between the three main players in the geopolitical arena, Japan, China and the United States. The hype surrounding the 'strategic partnership' between China and the United States under the Clinton administration created jitters in Tokyo, whereas the shift to 'strategic competition' under the Bush administration led to substantial wariness in Beijing. Likewise, a Sino-Japan tie-up or currency bloc would certainly receive a less-than-wholehearted blessing from the US government.

On the question of the future for Asian currencies, Wakatsuki argued that over a ten-year time horizon, the three major currencies, the yen, renminbi and won, would almost certainly be floating independently. China would shift to a floating, albeit heavily managed, regime before long, even if full capital account liberalization were to take longer than anticipated due to the non-performing assets problem within the banking system. While Wakatsuki agreed with Chen that yen fluctuations have been large of late, he argued that the detrimental effects of these would be much reduced if a strong link between the yen, the won and perhaps the Taiwan dollar were to be established.

On the relationship between the Asian currencies and the dollar, Wakatsuki maintained that the dollar's supremacy would be largely unchanged over a 10-year time span. As the renminbi moves to a floating regime, some countries could indeed weaken their ties to the dollar and increase links to the renminbi, perhaps in the form of a basket, but a significant weight would continue to be given to the dollar. The influence of the United States in Asia is not merely economic, noted Wakatsuki. The US presence in Asia is regarded in many countries as the linchpin for peace and security in the region and serves as a counterbalance to the growing military power of China. Under these circumstances, the United States would necessarily continue to influence the exchange rate regime choice of the region's countries. Nonetheless, even if the US dollar's supremacy were to be maintained, it would face challenges, from two sides in particular. One challenge may come from the rise of the euro. Since it is evident that the large US current account deficit is not sustainable, the dollar will come under some pressure and this will provide incentives for Asian countries to further diversify their reserves in favour of the euro. In addition, the continued enlargement of the euro area will increase the importance and attractiveness of the EU market for Asia and the euro may become the preferred international currency. Furthermore, a challenge might well emerge from China. Over the period under discussion, the renminbi might become a more internationally used currency, if not a fully qualified global currency. Its role would be further enhanced if China were to endeavour to create a genuine Greater China economic zone, comprising Hong Kong, Taiwan and possibly some other neighbouring countries, with the renminbi as a common currency.

The idea of establishing an Asian Monetary Fund is clearly one that has gained prominence in the minds of Asian policy-makers. As mentioned earlier, there is a feeling of distrust and concern among Asian countries that the IMF assistance proferred during the 1997/8 financial crisis was not appropriately prescribed and that in effect, the cure was worse than the disease. Some of the conditions prescribed by the IMF were seen as far too draconian and unrealistic. It was also noted at the time that, apart from the IMF, the only country that offered actual funds to meet the urgent need for liquidity at the time was Japan. Other G7 countries only offered hard-to-use secondary lines of defence. Although the Asian Monetary Fund proposed by Japan in 1997 was eventually aborted, it was enthusiastically supported by several countries in the region.

Obviously the Asian countries do not deny the useful role played by the British West Indies, but there is a feeling that regional facilities will provide greater assurance and security. As the countries hit by the crisis have recovered, economically, and have accumulated sufficient reserves, and as the memories of hardship have faded, the enthusiasm for the Asian Monetary Fund has clearly faded, but, noted Wakastuki, since the plan does not involve the transfer of any sovereignty, the idea still has some chance of materializing. The ongoing project to enhance Asian bond facilities and recent developments of so-called Asian bond facilities II constitute for some a good prototype or model for an Asian Monetary Fund further down the road.

Ulrich Kohli
Alternate Member of the Governing Board, Swiss National Bank, Zurich
Ulrich Kohli noted that three out of the four speakers had explicitly assumed, in their scenarios, that capital controls of some form would still be in use in ten years. In terms of predictions for exchange rate arrangements, he noted however that a diversity of views were expressed, from floating to fixed nominal to pegged real exchange rates. For his part, Kohli argued that, with the Balassa-Samuelson effect in play, real rates would likely change a great deal over time, and he was more in favour of flexible rates in order to accommodate this.

Finally, Kohli noticed that there was considerable agreement across the speakers that an Asian Monetary Union was not likely, even within a ten-year time span. Indeed, he noted, listening to both Williamson and Chen outline the situation in China, that there was certainly room to question whether China itself constituted an optimal currency area.

Avinash Persaud
Chairman, Intelligence Capital Limited & Investment, and Director, GAM London Limited, London
Avinash Persaud jumped into the debate, drawing on his experience as a market participant. He noted what he called a few 'rules' of foreign exchange that he had come to acknowledge during this experience. The first such 'rule' was that, if one were to look at the 30 most liquid foreign exchange markets, one could argue that the more open the economy, the more the authorities were likely to manage the exchange rate. Obviously there are exceptions, noted Persaud, notably the EMU, as well as others in Asia. However, applying this rule to China has some interesting implications. China is, perhaps surprisingly, a fairly open economy - the sum of its exports and imports as a percentage of GDP are well above 40%. Therefore some form of managed exchange rate, such as a peg, would seem to make sense, although this does not mean that the level of the peg would remain unchanged over time.

However, an open economy is probably not China's destiny, stated Persaud. One would expect, over time, with the greater development of the hinterland, that China will be a large, fairly closed economy relative to the other economies in the region. That is when the conditions for a full float, or a more meaningful float, will be in place. Thus, the conditions for a floating regime are not just about the maturity of the local financial system, but are also about the structure of the economy, and, in the case of China, about moving away from its current export-oriented focus.

The other 'rule' he had learnt was that, among the various features considered desirable in a reserve currency, key features have been economic size and size as a traded currency. What this tells us, therefore, is that before the end of this century, China has a very good chance of being the world's reserve currency. Clearly, a number of institutional changes will need to occur before this can happen, but it is a more than likely scenario.

Persaud provided some thoughts on arrangements in other countries in the region. The countries in South East Asia are fairly open, small economies, he noted, and are most likely to continue to manage their exchange rates, much as they are doing today. The logic behind this is that these economies do not like external factors derailing their domestic policies. Nonetheless, he suggested , their currencies will most likely move from being managed against the dollar to being managed against the renminbi.

In a final, short comment, Persaud also urged participants to include India in their thinking. He suggested that it would not be wise to dismiss the idea that India may, in the future, hold one of the world's major reserve currencies, perhaps even before China, if only because, as many forget, India will have the world's largest economy on the basis of population size before long.

Hermann Remsperger
Member of the Board, Deutsche Bundesbank, Frankfurt
Hermann Remsperger raised three questions relating to the floating exchange rate system prognosis. He noted that Johnson had made a strong case in favour of a floating exchange rate system, and he asked whether this was a long-term outcome, or whether the conditions for moving to a floating exchange rate regime were currently fulfilled.

Remsperger's second question waswhether China would really be adversely affected by fluctuations in its currency, given the high import content of China's exports.

A third and last question focused on the possible consequences of a floating exchange rate for China. While it is often assumed that the natural consequence of a floating exchange rate regime for China would be a stronger currency, it could well be, if one were to assume that the capital account were liberalized simultaneously, that the consequences in terms of an appreciation become less clear cut. Perhaps the immediate reaction to a floating rate would not be an appreciating, but rather a depreciating currency. He asked the panelists to comment on this.

Karen Johnson
Director, International Finance Division, Federal Reserve Board, Washington, DC
Karen Johnson immediately took up the clarification sought by Remsperger, suggesting that, in fact, the 'preconditions' argument was not a very powerful one when considering China's exchange rate regime. Using Mexico as an example, she noted that Mexico could not have floated under worse conditions if it had tried. Indeed, the currency was floated at a time when reserves were low and the financial system in disarray, and the decision was certainly taken as a last resort. Yet in retrospect, argued Johnson, Mexico was clearly grateful to have been forced to make the step. Indeed, the regime had worked better than anyone could have foreseen. This casts some doubt on the argument that certain preconditions have to be met to float a currency.

That said, continued Johnson, the key concern with respect to China was resource allocation. She agreed that there was certainly no telling whether the renminbi, if floated, would appreciate or depreciate. However, what would certainly follow would be a greater role for the market in setting prices, including the exchange rate, and thus a better allocation of resources. That alone, argued Johnson, constituted a powerful argument in favour of a float for China.

With respect to the second question raised by Remsperger, Johnson argued that it constituted exchange rate illusion to expect that if the nominal exchange rate were stabilized, risk would be reduced and greater stability introduced. What really mattered was the real exchange rate, and what really mattered for the real exchange rate was the effect that it had on resource allocation. The appearance of stability in the nominal exchange rate does not necessarily deliver a resilient economy. Rather stability is the ability to deal with shocks. And what you want in order to generate such stability is resilience. You are clearly kidding yourself, claimed Johnson, if you think that resilience can be achieved by pegging the nominal exchange rate.

John Williamson
Senior Fellow, Institute for International Economics, Washington, DC
John Williamson reacted strongly to Johnson's comments about Mexico. Mexican real wages, he pointed out, fell by 20% in the 1994–5 crisis, which was not the way in which any country would want to introduce a flexible exchange rate regime. Admittedly, it worked out over time, but there was a real price to pay because the float was introduced without any of the preconditions that most would recognize to be necessary in place.

Williamson commented on the idea outlined in the report of the basket-band-crawl (BBC) regime. He agreed that the basket was very relevant to current circumstances, noting that, as Chen had mentioned, a common basket deals with the problem of maintaining stability vis-à-vis other competitive economies. A basket also maintains stability in the face of common shocks, such as changes in G3 currencies. Nothing is more exogenous to the East Asian countries than changes among the three major currencies. Thus, something that can be done to avoid changes in competitiveness stemming from such shocks would be of real value.

Such a system would furthermore allow for a great deal of flexibility. If there is 'Balassa-Samuelson' type technical progress, such a system would not preclude real appreciation in those countries with faster progress. It would also not prevent idiosyncratic adjustments in response to balance of payments developments in particular countries. But what such a system would not do is provide a possible transitional mechanism to monetary union. Countries that have had an intermediate regime of this type have generally ended up floating, and he noted that they have done so without having to undergo the devastating crisis of the type Mexico faced. Examples include Poland, Chile, Colombia and Israel. Perhaps, suggested Williamson, East Asian countries could also envisage such a system as a transition to a freely floating regime.

Yung Chul Park
Research Professor, Graduate School of International Studies, Seoul National University, Seoul
Park continued with the discussion on floating, raising a couple of practical questions. First, East Asian economies would be reluctant to let their currencies float freely largely because of the shallowness and illiquidity of their foreign exchange markets. Even if they were to adopt a pure floating system, there is the question of who would be enforcing the rules of floating and through what mechanisms. Second, given the deepening of vertical industrial integration in East Asia that is often compared with a conveyor, belt carrying components, parts and semi-assemblies supplied by Japan, Taiwan, and other neighbouring economies to the final factory in China, would floating be an ideal and practical collective regional exchange regime in the region ? As an alternative regime, they could consider a collective exchange regime in which they could allow their exchange rates move freely within a large band against a common basket of major currencies.

Hans Genberg
Executive Director, Research, Hong Kong Monetary Authority, Hong Kong SAR
Hans Genberg drew the panel back to the issue of monetary arrangements, as

opposed to exchange rate arrangements. Floating, he noted, is not a monetary policy, because it provides no guide to what the central bank should do, only what it should not do, i.e. fix the exchange rate. In terms of monetary policy, then, what would the panel suggest for the East Asian countries? Should countries follow a pure inflation-targeting regime? And if so, what would be the role of the exchange rate in this regime? For example, in countries such as Malaysia and Vietnam, which have substantial trade with US dollar based economies such as China, Hong Kong, and the United States, it may be appropriate to include the nominal exchange rate in a monetary policy 'rule' even if the ultimate objective of monetary policy is a stable inflation rate.

Real exchange rate targeting raises additional difficult issues. First of all, if one were to adopt a policy of real exchange rate targeting, what would provide the nominal anchor for the economy? In addition, how would one ensure that the resulting system would be dynamically stable?

Genberg also noted that, in Europe, much of the impetus towards exchange rate fixing among the smaller countries in the region stemmed from increased intra-regional trade, which, they believed, required stable bilateral exchange rates. However, one country, Switzerland, did not peg, and yet continued to post strong economic growth. To what extent would it be in the interest of the smaller Asian countries to follow in the footsteps of the smaller European countries that chose to pursue mutually fixed exchange rate or Switzerland that has allowed the franc to float?

Märten Ross
Deputy Governor, Bank of Estonia, Talinn
Märten Ross emphasized the role of politics in the choice of exchange rate arrangements. The lessons from Europe, he suggested, tell us that it was not only economic rationale nor friendship among the Europeans that led to the common currency. To considerable extent it was also a certain uneasiness at having to follow Deutsche Bundesbank policy, which made it easier for policy-makers in Europe to come to agreement on a common currency. In Asia, where the renminbi will clearly have a major role to play, if not in ten then in 20 years, the same political game may well play out, he suggested – there may well be some discomfort at following the policies of the People's Bank of China. In this context, policy-makers in the region would have to start thinking about floating, having a nominal external anchor from outside the region, or, as in Europe, forming a currency union.

William R. White
Economic Advisor, Monetary and Economics Department, Bank for International Settlements, Basel
William R. White raised a question on the 'Mexican' scenario presented by Johnson. When the Mexicans floated, he noted, they essentially destroyed the banking system and endured negative credit growth for years. They nonetheless managed to rebuild their system, largely because they were receiving intrafirm credit from the US. What would be the result if the Chinese were to follow a similar route to that taken by the Mexicans, particularly in view of the fact that China has an even bigger NPL problem than that faced by Mexico at the time?

Angel Ubide
Director of Global Economics, Tudor Investment Corporation, Washington, DC
Following on from White's comment, Angel Ubide put the discussion in the context of the increased regionalization of the world economy, noting that Mexico

was, in the long run, successful in its decision to float largely because there was a 'big brother' next door and because the decision to float was taken as the process of integration into NAFTA was itself occurring.

Eastern Europe has clearly decided that it too is moving into some form of regional arrangement, and Southeast Asia is also, albeit slowly, moving towards some sort of regional arrangement. As noted earlier, in a world of increased capital flows and economic links, either a country belongs to some regional arrangement or it has a problem. Any discussion then, of specific exchange rate arrangements needs to acknowledge a context of regionalism, specifically the drive towards three regional blocks.

Robert N. McCauley
Senior Advisor, Monetary and Economic Department, Bank for International Settlements, Hong Kong
China was actually on a silver standard until the 1930s, noted Robert McCauley, and when it was discussing the transition from a commodities standard, both American and British officials competed to try to get China to orient its currency towards the dollar and the pound, respectively. Ironically, noted McCauley, the situation has today been reversed. The authorities of the major international currencies are today somewhat reluctant to have China hooked up to their currency. McCauley questioned what has changed. Is it global circumstances, or is there something in our understanding of currency markets that has changed?

Vít Bárta
Advisor to the Vice-Governor, Czech National Bank, Prague
Picking up on an earlier comment by Ocampo, Vít Bàrta called for greater clarification as regards deflationary biases in the international monetary system. He noted, as was suggested earlier in the day, that there is good deflation, bad deflation, and ugly deflation. Given that Asia is today the fastest growing region in the world, why would deflation turn ugly?

Concluding Remarks, Panel

Pochih Chen
Chairman, Taiwan Thinktank, Taipei
Pochih Chen reacted, in his final comments, to the Mexico analogy suggested by his fellow panelist. Clearly, noted Chen, the Mexican example did not apply to China, if only because, as was mentioned, China does not have a so-called 'big brother' as neighbour.

Karen Johnson
Director, International Finance Division, Federal Reserve Board, Washington, DC
Notwithstanding the reactions from the floor, Karen Johnson defended her 'Mexican' example, although she did note the validity of many of the comments made. She stressed that Mexico had not made an intellectual decision to move to a floating exchange rate system at the time, only to then succumb into crisis; Mexico found itself in a crisis and a floating rate was then the only option open to it. To say that the collapse of the banking system or the collapse of real wages was due to the move to floating is somehow to reverse cause and effect, she argued. Broadly speaking, suggested Johnson in a final remark, the experience of Latin America, including Brazil and Argentina and other countries in the region, has shown that exchange rate stabilization does not work.

Jose-Antonio Ocampo
Under Secretary-General for Economic and Social Affairs, United Nations Economic and Social Council, Geneva
With respect to exchange rate targetting, Jose-Antonio Ocampo noted that he was essentially thinking about some form of intermediate regime with an exchange rate target of some sort, but mixed with an inflation target, and even perhaps mixed with some degree of output targetting. He pointed out that one cannot really think of intermediate regimes as being anything other than regimes that have an exchange rate target of some sort.

Finally, Ocampo joined Chen and others in disagreeing with the 'Mexico' example outlined by Johnson. He noted that when Mexico floated, it had a totally open capital account. This is not the case in China, far from it. Furthermore, not only did Mexico's decision to float depress wages, but if one looks at Mexico's experience within NAFTA, it is a slow-growing economy. It is a booming export economy but with very slow growth. The domestic market has not grown. If this is the route for China, it can only be a route to disaster, he stated. And not only for China, he ventured, but for the world economy as a whole.

Data Appendix

Table A.1 Macroeconomic indicators for East Asia

China	1997	1998	1999	2000	2001	2002	2003	2004
GDP growth rate	8.8	7.8	7.1	8.0	7.5	8.3	9.5	9.5
Inflation (based CPI)	2.8	-0.8	-1.4	0.3	0.5	-0.8	1.2	3.9
Saving and Investment (in % of GDP)								
Gross fixed capital investment	38.0	37.4	37.1	36.4	38.0	39.2	42.4	43.9
Gross national savings	42.1	40.7	39.3	38.3	39.5	41.9	45.5	48.0
Public Finances								
General government balance (in % of GDP)	-1.2	-1.6	-2.5	-3.1	-4.4	-2.9	-2.4	-1.5
Monetary Sector								
M2 (growth rate)	20.7	14.9	14.7	12.3	15.0	19.4	19.7	14.8
Interest rate	8.6	4.6	3.2	3.2	3.2	2.7	2.7	3.3
External Sector (in % of GDP)								
Current account balance	4.1	3.3	2.1	1.9	1.5	2.7	3.1	4.0
Exchange Rates								
Nominal Effective Exchange Rate	95.1	99.5	97.3	100.0	104.5	103.6	96.5	92.0
Real Effective Exchange Rate	98.8	100.8	97.5	100.0	104.3	102.6	96.7	95.0

Table A.1 Macroeconomic indicators for East Asia (contd.)

Hong Kong	1997	1998	1999	2000	2001	2002	2003	2004
GDP growth rate	5.1	-5.0	3.4	10.2	0.5	1.9	3.2	8.1
Inflation (based CPI)	5.8	2.9	-4.0	-3.7	-1.6	-3.0	-2.6	-0.4
Saving and Investment (in % of GDP)								
Gross fixed capital investment	34.5	29.2	25.3	28.1	25.9	23.4	22.8	23.0
Gross national savings		30.7	31.7	32.4	32.0	31.2	33.2	32.8
Public Finances								
General government balance (in % of GDP)	6.5	-1.8	0.8	-0.6	-5.0	-4.9	-3.3	1.7
Monetary Sector								
M2 (growth rate)	10.1	11.6	8.8	7.8	-2.7	-0.9	8.4	9.3
Interest rate	7.0	6.3	7.0	8.0	3.3	2.8	2.5	3.8
External Sector (in % of GDP)								
Current account balance		1.5	6.4	4.3	6.1	7.9	10.4	9.8
Exchange Rates								
Nominal Effective Exchange Rate	96.3	101.8	98.9	100.0	104.4	103.8	98.2	94.3
Real Effective Exchange Rate								

Indonesia								
GDP growth rate	4.7	-13.1	0.8	4.9	3.8	4.4	4.9	5.1
Inflation (based CPI)	6.2	58.4	20.5	3.7	11.5	11.9	6.6	6.2
Saving and Investment (in % of GDP)								
Gross fixed capital investment	31.8	16.8	11.4	22.2	22.0	20.9	17.6	22.8
Gross national savings	29.5	21.1	15.5	27.6	26.9	25.5	21.1	
Public Finances								
General government balance (in % of GDP)	-0.7	-2.9	-1.1	!	-1.2			
Monetary Sector								
M2 (growth rate)	23.2	62.3	11.9	15.6	13.0	4.7	8.1	8.2
Interest rate	20.0	39.1	25.7	12.5	15.5	15.5	10.6	6.4
External Sector (in % of GDP)								
Current account balance	-2.3	4.3	4.1	5.3	4.9	4.5	3.5	
Exchange Rates								
Nominal Effective Exchange Rate								
Real Effective Exchange Rate	95.5	48.1	68.1	64.2	63.4	77.9	83.4	78.5

Table A.1 Macroeconomic indicators for East Asia (contd.)

Japan	1997	1998	1999	2000	2001	2002	2003	2004
GDP growth rate	1.8	-1.2	0.2	2.9	0.4	-0.5	1.4	2.7
Inflation (based CPI)	1.7	0.7	-0.3	-0.7	-0.7	-0.9	-0.3	0.0
Saving and Investment (in % of GDP)								
Gross fixed capital investment	28.7	26.9	26.0	26.3	25.8	23.9	24.0	
Gross national savings	30.9	29.9	28.6	28.8	27.9	26.7	27.2	
Public Finances								
General government balance (in % of GDP)								
Monetary Sector								
M2 (growth rate)	3.1	4.1	3.4	1.1	2.2	3.4	1.8	1.6
Interest rate	0.50	0.50	0.50	0.50	0.10	0.10	0.10	0.10
External Sector (in % of GDP)								
Current account balance	2.2	3.0	2.6	2.5	2.1	2.8	3.2	
Exchange Rates								
Nominal Effective Exchange Rate	81.3	76.5	89.4	100.0	90.5	85.7	85.4	87.1
Real Effective Exchange Rate	86.7	81.3	92.6	100.0	88.7	80.6	78.1	78.5

Korea	1997	1998	1999	2000	2001	2002	2003	2004
GDP growth rate	4.7	-6.9	9.5	8.5	3.8	7.0	3.1	4.6
Inflation (based CPI)	4.4	7.5	0.8	2.2	4.1	2.7	3.6	3.6
Saving and Investment (in % of GDP)								
Gross fixed capital investment	35.6	30.3	29.7	31.1	29.5	29.1	29.9	29.5
Gross national savings	34.0	42.0	35.2	33.5	31.2	30.1	31.9	33.6
Public Finances								
General government balance (in % of GDP)	-1.4	-3.9	-2.5	1.1	1.2	3.3	1.1	0.7
Monetary Sector								
M2 (growth rate)	14.1	27.0	27.4	25.4	13.2	11.0	6.7	-0.6
Interest rate	5.0	3.0	3.0	3.0	2.5	2.5	2.5	2.0
External Sector (in % of GDP)								
Current account balance	-1.6	11.7	5.5	2.4	1.7	1.0	2.0	4.1
Exchange Rates								
Nominal Effective Exchange Rate								
Real Effective Exchange Rate	96.0	79.5	86.9	90.0	87.6	93.7	95.5	97.1

Table A.1 Macroeconomic indicators for East Asia (contd.)

Malaysia	1997	1998	1999	2000	2001	2002	2003	2004
GDP growth rate	7.3	-7.4	6.1	8.9	0.3	4.1	5.3	7.1
Inflation (based CPI)	2.7	5.3	2.7	1.5	1.4	1.8	1.1	1.5
Saving and Investment (in % of GDP)								
Gross fixed capital investment	43.0	26.7	22.4	27.3	23.9	23.8	21.4	22.5
Gross national savings	37.0	39.9	38.3	36.7	32.2	31.3	34.3	35.1
Public Finances								
General government balance (in % of GDP)	2.4	-1.8	-3.2	0.7	-0.3	-0.7	-0.4	
Monetary Sector								
M2 (growth rate)	18.2	-1.5	16.3	11.6	2.4	3.7	9.6	19.3
Interest rate	7.6	8.5	3.4	2.7	2.8	2.7	2.7	2.7
External Sector (in % of GDP)								
Current account balance	-5.9	13.2	15.9	9.4	8.3	7.6	12.9	12.6
Exchange Rates								
Nominal Effective Exchange Rate	125.3	96.4	97.4	100.0	105.8	105.0	98.0	93.3
Real Effective Exchange Rate	119.4	94.9	97.6	100.0	105.5	105.7	97.1	91.9

Philippines	1997	1998	1999	2000	2001	2002	2003	2004
GDP growth rate	5.2	-0.6	3.4	4.0	3.4	5.5	4.9	5.0
Inflation (based CPI)	5.6	9.3	5.9	4.0	6.8	3.0	3.4	6.0
Saving and Investment (in % of GDP)								
Gross fixed capital investment	24.8	20.3	18.8	21.2	19.0	17.6	16.6	17.0
Gross national savings	19.5	22.7	28.2	29.4	20.8	23.3	18.4	19.4
Public Finances								
General government balance (in % of GDP)	0.1	-1.9	-3.8	-4.1	-4.0	-5.3	-4.6	-3.9
Monetary Sector								
M2 (growth rate)	23.1	8.6	16.9	8.1	3.6	10.4	3.6	9.9
Interest rate	14.6	12.4	7.9	13.8	8.3	4.2	5.5	8.4
External Sector (in % of GDP)								
Current account balance	-5.3	2.4	9.5	8.2	1.9	5.7	1.8	2.4
Exchange Rates								
Nominal Effective Exchange Rate	141.0	107.1	109.9	100.0	91.1	89.6	79.5	73.1
Real Effective Exchange Rate	120.6	98.6	107.3	100.0	95.1	95.5	85.9	82.2

Table A.1 Macroeconomic indicators for East Asia (contd.)

Singapore	1997	1998	1999	2000	2001	2002	2003	2004
GDP growth rate	8.6	-0.9	6.9	9.7	-1.9	2.1	1.1	9.9
Inflation (based CPI)	2.0	-0.3	0.0	1.4	1.0	-0.4	0.5	1.7
Saving and Investment (in % of GDP)								
Gross fixed capital investment	39.2	32.3	32.0	32.0	24.9	21.2	13.4	18.3
Gross national savings	54.9	55.0	50.6	46.4	43.6	42.6	44.2	44.4
Public Finances								
General government balance (in % of GDP)	9.6	16.9	10.4	11.3	-0.3	-1.6	6.5	
Monetary Sector								
M2 (growth rate)	10.3	30.2	8.5	-2.0	5.9	-0.3	8.1	6.2
Interest rate								
External Sector (in % of GDP)								
Current account balance	15.7	22.7	18.6	14.3	18.7	21.4	30.9	26.1
Exchange Rates								
Nominal Effective Exchange Rate	105.7	105.0	99.7	100.0	101.4	100.5	96.8	95.5
Real Effective Exchange Rate	110.7	106.5	99.7	100.0	100.8	98.0	93.9	92.8

Taiwan	1997	1998	1999	2000	2001	2002	2003	2004
GDP growth rate	6.4	4.3	5.3	5.8	-2.2	3.9	3.3	5.7
Inflation (based CPI)	0.9	1.7	0.2	1.3	0.0	-0.2	-0.3	1.6
Saving and Investment (in % of GDP)								
Gross fixed capital investment	24.2	24.9	23.4	22.8	17.7	16.7	16.6	20.7
Gross national savings	26.6	26.2	26.3	25.7	24.2	25.8	26.9	26.8
Public Finances								
General government balance (in % of GDP)	-3.8	-3.4	-6.0	-4.7	-6.7	-4.5	-2.9	-3.4
Monetary Sector								
M2 (growth rate)	8.0	8.6	8.3	6.5	4.4	2.6	5.8	7.4
Interest rate								
External Sector (in % of GDP)								
Current account balance	2.4	1.3	2.9	2.9	6.5	9.1	10.2	6.1
Exchange Rates								
Nominal Effective Exchange Rate								
Real Effective Exchange Rate								

Table A.1 Macroeconomic indicators for East Asia (contd.)

Thailand	1997	1998	1999	2000	2001	2002	2003	2004
GDP growth rate	-1.4	-10.5	4.4	4.8	2.2	5.3	6.9	6.1
Inflation (based CPI)	5.6	8.1	0.3	1.6	1.6	0.6	1.8	2.8
Saving and Investment (in % of GDP)								
Gross fixed capital investment	33.7	20.4	20.5	22.8	24.1	23.9	25.0	27.1
Gross national savings	31.7	33.2	30.6	30.4	29.5	29.4	30.6	31.6
Public Finances								
General government balance (in % of GDP)	-0.3	-2.8	-3.3	-2.2	-2.4	-1.4	0.4	
Monetary Sector								
M2 (growth rate)	16.5	9.7	5.4	3.4	2.4	1.4	6.6	5.1
Interest rate								
External Sector (in % of GDP)								
Current account balance	-2.0	12.7	10.1	7.6	5.4	5.5	5.6	4.5
Exchange Rates1)								
Nominal Effective Exchange Rate								
Real Effective Exchange Rate	93.7	82.4	85.6	79.6	78.1	82.1	80.4	

Source: IMF, International Financial Statistics, World Bank Indicators 2003, Asian Development Bank (www.adb.org), and Bank of Taiwan (www.bot.com.tw)

Table A.2 Current account surpluses

	2000	2001	2002	2003	2004	Total	Share
China	20,518	17,401	35,422	45,875	68,659	119,216	12.84
Hong Kong	7,083	9,941	12,596	16,211	16,039	45,831	4.94
Indonesia	7,992	6,901	7,824	8,106	3,108	30,823	3.32
Japan	119,660	87,798	112,447	136,215	17,209	456,120	49.12
Korea	12,251	8,033	5,394	12,321	27,613	37,998	4.09
Malaysia	8,488	7,287	7,190	13,381	14,871	36,346	3.91
Philippines	6,258	1,323	4,383	1,396	2,080	13,360	1.44
Singapore	13,257	16,086	18,909	28,184	27,879	76,436	8.23
Taiwan	8,851	18,217	25,630	29,258	18,658	81,956	8.83
Thailand	9,313	6,192	7,014	7,953	7,281	30,472	3.28
Sum	213,672	179,178	236,808	298,899	203,398	928,557	100

Source: IMF, International Financial Statistics

Endnotes

1 This group of countries (Japan, China, South Korea, Taiwan, Singapore, India and, as the seventh central bank, the Hong Kong Monetary Authority) represents 40% of global-ex-US GDP, and possesses 60% of global-ex-US central bank reserves

2 On 21 July 2005, the PBOC announced a change in China's exchange rate arrangement, but in its early days of operation, the behaviour of the RMB/US$ exchange rate was not very different from what it had been in the old arrangement, apart from the initial 2.1% appreciation. See Box 1 at the end of the chapter for the PBOC statement that accompanied the change.

3 The Shumer-Graham sponsored bill in the US Congress proposed a 27.5 percent tariff on Chinese imports

4 Market participants have been forecasting that Chinese reserves will reach $1,000bn by 2006, see *Financial Times*, July 20, 2005.

5 See also Figure 2.9 which shows that reserve accumulation has been larger than current account surpluses as well for East Asia (less Japan) as a whole.

6 South Korea, Taiwan, Hong Kong SAR, Singapore and Malaysia

7 The IMF has undertaken considerable empirical research into the impact of capital account liberalization on developing countries, and has recently come to the view that such moves are not a precondition for economic success - as demonstrated by China and India - and can cause serious financial and macroeconomic difficulties if institutional and policy frameworks are not significantly reformed and improved beforehand (Prasad et al., 2003)

8 See Torvik (2001) for a good discussion of the Dutch disease literature.

9 According to the president of the National Association of US Manufacturers, on the day of the announcement of the new exchange rate arrangement in China: 'Today's announcement by the Chinese authorities has the potential for beginning to correct the huge trade imbalances that have been created by distorted currencies'.

10 See Section 4.3.2.

11 It has also been argued that central bank investment in US government debt has held down risk-free yields, which have further pumped up the value of interest-rate sensitive dollar assets like property, corporate bonds and stocks, further boosting consumption. The empirical evidence for this effect is questioned in section 3.2.3.

12 Kumar and Persaud (2002).

13 Rose and Glick (1998).

14 See, Monthly *ASEAN Statistical Indicators*, June 2005.

15 See Box 2.1 for the statement released by the Peoples Bank of China on July 21, 2005

16 See Anthony and MacDonald (1999).

17 Mr. Xia Bin, of the Development Research Centre under the State Council, China's Cabinet, waived aside US calls for greater revaluation by saying the scale of Thursday's move was entirely appropriate - and he warned against assuming that more will come soon. 'I hope that some "hot money players" and some speculators do not harbour unrealistic fantasies and do not come once again to gamble on the exchange rate system,....I don't think...there will be any clear appreciation in the second half of the year. Don't harbour illusions.' Quoted in *Financial Times*, July 23, 2005.

18 It is very partial, however, to compare the scale of the reserve accumulation and the scale of the sale of domestic assets in a year, overlooking the effect of higher reserve requirements on the demand for reserves and the need for an increase in monetary base to meet growth in cash demand. See Higgins and Klitgaard (2004).

19 At the margin, such a mismatch introduces duration risk that would become evident in the event of a parallel upward shift of domestic and international yield curves. But a full assessment of the central bank's duration risk depends critically on the treatment of the outstanding note issue.

20 Our rationale for assuming these alternatives is based on institutional plausibility rather than on optimality (in the sense of achieving the highest possible gain). In theory, the first next-best option is always the highest-interest alternative available. If the first alternative somehow cannot accommodate the entire stock of foreign reserves to be disposed of, then the next-most-costly alternative should be adopted, etc.

21 If our calculations were extended beyond March 2004 they would show that the government, instead of the central bank, would bear the marginal opportunity cost under the Market Stabilization Scheme.

22 In particular, trading of the euro against the yen, which some considered would expand after the inception of the euro (Portes and Rey (1999), represented only 3% of activity in April 2004, up from the 2% observed before the euro (BIS (2005b), p 10). Euro/sterling represented 2%, euro/Swiss franc 1% and all others 2%. If one excludes dollar/euro transactions, then the dollar was on one side in 61% of all transactions, while the figure for the euro was 9%.

23 BIS (2005c), p 88 .

24 Such a position is alluded to by Kubarych (1984).

25 Identified holdings amounted to $1.659trn in March 2000, 91% of an estimated $1.830trn in dollar holdings then. If unidentified holdings are mostly invested in eurodollar bonds offshore, then the short-term share could be about a third.

26 Since this analysis is performed on US data on foreign holdings of securities, it neglects the effect of the official intervention on the value of the dollar, and the knock-on effects of the dollar's value on equity and fixed income markets. Thus, this exercise is not a fully elaborated counterfactual analysis.

27 Similarly, in spring of 1987, strong dollar-buying by central banks, against the backdrop of cutbacks in Treasury bill issuance owing to stronger than expected tax revenues, led to a widening of the spread between Treasury bills and eurodollar yields.

28 This does not include domestic bonds bought in domestic currency. For instance, banks in the United States increased their holdings of Treasury, agency, and corporate bonds by $ 142bn and $160bn in 2003 and 2004, respectively (Board of Governors of the Federal Reserve System, 2005).

29 Even these data are not comprehensive; central banks can and do buy and hold dollar bonds offshore (McCauley and Fung, 2003).

30 As pointed out by Crandall (2005), the stock estimates derived from the TIC data jump up at the dates for which survey evidence become available, suggesting that the TIC data systematically underreport official holdings. By country (including both official and private holdings), the survey implied the largest revision for China in the 2002 survey ($15bn), the second largest after Korea's $20 billion in the 2003 survey ($9bn) and the largest again in the 2004 survey ($19bn).

31 It might be answered that private purchases are more likely to be hedged through forward sales of dollars against euro or yen. But there is no reason why such positioning, like a domestic investor buying a Treasury note with Libor-based funding, cannot affect the ten-year yield.

32 The rest of the world is treated as a residual. It thus includes the global current account discrepancy.

33 See, for example, Bergsten (2004, 2005) and Goldstein (2004).

34 At this point it may be useful to quote Obstfeld and Rogoff (2004). On page 3 they note: "First, our framework should not be thought of as asking the question: 'How much depreciation of the dollar is needed to rebalance the current account?' Though wildly popular, this view is misguided. In fact, most empirical and theoretical models (including ours) suggest that even

very large autonomous exchange rate movements will not go far toward closing a current account gap of the magnitude presently observed in the case of the United States. The lion's share of the adjustment has to come from saving and productivity shocks that help equilibrate global net saving levels, and that imply dollar change largely as a by-product (though our model of course implies simultaneous determination of exchange rates and current accounts)."

35 On the pattern and evolution of trade in the region, see Zebregs (2004).

36 See Ho, Ma and McCauley (2005) and Park and Wyplosz (2004) for discussions about exchange rate policy in the region.

37 For a description with implications for Asia, see Wyplosz (2004).

38 Park (2004) and Ito and Park (2004) review the empirical literature.

39 White noted that the concern of many over the US twin deficits (particularly in view of the growing US fiscal deficit), but argued that the fiscal deficit was actually declining throughout most of the 1990s, even as the current account was deteriorating. The key concern, he thus argued, was really to do with US household savings.

40 See attached Figures D1-3. The ligher line on the graphs represents Mexico's real effective exchange rate, using a formula equivalent to that used to calculate the weighted average dollar. For Mexico, the weight on the dollar is naturally high, and the real effective peso reflects the influence of the dollar rising up to early 2002. Graphing the same data for a more recent period and a finer scale, Johnson showed that there hads indeed been some movements of the real effective exchange rate against the dollar. However, this was not of the sort that actually damaged the trading relationship.

References

Abaroa, P. E. (2004), 'The International Investment Position of the United States at Year-end 2003', *Survey of Current Business* (July), pp. 30-9.
Anderson, J. (2004), 'Asia Sterilization Update', *Asian Economic Comment* (1 November). UBS Investment Research. [[not in text]]
Anthony, M. and MacDonald, R. (1999). 'The Width of the Band and Exchange Rate Mean-Reversion: Some Further ERM Results', *Journal of International Money and Finance* 18(3) (June), pp. 411-28.
ASEAN (2005), Monthly ASEAN Statistical Indicators, June.
Bank for International Settlements (BIS) (2005a), *Quarterly Review* (March).
Bank for International Settlements (2005b), *The Triennial Central Bank Survey: Foreign Exchange and Derivative Markets Activity in 2004* (March).
Bank for International Settlements (2005c), *75th Annual Report* (27 June).
Bank of Japan (2002), 'Japan's International Investment Position at Year-end 2001', *Bank of Japan Quarterly Bulletin* (August), pp. 131-62.
Bank of Japan (2003), 'Japan's International Investment Position at Year-end 2002', *Bank of Japan Quarterly Bulletin* (August), pp. 153-86.
Bank of Japan (2004), 'Japan's International Investment Position at Year-end 2003', *Bank of Japan Quarterly Bulletin* (August), pp. 87-90.
Benassy-Quéré, Agnès (1996), 'Exchange Rate Regimes and Policies in Asia', Centre d'études prospectives et d'informations internationales, Document de Travail No. 96-07(July).
Bergsten, Fred (2004), 'The IMF and Exchange Rates', Testimony before the Committee on Banking, Housing, and Urban Affairs (19 May), Washington, DC, United States Senate.
Bergsten, Fred (2005), 'An Action Plan to Stop the Market Manipulators Now', *Financial Times* (15 March).
Bernanke, Ben S. (2005), 'The Global Saving Glut and the U.S. Current Account Deficit', remarks at the Sandridge Lecture, Virginia Association of Economics, Richmond, VA.
Bernanke, B., Reinhart, V. and Saks, B. (2004), 'Monetary Policy Alternatives at the Zero Bound: An Empirical Assessment', Board of Governors of the Federal Reserve System Finance and Economics Discussion Series No. 2004-48, Washington, DC.
Blanchard, Olivier, Giavazzi, Francesco and Sa, Filipa (2005), 'The US Current Account and the Dollar', NBER Working Paper No. 11137, Washington, DC, National Bureau of Economic Research, February.
Board of Governors of the Federal Reserve System (2005), Flow of Funds Accounts of the United States (1st quarter, 9 June), Washington, DC.
Brook, Anne-Marie, Sédillot, Franck and Ollivaud, Patrice (2004), 'Channels for narrowing the US current account deficit and implications for other

economies', OECD Economics Department Working Papers, No. 390, May.
Calvo, G. A. (1991), 'The Perils of Sterilization', IMF Staff Papers, 38(4), Washington, DC, International Monetary Fund, pp. 921-6.
Cline, William R. (forthcoming), 'The United States as a Debtor Nation: Risks and Policy Reform', photcopy. Institute for International Economics, Washington, DC.
De Jonquieres, Guy (2005), *Financial Times* (18 February). Needs title of article.
Dominguez, Kathryn M. and Frankel, Jeffrey A. (1994), *Does Foreign Exchange Intervention Work?,* Washington, DC, Institute for International Economics.
Dooley, Michael, Folkerts-Landau, David and Garber, Peter (2003), 'An Essay on the Revived Bretton Woods System', NBER Working Paper No. 9971. Washington, DC, National Bureau of Economic Research.
Eichengreen, Barry (1998), 'The Euro as a Reserve Currency', *Journal of the Japanese and International Economies* 12(4) (December), pp. 483-506.
Eichengreen, Barry and Frankel, Jeffrey A. (1996), 'Implications of the Future Evolution of the International Monetary System', in Michael Mussa, James M. Boughton and Peter Isard (eds), *The Future of the SDR: In Light of Changes in the International Financial System,* Washington, DC, International Monetary Fund, pp. 337-78.
Frankel, J. A. (1995), 'Still the Lingua Franca: The Exaggerated Death of the Dollar', *Foreign Affairs* 74(4) (July-August), pp. 9-16.
Frankel, J. A and Wei, Shang-Jin (1994), 'Yen Bloc or Dollar Bloc? Exchange Rate Policies of the East Asian Economies', in Takatoshi Ito and Anne Krueger (eds), *Macroeconomic Linkage: Savings, Exchange Rates, and Capital Flows,* Chicago, IL, University of Chicago Press, pp. 295-329.
Garzarelli, Francesco (2004), 'How Much Is Asian Buying Worth?', *Institutional Portal Global Markets Research Daily* (9 December), Goldman Sachs.
Goldstein, Morris (2004), 'Adjusting China's Exchange Rate Policies'. Available online at: *www.iie.com/publications/wp/wp04-1.pdf*
Gourinchas, P.-O. and Rey, H. (2005), 'International Financial Adjustment', NBER Working Paper No.11155, Cambridge, MA, National Bureau of Economic Research.
Higgins, M. and Klitgaard, T. (2004), 'Reserve Accumulation: Implications for Global Capital Flows and Financial Markets', *Current Issues in Economics and Finance* 10(10) (September/October), New York, Federal Reserve Bank of New York.
Ho, Corinne, Ma, Guonan and McCauley, Robert N. (2005), 'Trading Asian Currencies,' *BIS Quarterly Review* (March), pp. 49-58.
Ho, Corinne and McCauley, Robert N. (2005), 'Resisting Exchange Rate Appreciation and Accumulating Reserves: What Are the Consequences for the Domestic Financial System?', paper presented to Korea Institute of Finance seminar, Seoul (6 January).
International Monetary Fund (2004), *World Economic Outlook* (April).
Ito, Takatoshi and Park, Yung Chul (2004), 'Exchange Rate Regimes in East Asia', in Asian Development Bank (ed.), *Monetary and Financial Integration in East Asia, The Way Ahead,* Vol. 1, Basingstoke, Palgrave Macmillan, pp. 143-88.
Kasman, Bruce and Malik, Hussein (2004), 'Special Topic: The Asian Currency-Policy Link to US Interest Rates', *Fixed Income Markets Weekly* (6 February), pp. 1-4. New York, JP Morgan.
Kawai, M. (2002), 'Exchange Rate Arrangements in East Asia: Lessons from the 1997-98 Currency Crisis', *Monetary and Economic Studies* 20, no S-1 (December), Tokyo, Bank of Japan, Institute for Monetary and Economic Studies.
Kawai, Masahiro and Akiyama, Shigeru (1998), 'Roles of the World's Major

Currencies in Exchange Rate Arrangements', *Journal of the Japanese and International Economies* 12(4) (December), pp. 334-87.

Kindleberger, C. P. (1965), 'Balance-of-payments Deficits and the International Market for Liquidity', *Essays in International Finance* (May), Princeton, NJ, Princeton University.

Kubarych, R. (1984), 'Financing the U.S. Current Account Deficit', *Federal Reserve Bank of New York Quarterly Review* 9(9) (Summer), pp. 24-31.

Kumar, M. S. and Persaud, A. (2002), 'Pure Contagion and Investors' Shifting Risk Appetite: Analytical Issues and Empirical Evidence', *International Finance,* Vol. 5, 401-436

Latter, T. (2005) 'Asian Monetary Union – Where Do We Go From Here?', Occasional Paper No. 2, Hong Kong Institute for Monetary Research, Hong Kong.

Lau, Lawrence and Stiglitz, Joseph (2005), 'China's Alternative to Revaluation', *Financial Times*, April 24.

Lee Jong-Wha, McKibbin, Warwick J. and Park, Yung Chul (2004), 'The Transpacific Imbalance: Causes and Cures', *Brookings Discussion Papers in Internatonal Economics* No 162, Washington, The Brookings Institution.

Ma, Guonan and McCauley, Robert N. (2004), 'Maîtriser la Croissance en Chine dans un Contexte de Mobilité Internationale des Capitaux' ('Reining in China's Growth in a World of Increased Capital Flows), *Revue d'économie financière* 77 (special issue, Patrick Artus and Françoise Lemaine (eds), 'Le Devenir Financier de la Chine' (China's Financial Future), pp. 763-785

Malcolm, J. (2005), 'Anticipating the spillover from CNY reval', Deutsche Bank, Asian FX Strategy Notes, 4 January.

McCauley, Robert N. (1997), 'The Euro and the Dollar', Princeton University *Essays in International Finance* No. 205 (November), Princeton, NJ, Princeton University.

McCauley, RObert N. (2005), 'Distinguishing dollar reserves from official holdings in the United States', BIS *Quarterly Review*, September, pp. 57-72

McCauley, Robert N. and Fung, Ben (2003), 'Choosing Instruments in Managing Dollar Foreign Exchange Reserves', *BIS Quarterly Review* (March), pp. 39-46.

McCauley, Robert N. and Jiang, Guorong (2004), 'Treasury Yields and Foreign Official Holdings of US Bonds,' *BIS Quarterly Review* (March), pp. 11-12.

McKibbin W. J. and Stoeckel, A. (2004), 'What if China Revalues Its Currency?', EconomicScenarios 7 (February), 8 pages. Available only online at: *www.economicscenarios.com*

Obstfeld, Maurice and Rogoff, Kenneth (2004), 'The Unsustainable US Current Account Position Revised', NBER Working Paper No.10869, Cambridge, MA, National Bureau of Economic Research.

Ogawa, E. and Ito, T. (2000), 'On the Desirability of a Regional Basket Currency Arrangement', NBER Working Papers 8002, Washington, DC, National Bureau of Economic Research.

Ogawa, E. and Ito, T. (2002), 'On the Desirability of a Regional Basket Currency Arrangement,' *Journal of the Japanese and International Economies* 16(3), pp. 317-34.

Park, Yung Chul (2004), 'Regional Financial Integration in East Asia: Challenges and Prospects', paper presented at the United Nations Seminar on Regional Financial Arrangements, New York (14-15 July).

Park, Yung Chul and Wyplosz, Charles (2004), 'Exchange Arrangements in Asia: Do They Matter?,' paper presented at the KIEP Conference on Monetary and Exchange Rate Arrangement in East Asia, Seoul, August.

Portes, Richard and Rey, Hélène (1999), 'The determinants of cross-border equity

flows: the geography of information', CEPR Discussion Paper No. 2225, London, CEPR.
Prasad, Esvar and Wei, Shang-jin (2005), 'The Chinese Approach to Capital Controls', IMF Working Paper WP05, April, Washington, DC, International Monetary Fund.
Prasad et al. (2003), 'The Effects of Financial Globalization on Developing Countries: SOme Empirical Evidence', IMF Occasional Paper No 220, Washing, DC, International Monetary Fund.
Preeg, E. H. (2003) 'Exchange Rate Manipulation to Gain an Unfair Competitive Advantage: The Case Against Japan and China', in F. Bergsten and J. Williamson (eds), *Dollar Overvaluation and the World Economy*, Special Report No.16, Washington, DC, Institute for International Economics.
Rose, Andrew K. and Glick, Reuven (1998). 'Contagion and Trade: Why Are Currency Crises Regional', CEPR Discussion Paper No. 1947.
Roubini, N. and Setser, B. (2005), 'Will the Bretton Woods 2 Regime Unravel Soon? The Risk of Hard Landing in 2005-2006', processed (February).
Tille, C. (2002), 'The Impact of Exchange Rate Movements on US Foreign Debt', *Current Issues in Economics and Finance* 9(1), pp. 1-7, New York, Federal Reserve Bank of New York.
Tille, C. (2004), 'Financial Integration and the Wealth Effect of Exchange Rate Fluctuations', Federal Reserve Bank of New York, mimeo. Available at *http://web.gc.cuny.edu/economics/SeminarPapers/march1.pdf*
Torvik, R. (2001) 'Learning by Doing and the Dutch Disease', *European Economic Review* 4, pp. 285-306.
Truman, E. (2005) 'Postponing Global Adjustment: An Analysis of the Pending Adjustment of Global Imbalances', Working Paper 05-6, Washington, DC, Institute for International Economics.
US Department of Commerce, Bureaau of Economic Analysis, *http://www.bea.gov/bea/di1.htm*
US Treasury, Federal Reserve Bank of New York, Board of Governors of the Federal Reserve System (2004), 'Report on foreign portfolio holdings of U.S. securities as of June 30, 2003' (August). Available online at: *www.ustreas.gov/tic/shl2003r.pdf*
Wolf, M. (2005) 'Capital Flow Must Change Course', *Financial Times* (26 June).
Wyplosz, Charles (2004), 'Regional Exchange Rate Arrangements: Lessons from Europe for East Asia', in Asian Development Bank (ed.), *Monetary and Financial Integration in East Asia, The Way Ahead*, Vol. 2, Basingstoke, Palgrave Macmillan, pp. 241-84.
Zebregs, Harm (2004), 'Intraregional Trade in Emerging Asia', IMF Policy Discussion Paper, PDP/04/1 (April), Washington, DC, International Monetary Fund.